Manual for the
CHILD BEHAVIOR CHECKLIST/4-18

and
1991 PROFILE

Thomas M. Achenbach
Department of Psychiatry
University of Vermont

Ordering Information

This book and all materials related to the Child Behavior Checklist can be ordered from: Child Behavior Checklist

1 South Prospect St.

Burlington, VT 05401-3456

Fax: 802/656-2602

Proper bibliographic citation for this *Manual*:

Achenbach, T.M. (1991). *Manual for the Child Behavior Checklist/4-18 and 1991 Profile.* Burlington, VT: University of Vermont Department of Psychiatry.

Related Books

Achenbach, T.M. (1991). *Manual for the Teacher's Report Form and 1991 Profile.* Burlington, VT: University of Vermont Department of Psychiatry.

Achenbach, T.M. (1991). *Manual for the Youth Self-Report and 1991 Profile.* Burlington, VT: University of Vermont Department of Psychiatry.

Achenbach, T.M. (1992). *Manual for the Child Behavior Checklist/2-3 and 1992 Profile.* Burlington, VT: University of Vermont Department of Psychiatry.

Achenbach, T.M. (1993). *Empirically based taxonomy: How to use syndromes and profile types derived from the CBCL/4-18, TRF, and YSR.* Burlington, VT: University of Vermont Department of Psychiatry.

Achenbach, T.M. (1997). *Manual for the Young Adult Self-Report and Young Adult Behavior Checklist.* Burlington, VT: University of Vermont Department of Psychiatry.

Achenbach, T.M., & McConaughy, S.H. (1997). *Empirically based assessment of child and adolescent psychopathology. Practical applications.* (2nd ed). Thousand Oaks, CA: Sage.

McConaughy, S.H., & Achenbach, T.M. (1994). *Manual for the Semistructured Clinical Interview for Children and Adolescents.* Burlington, VT: University of Vermont Department of Psychiatry.

Library of Congress #90-72107   ISBN 0-938565-08-7

Printed in the United States of America 12 11 10 9

USER QUALIFICATIONS

Because the Child Behavior Checklist (CBCL) is designed to be filled out by parents and parent surrogates, no special qualifications are needed for administering it, beyond the tact and sensitivity that are necessary in all dealings with parents. When it is given to a parent, its purpose should be explained in terms of obtaining a picture of the child's behavior as the parent sees it. It is important to tell parents that the CBCL is designed for a wide variety of children and that some of the items may not apply to their child. The parent should be assured of confidentiality, which should be strictly guarded. Whoever gives the CBCL to the parent should be available to answer questions about the meaning of items. Answers to parents' questions should be objective and factual, rather than probing or interpretive.

Whenever possible, it is highly desirable to have the child's mother and father or another adult who lives with the child independently fill out separate CBCLs for the sake of comparing their views (see Chapter 9 for further details). Hand scoring the CBCL requires that the instructions (Appendix A) be followed carefully, including rules for scoring items that request descriptions of behavior. Our computer-scoring programs provide instructions that can be followed by users familiar with basic computer procedures.

Although the administration and scoring of the CBCL do not require special skills, proper clinical and research use require knowledge of the theory and methodology of standardized assessment procedures, as well as supervised training in working with parents and children. The training required will differ according to the ways in which the CBCL is to be used, but graduate training of at least the Master's degree level would ordinarily be expected. However, no amount of prior training can substitute for professional maturity and a thorough familiarity with the procedures and cautions presented in this *Manual*.

All users should understand that the CBCL is designed to provide standardized *descriptions* of behavior rather than diagnostic inferences. High scores on CBCL problem scales should not automatically be equated with any particular diagnosis or inferred disorder. Instead, the responsible professional will integrate parents' CBCL descriptions of their child with other types of data obtained in the comprehensive evaluation of the child and family and will not label individuals solely on the basis of scale scores.

PREFACE

This *Manual* provides basic information needed for understanding and using the Child Behavior Checklist for Ages 4-18 (CBCL/4-18) and its scoring profile. It also outlines the CBCL's relations to other instruments that we have developed, especially the Youth Self-Report (YSR) and Teacher's Report Form (TRF). The Reader's Guide following this Preface offers an overview of the contents to aid users in quickly locating the material they seek.

To aid users in moving between the CBCL/4-18, YSR, and TRF, the *Manuals* for the three instruments follow similar formats. In addition, the *Integrative Guide for the 1991 CBCL/4-18, YSR, and TRF Profiles* details relations among the profiles for the three instruments and the procedures for deriving syndromes that are common to all three.

The pre-1991 profiles for scoring the CBCL, YSR, and TRF were developed separately as data were accumulated for each one. The syndrome scales of each profile were designed to capture the patterns of problems specifically identified for each sex within particular age ranges on each instrument taken separately.

The pre-1991 syndrome scales functioned well for describing and assessing patterns that were empirically derived for specific sex/age groups as seen by a particular type of informant. The 1991 editions are designed to advance both the conceptual structure and the practical applications of empirically based assessment by focusing more precisely on the syndromes that are common to both sexes and different age ranges, according to parent-, self-, and teacher-reports.

The 1991 profiles for scoring data from all three sources include a common set of eight syndromes that are normed on the same national sample. However, to reflect important sex and age differences, the syndromes are normed separately for each sex within particular age ranges, according to reports by each type of informant. In addition, items found to be associated with a syndrome in ratings by a particular type of informant are retained for scoring by that type of informant. Some additional syndromes and competence scales are also specific to particular sex/age groups as seen by a particular kind of informant. For example, a syndrome designated as *Sex Problems* was found in parents' CBCL ratings of 4-11-year-olds, but was not found in parents' ratings of 12-18 year-olds, nor in teacher- or self-ratings. The *Sex Problems* syndrome is therefore scored only from CBCL ratings for 4-11-year-olds.

PREFACE

Although this *Manual* was written by a single author, the first person plural "we" is used throughout. This reflects the author's feeling that the work is a joint product of many coworkers, especially the following: Neil Aguiar, Janet Arnold, Jill Brown, Bruce Compas, Craig Edelbrock, Judy Ewell, Catherine Howell, Lynda Howell, David Jacobowitz, Stephanie McConaughy, Susan Oakes, Vicky Phares, Michael Sawyer, Catherine Stanger, Gavin Stewart, Frank Verhulst, and John Weisz. I deeply appreciate the contributions of all these people, plus the many others who have contributed through their own work and comments.

Much of the work reported here has been supported by University Associates in Psychiatry, a nonprofit health services and research corporation of the University of Vermont Department of Psychiatry. I am also grateful for the Spencer Foundation's support of our recent research on teachers' reports, for support from the March of Dimes Birth Defects Foundation, and for the National Institute of Mental Health's support of research that has contributed to this effort.

READER'S GUIDE

CONTENTS

Chapter 1
The Child Behavior Checklist
for Ages 4-18

This is a revision of the *Manual for the Child Behavior Checklist and Revised Child Behavior Profile* (Achenbach & Edelbrock, 1983). The current revision is necessitated by changes in the 1991 scoring profile, new national norms through age 18, and new provisions for coordinating data from parent-, self-, and teacher-reports. To reflect the extension of norms through age 18, the 1991 edition of the instrument is designated as the Child Behavior Checklist for Ages 4-18 (CBCL/4-18). For brevity, the words "child" and "children" will be used to include adolescents throughout this Manual.

Some small changes in wording were made in the 1988 and 1991 editions of the CBCL, but these do not affect scoring. The main changes involve deletion of the words "child" and "children" from items where they would seem inappropriate for subjects as old as 18. Also, problem item *42.* has been changed to *Would rather be alone than with others*, from the pre-1991 version *Likes to be alone*. All pre-1991 editions (designated as the CBCL/4-16) can be scored on the 1991 profile. Conversely, the 1991 edition of the CBCL/4-18 can be scored on the earlier versions of the profile, except that the pre-1991 versions do not include norms for ages 17 and 18. Continuity can thus be maintained in scoring data obtained at any time with any version of the CBCL/4-16 and CBCL/4-18. (Chapter 11 describes the Child Behavior Checklist for Ages 2-3, which is scored on a profile normed for 2-3-year-olds.)

To aid readers who are unfamiliar with the CBCL, as well as those who are familiar with it, this *Manual* first presents the multiaxial assessment model on which the CBCL is based. Thereafter, the instrument itself is described. Chapter 2 presents the scales for scoring the competence items on the 1991 profile, while Chapter 3 presents the scales for scoring the problem items. Internalizing and Externalizing groupings of problem scales are presented in Chapter 4. Chapter 5 deals with reliability, stability, and interparent agreement data for the CBCL/4-18. Chapter 6 provides evidence for validity and the basis for scale score cutpoints that distinguish between the normal, borderline, and clinical ranges.

Statistical and graphic comparisons of item scores obtained by referred and nonreferred children are presented in Chapter 7. Chapter 8 presents relations between the 1991 profile and the preceding edition. Applications in practical and research contexts are presented in Chapters 9 and 10, respectively. Chapter 11 describes closely related instruments, including the CBCL/2-3, Youth Self-Report (YSR), Teacher's Report Form (TRF), Semistructured Clinical Interview for Children and Adolescents (SCICA), Young Adult Behavior Checklist (YABCL), and Young Adult Self-Report (YASR). Chapter 12 provides answers to commonly asked questions. Instructions for hand scoring the 1991 CBCL/4-18 profile can be found in Appendix A, while psychometric data on the item and scale scores are displayed in Appendix B through D.

MULTIAXIAL EMPIRICALLY BASED ASSESSMENT

Parents (and parent surrogates) are typically among the most important sources of data about children's competencies and problems. They are usually the most knowledgeable about their child's behavior across time and situations. Furthermore, parental involvement is required in the evaluation of most children, and parents' views of their children's behavior are often crucial in determining what will be done about the behavior. Parents' reports should therefore be obtained in the assessment of children's competencies and problems whenever possible.

Beside parents, other sources of data are also important for the assessment of most children. For children attending school, teachers may be second only to parents as key adults in children's lives. Teachers can observe aspects of children's functioning that are not evident to parents or clinicians, and their views of a child are also influential in determining what will be done to help the child.

Direct assessment of children via observations in natural settings, clinical interviews, and structured self-reports provide additional perspectives for which we have developed empirically based scoring systems whose findings can be compared with those obtained from parent- and teacher-reports. Comprehensive assessment of children should also employ standardized tests of ability, achievement, perceptual-motor functioning, and speech-language skills, as well as relevant medical diagnostic procedures. Table 1-1 summarizes five assessment axes that are relevant to most children, although other kinds of assessment may also be feasible and relevant as well. As detailed elsewhere, the value of any one assessment procedure, such as the CBCL, can be greatly enhanced by meshing it with the other types of procedures (Achenbach, 1991a).

COMPETENCE ITEMS OF THE CBCL/4-18

Efforts to obtain professional help for a child are usually prompted by adults' concerns about the child's problems. However, the child's competencies may be

Table 1-1

Examples of Multiaxial Assessment Procedures

Approx. Age Range	Axis I Parent Reports	Axis II Teacher Reports	Axis III Cognitive Assessment	Axis IV Physical Assessment	Axis V Direct Assessment of Child
2-4	CBCL/2-3[a] CBCL/4-18 History Parent interview	Preschool records Teacher interview	Ability tests Perceptual-motor tests Language tests	Height, weight Medical exam Neurological exam	Observations during play Interview
5-11	CBCL/4-18 History Parent interview	TRF School records Teacher interview	Ability tests Achievement tests Perceptual-motor tests Language tests	Height, weight Medical exam Neurological exam	DOF[b] SCIC[c]
12-18	CBCL/4-18 History Parent interview	TRF School records Teacher interview	Ability tests Achievement tests Perceptual-motor tests	Height, weight Medical exam Neurological exam	DOF[b] YSR Clinical interview Self-concept measures Personality tests

[a]CBCL/2-3 = Child Behavior Checklist for Ages 2-3 (see McConaughy & Achenbach, 1988)
[b]DOF = Direct Observation Form (see McConaughy & Achenbach, 1988)
[c]SCIC = Semistructured Clinical Interview for Children (see McConaughy & Achenbach, 1990)

equally important in evaluating needs and prognosis. In our multiaxial assessment model, standardized tests are used to assess children's competence with respect to cognitive ability and knowledge of academic subject matter. Beside these kinds of competence, "social competence" has been widely espoused as a focus for assessment of children. However, prior to the CBCL, there had been little research to determine which competencies reportable by parents actually discriminate between children who are adapting successfully and those deemed to need help for behavioral/emotional problems.

After surveying the existing literature on assessment of competence to obtain candidate items, we pilot tested descriptions of positive characteristics in various formats. One approach was to construct bipolar scales with a problem at one end and its opposite at the other end. For example, "kind to animals" is the opposite of "cruel to animals." However, both characteristics might be true of a child: Some children are kind to some animals but cruel to others; or usually kind to a particular animal but occasionally cruel to it. A parent aware of both the kindness and cruelty would be apt to rate a bipolar item in the middle of the scale, thereby obscuring the occurrence of the opposite kinds of behavior.

For other bipolar items, both poles might represent problems. For example, the opposite of "acts too young for age" would be "acts too old for age."

For some problems, the most appropriate opposite is merely the negation of the problem. For example, the opposite of "fears going to school" is "does not fear going to school." Yet, bipolar items of this sort merely complicate the rating task without adding information about children's competencies.

A second approach is to write favorable items in the same format as the problem items but not restricted to opposites of the problem items. For example, "has a good sense of humor" is a favorable characteristic for which the negation or opposite is not necessarily a problem. We tested many items of this sort, but found that parents endorsed most of them for most children in clinical as well as nonclinical samples. This probably reflected social desirability effects, plus the fact that it is possible to think of at least *some* evidence for such characteristics in nearly all children.

A third approach is to use items of the type comprising the Vineland Social Maturity Scale (Doll, 1965; Sparrow, Cicchetti, & Balla, 1984). These items ask parents to indicate whether their child performs age-appropriate tasks, such as dressing, self-care, and making purchases at a store. Although these items are helpful for assessing the type of management needed by the retarded children for whom the Vineland Scale was primarily designed, our pilot work indicated that they did not discriminate effectively among nonretarded disturbed and nondisturbed children. Most children of normal intelligence are capable of the Vineland items designed for their chronological age level. Whether they actually demonstrate particular Vineland accomplishments may depend more on their opportunities and on their parents' behavior than on their own competence.

A fourth approach is to obtain parents' reports of the actual frequency with which their child engages in specific activities, such as a particular sport or hobby. However, because the frequency of each activity may be limited by opportunities to pursue it, the absolute frequency may not reflect a child's competence. For example, a good skier may have few opportunities for skiing. Yet, this type of competence may be at least as important as participating frequently but ineptly in neighborhood games that peers play continually.

To avoid the constraints of the foregoing approaches, we devised the items shown in Figure 1-1. Items I and II ask parents to specify the sports and nonsports activities (up

CHILD BEHAVIOR CHECKLIST FOR AGES 4–18

For office use only
ID #

CHILD'S NAME

PARENTS' USUAL TYPE OF WORK, even if not working now. *(Please be specific—for example, auto mechanic, high school teacher, homemaker, laborer, lathe operator, shoe salesman, army sergeant.)*

SEX   ☐ Boy   ☐ Girl   AGE   ETHNIC GROUP OR RACE

FATHER'S TYPE OF WORK: _____

TODAY'S DATE   Mo. _____ Date _____ Yr. _____

CHILD'S BIRTHDATE   Mo. _____ Date _____ Yr. _____

MOTHER'S TYPE OF WORK: _____

GRADE IN SCHOOL _____

NOT ATTENDING SCHOOL ☐

Please fill out this form to reflect *your* view of the child's behavior even if other people might not agree. Feel free to write additional comments beside each item and in the spaces provided on page 2.

THIS FORM FILLED OUT BY:

☐ Mother (name): _____

☐ Father (name): _____

☐ Other—name & relationship to child: _____

I. Please list the sports your child most likes to take part in. For example: swimming, baseball, skating, skate boarding, bike riding, fishing, etc.

☐ None

Compared to others of the same age, about how much time does he/she spend in each?

Compared to others of the same age, how well does he/she do each one?

	Don't Know	Less Than Average	Average	More Than Average		Don't Know	Below Average	Average	Above Average
a. _____	☐	☐	☐	☐		☐	☐	☐	☐
b. _____	☐	☐	☐	☐		☐	☐	☐	☐
c. _____	☐	☐	☐	☐		☐	☐	☐	☐

II. Please list your child's favorite hobbies, activities, and games, other than sports. For example: stamps, dolls, books, piano, crafts, cars, singing, etc. (Do **not** include listening to radio or TV.)

☐ None

Compared to others of the same age, about how much time does he/she spend in each?

Compared to others of the same age, how well does he/she do each one?

	Don't Know	Less Than Average	Average	More Than Average		Don't Know	Below Average	Average	Above Average
a. _____	☐	☐	☐	☐		☐	☐	☐	☐
b. _____	☐	☐	☐	☐		☐	☐	☐	☐
c. _____	☐	☐	☐	☐		☐	☐	☐	☐

III. Please list any organizations, clubs, teams, or groups your child belongs to.

☐ None

Compared to others of the same age, how active is he/she in each?

	Don't Know	Less Active	Average	More Active
a. _____	☐	☐	☐	☐
b. _____	☐	☐	☐	☐
c. _____	☐	☐	☐	☐

IV. Please list any jobs or chores your child has. For example: paper route, babysitting, making bed, working in store, etc. (Include **both** paid and unpaid jobs and chores.)

☐ None

Compared to others of the same age, how well does he/she carry them out?

	Don't Know	Below Average	Average	Above Average
a. _____	☐	☐	☐	☐
b. _____	☐	☐	☐	☐
c. _____	☐	☐	☐	☐

Figure 1-1. Competence Items I-IV of the CBCL/4-18.

V.   1. About how many close friends does your child have? ☐ None ☐ 1 ☐ 2 or 3 ☐ 4 or more
(Do not include brothers & sisters)

     2. About how many times a week does your child do things with any friends outside of regular school hours?
(Do not include brothers & sisters) ☐ Less than 1 ☐ 1 or 2 ☐ 3 or more

VI.   Compared to others of his/her age, how well does your child:

		Worse	About Average	Better	
a.	Get along with his/her brothers & sisters?	☐	☐	☐	☐ Has no brothers or sisters
b.	Get along with other kids?	☐	☐	☐	
c.	Behave with his/her parents?	☐	☐	☐	
d.	Play and work by himself/herself?	☐	☐	☐	

VII.   1. For ages 6 and older — performance in academic subjects: (If child is not being taught, please give reason)

        Not being taught because _____

	Failing	Below average	Average	Above average
a. Reading, English, or Language Arts	☐	☐	☐	☐
b. History or Social Studies	☐	☐	☐	☐
c. Arithmetic or Math	☐	☐	☐	☐
d. Science	☐	☐	☐	☐
e. _____	☐	☐	☐	☐
f. _____	☐	☐	☐	☐
g. _____	☐	☐	☐	☐

Other academic subjects — for example: computer courses, foreign language, business. Do **not** include gym, shop, driver's ed., etc.

     2. Is your child in a special class or special school? ☐ No   ☐ Yes — what kind of class or school?

     3. Has your child repeated a grade? ☐ No   ☐ Yes — grade and reason

     4. Has your child had any academic or other problems in school? ☐ No   ☐ Yes — please describe

       When did these problems start?

       Have these problems ended? ☐ No ☐ Yes — when?

Does your child have any illness, physical disability, or mental handicap? ☐ No   ☐ Yes — please describe

What concerns you most about your child?

Please describe the best things about your child:

Figure 1-1 (cont.). Competence Items V-VII of the CBCL/4-18.

to three each) that their child most likes to take part in. To estimate the quality and amount of the child's involvement in each activity, adjusted for peer group norms as perceived by the parents, parents are asked to indicate how much time the child spends in each and how well the child performs each one, as compared to others of the same age.

To score the amount and quality of participation independently of the sheer number of activities listed, one score is assigned for the *number* of activities, while a second score is computed for the mean of the *ratings* of amount and quality of participation. As a result, a child who likes only one sport, for example, gets a low score for number of sports, but can nevertheless get a high score for participating more often or more effectively in that sport than peers do. Similar principles apply to scoring the child's involvement in organizations (Item III), jobs and chores (Item IV), and friendships (Item V).

Item VI requests the parent's rating of how well the child gets along with siblings, peers, and parents, and how well the child plays and works alone. For Item VII, parents are to rate the child's performance in academic subjects and to indicate whether the child is in a special class or school, has repeated a grade, and has other school problems. Responses to items I-VII are scored on the competence scales of the profile described in Chapter 2.

Following the competence items on page 2 of the CBCL, as shown in Figure 1-1, unnumbered open-ended items request information on illnesses and handicaps, what concerns the parent most about the child, and the best things about the child. These items are designed to obtain information that may be more useful in open-ended than structured form. They are not scored on the profile.

PROBLEM ITEMS OF THE CBCL/4-18

To develop standardized procedures for assessing behavioral/emotional problems, we started with descriptions of problems that are of concern to parents and mental health professionals. These descriptions were derived from our earlier studies (Achenbach, 1966; Achenbach & Lewis, 1971), the clinical and research literature, and consultation with clinical and developmental psychologists, child psychiatrists, and psychiatric social workers.

We then pilot tested draft versions of the descriptions, instructions, and response scales with parents of children being evaluated in three guidance clinics in Connecticut. To improve the items, successive drafts of the instrument were discussed with parents and mental health workers and paraprofessionals who interviewed them. Parents were also asked to add items that were not already included in the draft instrument. We used this feedback in conjunction with analyses of response distributions to improve the item pool.

After successive revisions of pilot editions used in several clinical settings, we finalized the 118 problem items shown in Figure 1-2. To permit parents to include items not listed, we provided spaces for *other physical problems without known medical cause* (Item 56h) and *any problems your child has that were not listed above* (Item 113). Note that items are numbered 1-113, but that Item 56 includes physical problems *a* through *g*. The total number of specific problems listed is thus 118, plus space for "other physical problems" (Item 56h) and "any problems your child has that were not listed" (Item 113).

Items 2. *Allergy* and 4. *Asthma* are not counted toward the total problem score in the 1991 profile, because they did not discriminate significantly between clinically referred and nonreferred samples. If a parent circled 2 for the

Below is a list of items that describe children and youth. For each item that describes your child **now or within the past 6 months**, please circle the **2** if the item is **very true** or **often true** of your child. Circle the **1** if the item is **somewhat** or **sometimes true** of your child. If the item is **not true** of your child, circle the 0. Please answer all items as well as you can, even if some do not seem to apply to your child.

0 = Not True (as far as you know)　　　　1 = Somewhat or Sometimes True　　　　2 = Very True or Often True

0 1 2	1.	Acts too young for his/her age	
0 1 2	2.	Allergy (describe): _____	
		_____	
0 1 2	3.	Argues a lot	
0 1 2	4.	Asthma	
0 1 2	5.	Behaves like opposite sex	
0 1 2	6.	Bowel movements outside toilet	
0 1 2	7.	Bragging, boasting	
0 1 2	8.	Can't concentrate, can't pay attention for long	
0 1 2	9.	Can't get his/her mind off certain thoughts; obsessions (describe): _____	
0 1 2	10.	Can't sit still, restless, or hyperactive	
0 1 2	11.	Clings to adults or too dependent	
0 1 2	12.	Complains of loneliness	
0 1 2	13.	Confused or seems to be in a fog	
0 1 2	14.	Cries a lot	
0 1 2	15.	Cruel to animals	
0 1 2	16.	Cruelty, bullying, or meanness to others	
0 1 2	17.	Day-dreams or gets lost in his/her thoughts	
0 1 2	18.	Deliberately harms self or attempts suicide	
0 1 2	19.	Demands a lot of attention	
0 1 2	20.	Destroys his/her own things	
0 1 2	21.	Destroys things belonging to his/her family or others	
0 1 2	22.	Disobedient at home	
0 1 2	23.	Disobedient at school	
0 1 2	24.	Doesn't eat well	
0 1 2	25.	Doesn't get along with other kids	
0 1 2	26.	Doesn't seem to feel guilty after misbehaving	
0 1 2	27.	Easily jealous	
0 1 2	28.	Eats or drinks things that are not food— **don't** include sweets (describe): _____	
		_____	
0 1 2	29.	Fears certain animals, situations, or places, other than school (describe): _____	
		_____	
0 1 2	30.	Fears going to school	

0 1 2	31.	Fears he/she might think or do something bad
0 1 2	32.	Feels he/she has to be perfect
0 1 2	33.	Feels or complains that no one loves him/her
0 1 2	34.	Feels others are out to get him/her
0 1 2	35.	Feels worthless or inferior
0 1 2	36.	Gets hurt a lot, accident-prone
0 1 2	37.	Gets in many fights
0 1 2	38.	Gets teased a lot
0 1 2	39.	Hangs around with others who get in trouble
0 1 2	40.	Hears sounds or voices that aren't there (describe): _____
		_____
0 1 2	41.	Impulsive or acts without thinking
0 1 2	42.	Would rather be alone than with others
0 1 2	43.	Lying or cheating
0 1 2	44.	Bites fingernails
0 1 2	45.	Nervous, highstrung, or tense
0 1 2	46.	Nervous movements or twitching (describe):
		_____
0 1 2	47.	Nightmares
0 1 2	48.	Not liked by other kids
0 1 2	49.	Constipated, doesn't move bowels
0 1 2	50.	Too fearful or anxious
0 1 2	51.	Feels dizzy
0 1 2	52.	Feels too guilty
0 1 2	53.	Overeating
0 1 2	54.	Overtired
0 1 2	55.	Overweight
	56.	Physical problems without known medical cause:
0 1 2	a.	Aches or pains (**not** headaches)
0 1 2	b.	Headaches
0 1 2	c.	Nausea, feels sick
0 1 2	d.	Problems with eyes (describe): _____
0 1 2	e.	Rashes or other skin problems
0 1 2	f.	Stomachaches or cramps
0 1 2	g.	Vomiting, throwing up
0 1 2	h.	Other (describe): _____

Please see other side

Figure 1-2. Problem Items 1-56h of the CBCL/4-18.

0 = Not True (as far as you know)   1 = Somewhat or Sometimes True   2 = Very True or Often True

0 1 2	57.	Physically attacks people	0 1 2	84. Strange behavior (describe):_____
0 1 2	58.	Picks nose, skin, or other parts of body (describe): _____		_____
			0 1 2	85. Strange ideas (describe):_____
0 1 2	59.	Plays with own sex parts in public		_____
0 1 2	60.	Plays with own sex parts too much	0 1 2	86. Stubborn, sullen, or irritable
0 1 2	61.	Poor school work	0 1 2	87. Sudden changes in mood or feelings
0 1 2	62.	Poorly coordinated or clumsy	0 1 2	88. Sulks a lot
0 1 2	63.	Prefers being with older kids	0 1 2	89. Suspicious
0 1 2	64.	Prefers being with younger kids	0 1 2	90. Swearing or obscene language
0 1 2	65.	Refuses to talk	0 1 2	91. Talks about killing self
0 1 2	66.	Repeats certain acts over and over; compulsions (describe): _____	0 1 2	92. Talks or walks in sleep (describe): _____
				_____
			0 1 2	93. Talks too much
0 1 2	67.	Runs away from home	0 1 2	94. Teases a lot
0 1 2	68.	Screams a lot		
			0 1 2	95. Temper tantrums or hot temper
0 1 2	69.	Secretive, keeps things to self	0 1 2	96. Thinks about sex too much
0 1 2	70.	Sees things that aren't there (describe):		
			0 1 2	97. Threatens people
			0 1 2	98. Thumb-sucking
		_____	0 1 2	99. Too concerned with neatness or cleanliness
			0 1 2	100. Trouble sleeping (describe):_____
0 1 2	71.	Self-conscious or easily embarrassed		
0 1 2	72.	Sets fires		_____
0 1 2	73.	Sexual problems (describe):_____	0 1 2	101. Truancy, skips school
			0 1 2	102. Underactive, slow moving, or lacks energy
		_____	0 1 2	103. Unhappy, sad, or depressed
			0 1 2	104. Unusually loud
0 1 2	74.	Showing off or clowning	0 1 2	105. Uses alcohol or drugs for nonmedical purposes (describe): _____
0 1 2	75.	Shy or timid		
0 1 2	76.	Sleeps less than most kids		_____
0 1 2	77.	Sleeps more than most kids during day and/or night (describe): _____	0 1 2	106. Vandalism
			0 1 2	107. Wets self during the day
			0 1 2	108. Wets the bed
		_____	0 1 2	109. Whining
0 1 2	78.	Smears or plays with bowel movements	0 1 2	110. Wishes to be of opposite sex
0 1 2	79.	Speech problem (describe): _____	0 1 2	111. Withdrawn, doesn't get involved with others
			0 1 2	112. Worries
0 1 2	80.	Stares blankly		113. Please write in any problems your child has that were not listed above:
0 1 2	81.	Steals at home		
0 1 2	82.	Steals outside the home	0 1 2	_____
0 1 2	83.	Stores up things he/she doesn't need (describe): _____	0 1 2	_____
			0 1 2	_____

PLEASE BE SURE YOU HAVE ANSWERED ALL ITEMS.   PAGE 4   UNDERLINE ANY YOU ARE CONCERNED ABOUT.

Figure 1-2 (cont.). Problem Items 57-113 of the CBCL/4-18.

remaining 116 specific problem items and 2 for problems entered by the parent on Items 56h and 113, the total problem score would be 118 x 2 = 236.

The final list of items includes a broad range of problems that are reportable by parents. We tried to avoid redundancy among items, because we wished to prevent the artifactual correlations that arise when two or more items reflect the same problem.

For several items, we found that having the parent describe the behavior could help to avoid improperly scoring a problem that did not really fit the item or that should be scored elsewhere. An example is Item *46. Nervous movements or twitching (describe)*. We found that some parents scored this as present to reflect difficulty in sitting still. Because this behavior is more specifically covered by Item *10. Can't sit still, restless, or hyperactive,* we wished to avoid having the two items scored for the same problem. Item *46* therefore requests a description of the specific behavior. As indicated in the scoring instructions (Appendix A), a report of difficulty sitting still should be scored only on Item 10. As another example, for Item *66. Repeats certain acts over and over; compulsions (describe)*, descriptions such as "Won't take no for an answer" or "Keeps hitting brother" would not justify scoring compulsions as present. Appendix A provides guidelines for scoring the open-ended questions.

Descriptions are also clinically helpful on items that can include a broad range of deviant behavior. For example, the descriptions requested on Items *84. Strange behavior* and *85. Strange ideas* are helpful in clarifying what the parent has in mind. Where parents' descriptions indicate that they have scored an item inappropriately or scored more than one item for a particular behavior, only the item that most precisely describes the behavior is to be counted, as indicated in Appendix A.

Response Scale for Problem Items

A three-step response scale (0, 1, 2) was chosen because it is typically easier than a *present/absent* scale for most untrained raters. For each item that describes the child currently or within the last 6 months, parents are to circle the *2* if the item is *very true or often true* of their child; the *1* if the item is *somewhat or sometimes true* of their child; and the *0* if the item is *not true* of their child. The score of *1* can be used when mild or ambiguous instances of a problem would make a forced choice between present and absent difficult.

More finely differentiated response scales were rejected because fine gradations in problems are unlikely to be captured by a questionnaire. Furthermore, research has shown that more differentiated scales for scoring problem items are vulnerable to respondent characteristics that reduce the discriminative power of items below that obtained with the three-step scales (Achenbach, Howell, Quay, & Conners, 1991). In addition, multicategory response scales have not been found to increase the differentiation of syndromes empirically derived from ratings of behavioral/emotional problems (Achenbach & Edelbrock, 1978).

ADMINISTRATION OF THE CBCL/4-18

The CBCL can be filled out by most parents who have at least fifth grade reading skills. Some parents can complete it in as little as 10 minutes, although 15 to 17 minutes is more typical. If there is a question about a parent's reading skills or other problems in independently completing the CBCL, the following method of administration is suggested: An interviewer hands the parent a copy of the CBCL while retaining a second copy. The interviewer says, "I'll read you the questions on this form and I'll write down your answers." Parents who can read will usually start answering the questions without waiting for them to be read, but this procedure avoids the embarrassment or errors that may arise if a parent cannot read well. Even for parents who cannot read well, having the CBCL in front of them enables them to see the format of the questions to be asked in the same way as for parents who complete the form independently. For parents who do not speak English, there are translations into the languages listed in Chapter 10.

Parents who fill out the CBCL independently should have the opportunity to ask for clarification of items by a person familiar with the CBCL. If a parent requests clarification, the parent's questions should be answered as factually as possible, rather than being used as an opportunity to probe the parent's psyche. The emphasis should be on helping the parent use the items to describe the child's behavior as accurately as possible, with the addition of written comments as needed.

SUMMARY

The present revision of the *Manual for the Child Behavior Checklist* is necessitated by changes in the 1991 profile for scoring the CBCL, new national norms through age 18, and new provisions for coordinating data from parent-, self-, and teacher-reports. Pre-1991 editions of the CBCL — designated as the CBCL/4-16 — can be scored on the 1991 edition of the profile. Conversely, the 1991 edition of the CBCL — designated as the CBCL/4-18 — can be scored on pre-1991 editions of the profile, except that pre-1991 editions do not include norms for ages 17 and 18.

The CBCL is intended to serve as one component of *multiaxial empirically based assessment.* Other components include teacher reports, standardized tests, physical assessment, and direct assessment of the child, such as observations, interviews, and structured self-reports.

The CBCL is designed to record in a standardized format children's competencies and problems as reported by their parents or parent surrogates. It can be self-administered or administered by an interviewer. The 20 competence items obtain parents' reports of the amount and quality of their child's participation in sports, hobbies, games, activities, jobs and chores, and friendships; how well the child gets along with others and plays and works alone; and school functioning. Each of the 118 specific problem items and two open-ended problem items is scored on a 3-step response scale.

Chapter 2
Competence Scales

Prior to the CBCL, there had been little research to determine which competencies reportable by parents discriminate between children who are adapting successfully versus children needing help for behavioral/emotional problems. Chapter 1 described our efforts to develop standardized competence items that would discriminate significantly between children referred for mental health services and nonreferred children. The analyses performed to test the discriminative power of each CBCL competence item are reported in Chapter 7. In this chapter, we describe the competence scales that were constructed from the items that appear on pages 1 and 2 of the CBCL, as shown in Figure 1-1.

Because few 4- and 5-year-olds are in regular school situations where academic performance is evaluated, the school items are not scored for these ages. Furthermore, preliminary analyses of covariance (ANCOVA) — reported in Chapter 7 — indicated that differences between referred and nonreferred children on the other competence items were much smaller at ages 4-5 than at older ages. This is partly due to "floor effects" on some items, whereby the number of sports, organizations, and jobs or chores was too low at ages 4-5 to show much difference between referred and nonreferred children. Because many of the competence items did not discriminate well in the current samples of 4- and 5-year-olds, and because the school items are not scored at all for 4-5-year-olds, we have not normed the 1991 CBCL competence scales for ages 4 and 5. However, scores obtained by 4- and 5-year-olds for the individual

17

competence items can be entered on the hand-scored profile and are automatically computed by the computer-scoring program.

The analyses reported in Chapter 7 revealed that the number of nonsports activities scored from Item II yielded equal mean scores of 1.1 for referred and nonreferred children. The number of nonsports activities is therefore omitted from the Activities and total competence scales of the 1991 CBCL profile. As detailed in Chapter 7, all other competence items showed significantly (p <.01) higher scores for nonreferred than for referred children. These items are therefore included in the Activities, Social, and School scales. The scales are scored like those of the pre-1991 CBCL profile (Achenbach & Edelbrock, 1983), except that the number of nonsports activities is not counted and is displayed separately beneath the scales.

The nature of the competence items makes them less appropriate than our problem items for deriving scales through principal components analysis, as described for the problem items in Chapter 3. This is because scores on some competence items depend partly on other items. On items pertaining to sports, nonsports activities, organizations, and jobs and chores, for example, parents can rate the amount and quality of their child's participation only if they also report that the child participates in the specified type of activity.

The scoring rules are designed to minimize artifactual correlations between the *number* of activities of a particular type and *ratings* of quality and amount of participation. For example, a child reported to like one sport gets the same score (0) as a child reported to like no sports. However, only the child who likes at least one sport can get a score above 0 for amount and quality of participation. Thus, a score of 0 for number of sports can be accompanied either by a score of 0 or by a score above 0 for amount and quality of participation. Furthermore, because scores for amount and quality of participation are averaged over all sports reported, these scores do not automatically increase as the number of sports increases. Nevertheless, it would hardly make sense to use multivariate analyses to find out which of these intrinsically interdependent scores covary to form syndromes as was done with the problem items. Instead, we grouped items into three scales designated as *Activities*, *Social*, and *School* on the basis of their content.

Items are scored according to the instructions provided in Appendix A. The items of each scale are summed to yield a total raw score for that scale. If data are missing for one item of the Activities or Social scale, the mean of the other items of the scale is substituted for the missing item on that scale. However, if data are missing for any of the four items of the School scale, a total score should not be calculated for this scale. The total competence score is the sum of the raw scores for the Activities, Social, and School scales. It is scored only if raw scale scores were obtained from all three scales. This requires that no more than one item be missing for the Activities and Social scales and no items are missing from the School scale.

NORMING THE COMPETENCE SCALES

Normative data for the CBCL competence scales were drawn from a subset of nonhandicapped subjects in a national sample assessed in the spring of 1989. Details of the procedure for obtaining data on the 7- to 18-year-olds in the sample have been provided by McConaughy, Stanger, and Achenbach (1991). These subjects were chosen to be representative of the 48 contiguous states with respect to SES, ethnicity, region, and urban-suburban-rural residence. The data were obtained in a home interview survey. The interviewer handed the parent or parent-surrogate a copy of the CBCL and then read the CBCL items aloud and wrote down the respondent's answers on a second copy of the CBCL. After the CBCL, the interviewer asked questions about the subject's mental health and special education history, plus a variety of family variables (McConaughy et al., 1991).

Data for the 4- to 6-year-olds were obtained under a separate contract by identifying households in the survey that were occupied by children in this age range, in addition to the initial 7- to 18-year-old subject. If there was more than one nonhandicapped 4- to 6-year-old in the household, the interviewer selected the one whose birthday would occur next. An English-speaking parent or parent-surrogate of the 4- to 6-year-old (not always the same respondent as for the 7- to 18-year-old) was then asked to respond to the CBCL in the same manner as done for the older subjects. Of the 420 eligible 4- to 6-year-olds for whom CBCLs were sought, completed CBCLs were obtained for 398 (94.8%).

The 7- to 18-year-old subjects were drawn from a sample originally assessed in 1986, when a 92.1% completion rate was obtained. In the 1989 follow-up, CBCLs were completed for 90.2% of the 1986 subjects. Multiplying the 90.2% 1989 completion rate by the 92.1% 1986 completion rate yields an overall rate of 83.1% for completed assessments of subjects who had been targeted in the 1986 sample.

A normative sample of children was constructed by drawing from the pool of 4- to 18-year-olds all those who had not received mental health services or special remedial school classes within the preceding 12 months. This was done to provide a normative sample of children who were considered to be "healthy" in the sense that they had not recently received professional help for behavioral/emotional problems. This criterion may, of course, fail to exclude children who have significant problems that have not received professional attention for various reasons, including a lack of parental concern. On the other hand, the exclusion criterion of referral for help may inadvertently exclude children who do not have significant problems but whose parents might be overconcerned. Both these types of errors would reduce our ability to identify items and scale scores that discriminate between "healthy" and "disturbed" children.

Despite the inevitable error variance in our definitions of both "healthy" and "disturbed" children, most CBCL scale and item scores discriminated very well between referred and nonreferred children, as documented in Chapters 6 and 7. If a more accurate criterion of truly "healthy" versus truly "disturbed" could be applied in large representative samples like ours, still better discrimination might be found. However, as detailed elsewhere (Achenbach & Edelbrock, 1981), other criteria for distinguishing between normal and deviant children have not functioned better than referral status.

In our previous work, we used referral for mental health services as the criterion for distinguishing between referred and nonreferred children. In our current work, we added special education classes for behavioral/emotional problems to the criterion, because Public Law 94-142 (Education of the Handicapped Act, 1977, 1981) now mandates that schools provide special services for children having significant behavioral/emotional problems. As schools have assumed greater responsibility for providing such services, the schools have become primary sites for evaluating and dealing with problems that would previously have been candidates for mental health services outside of school.

Table 2-1 summarizes the demographic characteristics of the 4- to 18-year-olds who comprised the CBCL normative samples, after excluding those who had received mental health or special education classes during the previous 12 months. Note that all 4- and 5-year-olds were omitted from the competence scale norms as a result of the findings

Table 2-1
Demographic Distributions of CBCL
Normative Sample

		Boys		Girls		
		4-11	12-18	4-11	12-18	Combined[d]
	N =	581[b]	564	619[c]	604	2,368
SES[a]						
	Upper	35%	34%	39%	35%	36%
	Middle	47	44	44	44	45
	Lower	18	22	18	21	20
	Mean Score	5.6	5.4	5.7	5.5	5.5
	S.D. of Score	2.1	2.2	2.2	2.2	2.2
Ethnicity						
	White	73	72	74	74	73
	Black	15	17	17	16	16
	Hispanic	7	8	7	7	7
	Other	4	4	2	3	3
Region						
	Northeast	23	22	22	22	23
	North Central	27	27	26	28	27
	South	31	33	31	33	32
	West	20	18	21	18	19
CBCL Respondent						
	Mother	80	81	85	82	82
	Father	17	16	13	15	15
	Other	3	3	3	3	3

[a]Hollingshead (1975) 9-step scale for parental occupation, using the higher status occupation if both parents were wage earners; score 1-3.5 = lower; 4-6.5 = middle; 7-9 = upper. If occupational level was unclear, the mean of the two most likely scores was used, resulting in some half-step scores, such as 3.5.

[b]Competence scale norms exclude 123 4-5-year-old boys.

[c]Competence scale norms exclude 129 4-5-year-old girls.

[d]Scores for the combined samples are unweighted means of the 4 sex/age groups.

presented in Chapter 7. However, they were included in the norms for the problem scales reported in Chapter 3.

ASSIGNMENT OF PERCENTILES AND T SCORES TO COMPETENCE SCALES

Activities, Social, and School Scale Scores

Figure 2-1 illustrates the competence portion of the hand-scored 1991 CBCL profile for 8-year-old Jenny. As can be seen in Figure 2-1, percentiles are displayed on the left side of the competence profile and T scores are displayed on the right side. The percentiles enable the user to compare a child's raw score on each competence scale shown in the columns of the graphic display with percentiles for the normative samples of the child's sex and age range. The T scores, which are automatically calculated by the computer-scoring program, provide a metric that is similar for all scales. The remainder of this section can be skipped by readers uninterested in how T scores were assigned. The intervals on the left side of the profile encompass differing numbers of percentiles in order to correctly correspond to the T score intervals on the right side of the profile. (Chapter 10 discusses the use of raw scores versus T scores for statistical purposes.)

The percentiles indicated on the 1991 profile were derived according to a procedure designed to produce smoother, more normal distributions of percentile scores than were generated for the pre-1991 versions of the profile. According to this procedure, a raw score that falls at a particular percentile of the cumulative frequency distribution is assumed to span all the next lower percentiles down to the percentile occupied by the next lower raw score in the distribution (Crocker & Algina, 1986). To represent

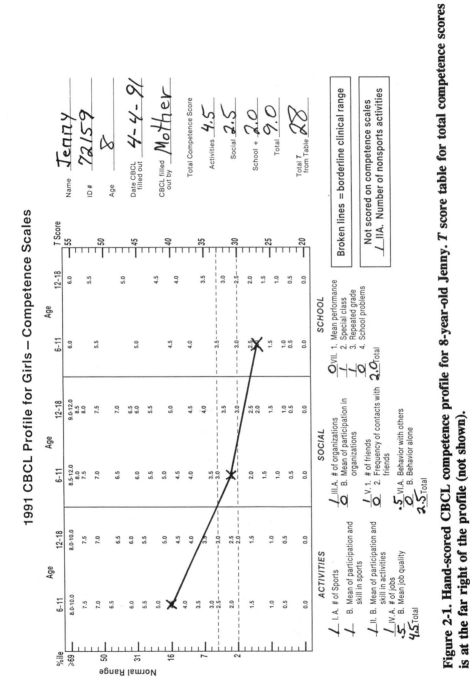

Figure 2-1. Hand-scored CBCL competence profile for 8-year-old Jenny. T score table for total competence scores is at the far right of the profile (not shown).

this span of percentiles, each raw score is assigned to the midpoint of the percentiles that it spans.

As an example, 13.2% of 6- to 11-year-old girls obtained a raw score of 4.0 or lower on the Activities scale of the profile shown in Figure 2-1. The next higher raw score, 4.5, was obtained by 4.2% of the girls. The *cumulative percent* of girls obtaining a raw score of 4.0 or lower was thus 13.2%, while the cumulative percent obtaining a raw score of 4.5 or lower was 13.2% + 4.2% = 17.4%. The interval from raw score 4.0 to raw score 4.5 thus spanned from a cumulative percent of 13.2% to a cumulative percent of 17.4%. To represent this interval in terms of a percentile at the midpoint of the interval, we took the cumulative percent at the top of the interval (17.4%) and subtracted the cumulative percent at the bottom of the interval (13.2%), i.e., 17.4% minus 13.2% = 4.2%. To obtain the midpoint, we then divided this difference in half and added it to the lower percent, i.e., 13.2 + 2.1 = 15.3. This corresponds to the following formula provided by Crocker and Algina (1986, p. 439):

$$P = \frac{cf_l + .5(f_i)}{N} \text{ X } 100\%$$

where P = percentile; cf_l is the cumulative frequency for all scores lower than the score of interest; f_i is the frequency of scores in the interval of interest; and N is the number in the sample.

After obtaining the midpoint percentile in this way, we used the procedure provided by Abramowitz and Stegun (1968) to assign a normalized T score of 40 to the 15.3rd percentile for the raw score of 4.5. In Figure 2-1, the raw score of 4.5 is therefore on the same line as the T score of 40 listed on the right side of the profile.

The main effect of using the midpoint percentile rather than the cumulative percentile on the syndrome scales was to provide a smoother, less skewed, and more differentiated basis for T scores.

The raw scores of the CBCL competence scales were *negatively skewed* in the normative samples. That is, a large proportion of nonreferred children received relatively high competence scores. Furthermore, *low* scores are clinically significant on the competence scales. To take account of the negatively skewed distributions and the need for finer differentiation between low scores than between high scores on the competence scales, we assigned T scores to the competence scales in the following ways:

1. At the top of each competence scale, we assigned a T score of 55 to all raw scores at the 69th percentile and above. We did this because a large percent of the subjects in our CBCL normative samples obtained the highest possible score on the School scale. This meant that a very small difference in raw scores (5.5 versus 6.0) could produce a disproportionately large difference in T scores. Furthermore, differences at the *high* end of the competence scales are unlikely to be important, since they are all well within the normal range.

2. At the low end of the scales, we based T scores on percentiles down to the second percentile (T score = 30). We then divided the remaining raw scores into equal T score intervals down to a T score of 20. Because there are not many raw scores below the second percentile of the competence scales, we assigned the low competence scores a range of only 10 T scores (29 through 20). Broken lines at T scores of 30 and 33 demarcate a borderline clinical range that spans from about the second to the fifth percentile of the normative sample. This range was chosen to approximate the same degree of deviance

from the middle of the normative sample as is represented by the borderline clinical range from $T = 67$ to $T = 70$ for the syndrome scales described in Chapter 3. The borderlines were chosen to provide efficient discrimination between demographically matched referred and nonreferred samples (described in Chapter 6), while minimizing the number of "false positives," i.e., normal children who score in the clinical range. If maximum discrimination is sought between deviant and nondeviant children without regard to the increase in false positives, cutpoints above $T = 33$ on the competence scales may improve discrimination in some samples.

Looking again at Jenny's profile in Figure 2-1, you can see that Jenny obtained a raw score of 2.5 on the Social scale. The left side of the profile shows that a raw score of 2.5 on the Social scale falls just above the 2nd percentile for 6-11-year-old girls. As shown on the right side of the profile, this is equivalent to a T score of 31. Because T scores from 30 to 33 are within the borderline clinical range demarcated by the broken lines on the profile, Jenny's score is low enough to be of concern, although it is not below $T = 30$, where deviance is indicated with more certainty. On the School scale, Jenny's raw score of 2.0 is well below the 2nd percentile and T score of 30, indicating considerable evidence for poor functioning in school, as compared to a normative sample of 6-11-year-old girls.

Total Competence Score

The CBCL total competence score is the sum of raw scale scores from the Activities, Social, and School scales. If any of the competence scale scores is missing, the total competence score is not computed.

Percentiles and T scores were assigned to the CBCL total competence score in the same way as done for the scores of the competence scales, except that *(a)* the top end of the total competence scale was not truncated at a T score of 55, and *(b)* T scores below 30 were assigned in equal intervals down to 10 instead of 20. Midpoint percentiles for the raw total competence score were computed in the manner described previously for the competence scales. Normalized T scores were then assigned from the 2nd percentile ($T = 30$) to the highest possible raw score, which was assigned a T score of 80. Raw scores below the second percentile were divided into equal intervals for assignment to T scores from 10 through 29. On the hand-scored profile, a table to the right of the graphic display lists the T score for each possible raw score. The computer-scoring program automatically computes the T score for the total competence score. T scores below 37 are considered to be clearly in the clinical range, whereas T scores from 37 to 40 are in the borderline clinical range. The borderline clinical range is indicated by broken lines in the box to the right of the hand-scored profile. The computer-scored profile displays a + with total competence scores that are in the borderline range and ++ with scores that are in the clinical range.

Table 2-2 presents the mean, standard deviation, and standard error of the raw scores and T scores obtained by our normative samples on each competence scale. Because of the skewed distributions, truncation of high T scores at $T = 55$, and assignment of low T scores in equal intervals, the mean T scores of the competence scales are below 50 and their standard deviations are less than 10. However, the mean of the total competence score is close to 50 and its standard deviation is close to 10 for all four groups shown in Table 2-2. The distributions would differ in clinical samples, of course. Appendix B presents the

Table 2-2
Competence Scale Scores for CBCL Normative Samples

Scale	Boys 6-11	Boys 12-18	Girls 6-11	Girls 12-18
N^b =	458	564	488	604
Activities				
Raw Score				
Mean	6.4	6.6	6.4	6.5
SD	1.7	1.7	1.8	1.8
SE[a]	.1	.1	.1	.1
T score				
Mean	48.0	47.7	47.8	47.8
SD	7.1	7.3	7.3	7.3
SE[a]	.3	.3	.3	.3
Social				
Raw Score				
Mean	6.9	7.5	6.9	7.3
SD	2.0	2.0	2.1	2.2
SE[a]	.1	.1	.1	.1
T score				
Mean	48.0	48.1	48.1	48.1
SD	7.3	7.2	7.2	7.2
SE[a]	.4	.3	.3	.3
School				
Raw Score				
Mean	5.1	4.8	5.3	5.1
SD	.9	1.1	.8	.9
SE[a]	.0	.0	.0	.0
T score				
Mean	48.4	48.3	48.4	48.3
SD	7.1	6.7	6.9	7.2
SE[a]	.3	.3	.3	.3
Total Competence				
Raw Score				
Mean	18.6	19.0	18.7	19.1
SD	3.3	3.5	3.6	3.6
SE[a]	.2	.2	.2	.2
T score				
Mean	50.3	50.3	50.2	50.4
SD	9.6	9.7	9.8	9.8
SE[a]	.5	.5	.5	.4

[a]SE = standard error of the mean. [b]Ns vary because of missing data for some scales; e.g., children not attending school would not have School scale or Total Competence scores because they lacked school data.

corresponding data for the competence scales in demographically matched referred and nonreferred samples.

SUMMARY

Scales entitled Activities, Social, and School are provided for scoring the competence items on pages 1 and 2 of the CBCL/4-18. The total competence score comprises the sum of the three scale scores. The competence scales are not scored for 4-5-year-olds, because children of these ages are seldom in school situations where academic performance is evaluated. Furthermore, the other competence items were not found to discriminate well between referred and nonreferred 4- and 5-year-old children. Because the number of nonsports activities did not discriminate between referred and nonreferred 6- to 18-year-olds either, this item is not scored in the 1991 competence scales.

The procedures for assigning percentiles and T scores to the 1991 scale scores were detailed and illustrated on the competence portion of the 1991 CBCL profile. The normative samples for the 1991 CBCL profile scales were described and their mean raw and T scores for each scale were presented.

Chapter 3
Syndrome and Total Problem Scales

Beside describing children in terms of many specific items, the CBCL is also designed to identify syndromes of problems that tend to occur together. In fact, a primary reason for developing the CBCL was to provide an empirical foundation for identifying syndromes from which to construct a taxonomy of childhood disorders. The word *syndrome* refers to problems that tend to occur together, without implying any particular model for the nature or causes of disorders. Rather than imposing *a priori* assumptions about what syndromes exist, we derived syndromes quantitatively from CBCL problem items scored for clinically referred children by their parents. (Findings for pre-1991 editions of the CBCL profile have been reported by Achenbach, 1978, and by Achenbach & Edelbrock, 1979, 1983.)

To derive the syndromes, we applied principal components analyses to the correlations among items. Like factor analysis, principal components analysis is used to identify groups of items whose scores covary with each other. However, in factor analysis, the obtained correlations among items are reduced to reflect only the variance each item has in common with all other items. The estimate of the item's "communality" (the variance it has in common with all other items) typically consists of the square of the item's multiple correlation with all other items. In principal components analysis, by contrast, the obtained correlation of each item with each other item is taken at face value rather than being reduced according to an estimate of communality.

Because we wanted to focus on the associations that were actually obtained among items in large samples, we did not want the associations among particular items to be differentially reduced by the degree to which the items happened to correlate with all other items. When the number of items is as large as we used, the results of principal components analyses are generally similar to the results of principal factor analyses in any event (Gorsuch, 1983).

PRE-1991 SYNDROMES

To reflect possible sex and age differences in the prevalence and patterning of problems, we performed separate principal components analyses for each sex within particular age ranges. For the pre-1991 editions of the profiles, the age ranges were 4 to 5, 6 to 11, and 12 to 16. We analyzed all items that were reported to be present for at least 5% of a clinical sample of a particular sex and age. This number ranged from 111 to 114 items for the six sex/age groups.

We applied orthogonal (varimax) and oblique (direct quartimin) rotations to the largest 7 to 15 components obtained for each sex/age group. We then compared all the orthogonal and oblique rotations within each sex/age group to identify sets of problems that tended to remain together in most of the analyses. Next, we chose the rotation that included the most representative sets of problem items found for a particular sex/age group. These items formed the basis for the syndrome scales for that sex/age group. Note that the pre-1991 syndrome scales for each sex/age group were based directly on the rotated components for that sex/age group alone, whether or not similar syndromes were found for other sex/age groups. Analogous procedures were followed in developing the pre-1991 syndrome scales for each sex/age group on the YSR and TRF.

In deriving the pre-1991 syndromes, we sought to capture possible differences in the patterning of problems for different sex/age groups, as seen by different informants. Our analyses of each group yielded some syndromes that were similar among different sex/age groups scored by different informants. However, the exact composition of these syndromes varied among the sex/age groups and informants.

The variations may have been partially due to some differences in the items that were analyzed, as even within a particular instrument, such as the CBCL, the items that failed to meet the 5% prevalence criterion varied among the sex/age groups. Differences in the item lists rated by different informants could have contributed to differences in the syndromes obtained from the CBCL, YSR, and TRF. Chance differences among samples could also have contributed to variations among syndromes.

When the focus was on each sex/age group as seen by each informant taken separately, the differences among syndromes did not pose major problems. Because the overall list of items on a particular instrument was the same for scoring all sex/age groups on that instrument, children of both sexes and different ages could be compared on each specific item, as well as on total scores computed by summing all items. By using standard scores derived from normative samples, different sex/age groups could also be compared with each other on those of the syndromes that were fairly similar from one sex/age group to another.

DERIVATION OF THE 1991 SYNDROMES

As the development and applications of our instruments have advanced, it has become more important to coordinate assessment of children of both sexes in different age ranges and as seen from different perspectives. A more uniform set of syndrome scales across sex/age groups and instruments would make it easier for practitioners to keep track of the syndromes being assessed. The common elements of syndromes derived from the different instruments for multiple sex/age groups would also provide the basis for taxonomic constructs that transcend specific instruments. Such constructs would serve as foci for research and theory from diverse perspectives.

To improve the coordination of assessment for both sexes across the age range spanned by the CBCL, we performed new principal components analyses of clinical samples of each sex at ages 4 to 5, 6 to 11, and 12 to 18. These samples included CBCLs that had been analyzed for the previous edition of the profile (Achenbach & Edelbrock, 1983), plus additional CBCLs obtained for children referred for mental health services since then.

The subjects were seen in 52 settings, including guidance clinics, private psychiatric and psychological practices, community mental health centers, university child psychiatric and psychological services, clinics for military dependents, health maintenance organizations, clinics in general hospitals, family service agencies, clinics operated by religious groups, and special education programs. Located throughout the eastern, southern, and midwestern United States, the settings provided a broad distribution of socioeconomic, demographic, and other client characteristics that should minimize selective factors affecting the caseloads of individual services. On Hollingshead's (1975) 9-step scale for parental occupation, the mean SES was 4.8 (sd = 2.1), averaged across the distributions for the six sex/age groups. Ethnic distribution averaged across the six sex/age groups was 89.2% white, 8.7% black, and 2.2% other. (The following sections can be skipped by readers uninterested in how the 1991 syndromes were derived.)

Principal Components Analyses

Two principal components analyses were performed on the sample for each sex/age group. One analysis resembled the analyses used to develop the previous edition of the profile. This analysis employed all problem items that were reported for at least 5% of a particular sex/age group. The open-ended items, *56h. Other physical problems* and *113. Other problems*, were not included, because their content varied across subjects according to what the respondents wrote in. Because our focus was now on syndromes that were common to multiple sex/age groups, we also included the following items that were reported for <5% of a particular sample but that had loaded highly on syndromes previously found for most sex/age groups: Boys 4-5 — *55. Overweight*; girls 4-5 — *51. Dizzy, 56d. Problems with eyes*; boys 6-11 — *101. Truancy*; girls 6-11 — none; boys 12-18 — *5. Behaves like opposite sex, 70. Sees things, 110. Wishes to be opposite sex*; girls 12-18 — none. Table 3-1 lists the sample sizes and the items that were excluded from the analyses for each sex/age group.

The second principal components analysis for each sex/age group was designed to identify syndromes that had counterparts in ratings by multiple informants. This analysis therefore employed only the 89 problem items that have counterparts on the YSR and TRF, as well as being on the CBCL.

Rotations of Principal Components

After performing principal components analyses, we subjected the largest 7 to 15 components from each analysis to orthogonal (varimax) rotations. (Rotations of principal components are transformations of their item loadings designed to approximate the ideal of "simple struc- ture" — that is, to divide all the items that were analyzed

Table 3-1
Low Prevalence Items Omitted from
Principal Components Analyses[a]

Group	N	Items
Boys 4-5	378	51. Dizzy; 101. Truancy; 105. Alcohol, drugs.
Girls 4-5	292	72. Sets fires; 78. Smears BM; 91. Talks about suicide; 101. Truancy; 105. Alcohol, drugs; 106. Vandalism.
Boys 6-11	1,339	78. Smears BM; 105. Alcohol, drugs; 110. Wishes to be opposite sex.
Girls 6-11	742	4. Asthma; 28. Eats things that aren't food; 59. Plays with sex parts in public; 72. Sets fires; 78. Smears BM; 105. Alcohol, drugs; 106. Vandalism.
Boys 12-18	1,060	6. BM outside toilet; 28. Eats things that aren't food; 59. Plays with sex parts in public; 78. Smears BM; 107. Wets during day.
Girls 12-18	644	6. BM outside toilet; 28. Eats things that aren't food; 59. Plays with sex parts in public; 60. Plays with sex parts too much; 72. Sets fires; 78. Smears BM; 107. Wets during day.

[a] Items *56h. Other physical problems* and *113. Other problems not listed above* were also excluded from all principal components analyses.

into relatively few tightly knit groups of strongly interrelated items.)

In all the analyses for the pre-1991 syndromes, the orthogonal (varimax) rotations had provided more stable and representative solutions than the oblique (direct quartimin) rotations. For this reason, and to minimize correlations among syndromes, only varimax rotations were performed to identify the 1991 syndromes. Although the varimax criterion for simple structure avoids correlations among rotated components, this does not preclude correlations among the sets of high loading items that are retained from the rotated components to form syndrome scales. In fact, as discussed later, the final syndrome scales do correlate positively with each other.

For each sex/age group, the 7- to 15-component rotations were examined to identify sets of items that consistently grouped together with high loadings on a rotated component. Four to five rotations were selected that included representative versions of these components. The items loading ≥.30 on these components were then listed side-by-side to identify the version of each component that included the maximum number of high loading items which also loaded highly on the other versions. (As done for the pre-1991 syndromes, we retained items loading ≥.30 for all syndromes except the one designated as *Aggressive Behavior*, for which the large number of high loading items argued for retaining items with loadings ≥.40. Items that loaded ≥.40 on the Aggressive syndrome and ≥.30 on a second syndrome were retained only for the second syndrome.)

After selecting the two to three best versions of each rotated component, we identified the rotation that included the largest proportion of the best versions of each component. The versions of the rotated components found in this rotation were used to represent the syndromes for the sex/age group for which the analysis was done.

Example of Syndrome Identification. As an example, we performed a principal components analysis of 115 problem items scored for the CBCLs of 1,339 6- to 11-year-old boys, excluding the three low prevalence items listed in Table 3-1. We then identified syndromes of items that tended to occur together, as reflected by their high loadings on a particular component. We selected the 11-, 12-, 13-, and 14-component rotations as including the best examples of these syndromes of high loading items.

One syndrome was designated as *Somatic Complaints*, because the items loading ≥.30 all involved somatic problems. From the versions of this syndrome found in the 11-, 12-, 13-, and 14-component rotations, we listed items that loaded ≥.30 on any of the four versions. We found that three of the four versions had exactly the same seven items loading ≥.30. On the remaining version, one of the seven items fell below .30 and was replaced by another item. Based on the Somatic Complaints syndrome, the three rotations that produced identical sets of high loading items all became equal candidates for retention. The same procedure was followed for each of the other syndromes that appeared in multiple rotations of the components for 6- to 11-year-old boys.

When we tabulated the number of syndromes whose best versions occurred in each rotation, we found that the 11- and 14-component rotations both had "best" versions of five syndromes and "second best" versions of one syndrome. The 12-component rotation had "best" versions of four syndromes and the 13-component rotation had "best" versions of three syndromes, while both these rotations had "second best" versions of two syndromes. All four rotations thus produced fairly similar results.

From the two top contenders — the 11- and 14-component rotations — we selected the 11-component rotation, because the versions of syndromes below the best and second best appeared slightly better than in the 4-component rotation. However, the contents of the syndromes retained from the 11-component rotation differed little from what would have been retained if the 14-component rotation had been selected. Furthermore, as explained in the following sections, the syndromes selected from the analyses of 115 items for 6- to 11-year-old boys contributed only a small part to the final selection of items for the 1991 CBCL syndrome scales.

Analysis of 89 Common Items

Recall now that a second principal components analysis was performed on the CBCL sample for each sex/age group. To identify "cross-informant" syndromes that were common to the CBCL, YSR, and TRF, the second principal components analyses employed only the 89 problem items that are common to the three instruments, minus the low frequency items listed in Table 3-1. Varimax rotations were performed on the largest 7 to 15 components obtained for each sex/age group. The procedures outlined earlier were then used to identify the syndromes that would serve as the CBCL candidates for the cross-informant syndromes. We thus obtained two sets of syndromes for each sex/age group. For boys 6 to 11, for example, one set was derived from the analyses of 115 items, while the second set was derived from the analysis of the 89 common items, minus the low frequency items shown in Table 3-1.

Derivation of Core Syndromes

The syndromes derived from the two sets of analyses for each sex/age group represent two alternative ways of viewing patterns of co-occurring problems. The analyses of all the items specific to the CBCL might detect patterns that are not detectable in the subset of items common to the CBCL, YSR, and TRF. The analyses of the common items, on the other hand, might identify patterns that are also detectable in YSR and TRF ratings.

To determine whether particular syndromes were evident only in the analyses of the full set of CBCL items, we compared the syndromes obtained from these analyses with the syndromes obtained from the analyses of the subset of common items. One syndrome, designated as *Sex Problems*, was found in the analyses of the full set of items for 4-5- and 6-11-year-olds of both sexes, but did not have a clear counterpart in the common-item subset. Eight other syndromes were found in the analyses of both the full set of items and the common-item subset. Table 3-2 lists the names of the syndromes and the mean of their eigenvalues obtained in the varimax rotation of the full set of items.

Table 3-2
Syndromes Retained from Principal
Components/Varimax Analyses of the CBCL

Internalizing		Neither Int nor Ext		Externalizing	
Withdrawn	(3.55)	Social Problems	(2.97)	Delinquent Behavior	(4.03)
Somatic Complaints	(3.89)	Thought Problems	(3.37)	Aggressive Behavior	(10.58)
Anxious/ Depressed	(5.45)	Attention Problems	(4.36)		
		Sex Problems[a] (2.75)			

Note. Internalizing and Externalizing groupings were derived from second-order analyses, as explained in Chapter 4. Mean of the eigenvalues for all sex/age groups in which the syndrome was found is shown in parentheses.
[a] Sex Problems syndrome was found only for ages 4-5 and 6-11.

There were some differences between the items comprising the versions of syndromes obtained from the analyses of the full set and those obtained from the common-item subset. There were also differences among the versions of each syndrome found for different sex/age groups. To identify *core syndromes* that underlay these variations, we made side-by-side lists of the items of the versions of a syndrome obtained from each sex/age group in both the full set and the common-item analyses. We then determined which items were found in the syndrome for a majority of the sex/age groups in which the syndrome was obtained. The Somatic Complaints syndrome, for example, was found for all six sex/age groups. We therefore constructed the core Somatic Complaints syndrome from items that were found in versions of this syndrome for at least four of the six sex/age groups. An item was counted as present for a particular sex/age group if it was found in either the full set or common-item version of the syndrome for that group. (Item *105. Uses alcohol or drugs for nonmedical purposes* was retained for the core *Delinquent Behavior* syndrome because it loaded very highly for 12-18-year-olds of both sexes although it was too uncommon among younger children for inclusion in their principal components analyses.)

The core syndromes were used in the following ways:

1. They provided the items for the 1991 syndrome scales. Thus, scales were constructed for the syndrome that was found only in the analyses of the full set and for the eight syndromes found in both the full set and common-item subset. The items comprising the core syndrome are used to score all the sex/age groups that are scored for that syndrome.

2. The core versions of the syndromes found in the common-item subset were compared with common-item core syndromes from the YSR and TRF to identify syndromes that were similar in two or more instruments.

Cross-Informant Syndromes

A major aim of the 1991 profiles is to provide common foci for assessing children from the perspectives of parent-, self-, and teacher-reports. These common foci consist of syndromes that were identified as having counterparts in the principal components analyses of the CBCL, YSR, and TRF. Core syndromes were constructed from the syndromes derived from the YSR and TRF by the method just described for the CBCL (details are provided by Achenbach, 1991b, 1991c).

To identify items that were common to the core syndromes of two or more informants, we made side-by-side lists of the items comprising the corresponding core syndromes from the different instruments. Items that were found on core syndromes for at least two of the three instruments were used to form a *cross-informant syndrome construct*. For example, items of the core Somatic Complaints syndromes derived from the CBCL, YSR, and TRF were listed side-by-side. Nine items were found to be common to the core Somatic Complaints syndrome from at least two of the three instruments. These nine items were used to define a cross-informant syndrome construct which could be assessed via the Somatic Complaints scales of the CBCL, YSR, and TRF.

The term "construct" is used to indicate that the common items represent a hypothetical variable. In statistical language, the term "latent variable" is used for variables of this sort. Because none of the core syndromes for the individual instruments included any additional items, the Somatic Complaints scales for all three instruments have the same nine items, although they are normed separately for the different informants, as described later.

For some cross-informant constructs, the core syndrome of a particular instrument did include items beside those that qualified for the cross-informant construct. Because these items were associated with the syndrome in ratings by a particular type of informant, they were retained for the syndrome scale to be scored by that type of informant. As an example, for the cross-informant construct designated as *Thought Problems*, the CBCL core syndrome included item *80. Stares blankly*. This item is not on the YSR, because it did not seem sensible to ask youths to report whether they stare blankly. It is on the TRF, but did not qualify for the TRF core syndrome. Because it was associated with the CBCL Thought Problems syndrome in a majority of the sex/age groups, it is scored on the CBCL Thought Problems scale even though it is not part of the cross-informant construct and is not scored on the YSR or TRF Thought Problems scales. Other items were also retained on particular scales for one instrument to capture aspects of a syndrome that might be evident to only one type of informant. Table 3-3 summarizes the steps in constructing the 1991 syndrome scales.

PROFILE FOR SCORING
THE 1991 SYNDROMES

The 1991 profiles for the CBCL, YSR, and TRF display the items of the eight cross-informant syndromes that are scored from the respective type of informant. To facilitate comparison among reports by the different informants, the syndromes are arranged in the same order on all three profiles. A cross-informant computer program is available that scores and compares data from any combination of father-, mother-, youth-, and teacher-reports (details are provided by Achenbach, 1991a).

For users who have access to only one type of informant, programs are also available that score only the CBCL, YSR, or TRF. The syndromes that were found in ratings by only one type of informant are not displayed on the profiles, because they comprise relatively rare problems and their distributions of scores do not lend themselves to a profile approach. However, the computer-scoring programs compute total scores and T scores for these scales, and the hand-scoring profiles provide spaces to enter the scores for them.

Figure 3-1 shows the problem scales of the girls' version of a computer-scored profile completed for 8-year-old Jenny. (Appendix A provides detailed hand-scoring

Table 3-3
Steps in Deriving 1991 CBCL Syndrome Scales

---

1. Two sets of principal components analyses were performed on CBCL problem items for clinically referred children of each sex at ages 4-5, 6-11, 12-18.

   a. Set 1—principal components analysis of all but low prevalence CBCL problem items.

   b. Set 2—principal components analysis of 89 problem items common to CBCL, YSR, TRF.

2. Varimax rotations of 7 to 15 components from each analysis.

3. Identification of groups of items that remained together throughout multiple rotations.

4. Selection of rotation that included the largest proportion of the best versions of groups of co-occurring items.

5. Derivation of *core syndromes* from items found in the versions of a syndrome for most sex/age groups.

6. Derivation of *cross-informant constructs* from items common to core syndromes for at least two of the three instruments (CBCL, YSR, TRF).

7. Construction of CBCL syndrome scales consisting of CBCL items for the eight cross-informant scales, plus *Sex Problems* scale scored only from CBCL.

8. Assignment of normalized *T* scores based on percentiles of normative samples, separately for each sex at ages 4-11 and 12-18.

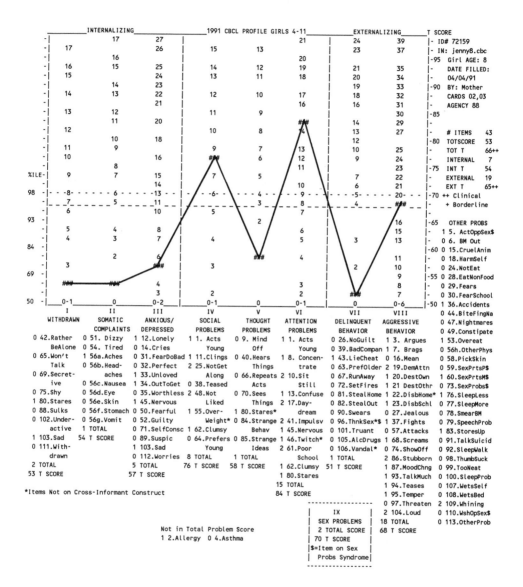

Figure 3-1. Computer-scored problem profile for 8-year-old Jenny.

instructions.) The eight syndromes displayed on the profile have counterparts that bear the same names on the 1991 profiles for the YSR and TRF. The names are intended as descriptive summaries of the items comprising the syndromes, rather than being diagnostic labels. Chapter 4 presents the basis for designating scales I-III as Internalizing and scales VII-VIII as Externalizing.

The items comprising each syndrome scale are listed under the title of the scale. A total scale score is computed by summing the 1s and 2s for the scale's items that were scored as describing the child. Asterisks indicate items on the CBCL version of a cross-informant syndrome scale that are not on the YSR or TRF versions. On syndrome scale *V. Thought Problems*, for example, the asterisk beside Item *80. Stares blankly* indicates that it was included in the core syndrome derived from the principal components analyses of the six sex/age groups scored on the CBCL, but not on the core syndromes scored on the YSR or TRF. Item 80 is therefore scored on the CBCL *Thought Problems* scale but not on the YSR or TRF *Thought Problems* scales.

On the right side of the profiles, *T* scores are shown that indicate how particular scale scores compare with scores obtained by normative samples of children. The precise *T* scores obtained by the child are computed and printed beneath the syndrome scales. Later sections of this chapter explain how the *T* scores were assigned. Items that are not scored on syndrome scales I-VIII are listed to the right of the profile under the heading *Other Problems*. These items do not constitute a separate scale, but they are included in the CBCL total problem score.

Beside the eight scales for scoring syndromes that have counterparts on the YSR and TRF, the CBCL profile provides space for scores on Scale *IX. Sex Problems* for ages 4-11. This scale is viewed as optional, because it was derived only from parents' CBCL ratings of 4-11-year-olds. Furthermore, the items of this scale have low prevalence rates and most children have very low scale scores. As a consequence, the *Sex Problems* scale does not lend itself to the specification of normal, borderline, and clinical ranges like those specified for scales I-VIII. Although T scores can be computed for the scale, these T scores merely provide guidelines as to whether the child scores at relatively low, medium, or high levels compared to normative samples of peers.

The computer-scoring program automatically computes and displays the raw total score and T score for the Sex Problems scale in the box shown in the lower right-hand corner of Figure 3-1. The six items of the scale are marked with $ on the computer-scored profile. Appendix A provides instructions and T scores for scoring the Sex Problems scale on the hand-scored profile.

As shown at the bottom of the profile in Figure 3-1, Items *2. Allergy* and *4. Asthma* are not included in the problem scales. This is because they did not discriminate significantly between referred and nonreferred children in parent-ratings (analyses are presented in Chapter 7), or in self-ratings either (Achenbach, 1991c). However, the scores for these scales are displayed, because it may be clinically important to know whether a child has allergies and/or asthma.

As detailed in Chapter 4, scores for Internalizing and Externalizing are computed by summing Scales I-III and VII-VIII, respectively. No items are included on both an Internalizing and Externalizing scale. The computer scoring program prints the raw scores and T scores for Internalizing and Externalizing to the right of the profile, as shown in Figure 3-1.

The total problem score is computed by summing all problem items on pages 3 and 4 of the CBCL, except Items *2. Allergy* and *4. Asthma*. If the parent has rated more than one problem item for *113. Other problems*, only the problem receiving the highest score is counted toward the total problem score. For example, if one additional problem was rated 1 and a second additional problem was rated 2, add 2 to the total problem score. As Figure 3-1 shows, the raw total problem score and its T score are printed to the right of the computer-scored profile, as is the total number of problem items scored present (excluding Allergy and Asthma).

ASSIGNING NORMALIZED T SCORES TO SYNDROME SCALES

(This section can be skipped by readers uninterested in how T scores were assigned.)

Lowest T Scores

For each syndrome scale, we computed percentiles using the same procedure and normative samples as were described in Chapter 2 for the competence scales. On some syndrome scales, more than 50% of the normative sample obtained scores of 0 or 1. On other syndrome scales, much smaller percentages of the normative sample obtained very low scores. If we assigned normalized T scores solely on the basis of percentiles, some scales would start at much lower T scores than other scales would. When displayed on a profile, the different starting points for the scales could lead to misleading impressions. For example, if a child obtained a raw score of 0 on a scale that started at a T score of 28 and a raw score of 0 on a scale that started at a T score of 50, it might appear that the child scored higher on the second scale than on the first. Yet, the child had no problems on either scale.

To avoid misleading impressions of this sort and to prevent over-interpretation of differences among scores in the low normal range, we truncated the assignment of T scores to the syndrome scales. According to the midpoint percentiles, no syndrome scales would have required starting at a T score higher than 50, which is equivalent to the 50th percentile. To equalize the starting points of all the syndrome scales, we assigned a T score of 50 to all raw scores that fell at midpoint percentiles $\leq$50. As an example, on Scale *V. Thought Problems* for girls 4-11, only a raw score of 0 fell $\leq$50th percentile. On Scale *VIII. Aggressive Behavior*, by contrast, raw scores of 0-6 were all $\leq$50th percentile. All these scores were therefore assigned a T score of 50, as shown in Figure 3-1.

The assignment of a T score of 50 to several raw scores reduces the differentiation among low scores on scales such as the *Aggressive Behavior* scale. Loss of this differentiation is of little clinical importance, because it involves small differences that are all at the low end of the normal range. If differentiation at the low end is nevertheless desired for assessing differences that are within the normal range, raw scale scores may be used in place of T scores. For statistical analyses, raw scores are usually preferable, because they directly reflect all differences among individuals without any truncation or other transformations.

On scales comprising low prevalence items, a large percentage of the normative sample obtained the second lowest possible raw score on the scale. This produced a large gap between the percentiles of the lowest score and the second lowest score. If the second lowest score qualified for a T score >55, we limited the gap between the T score of 50 and the next T score by assigning it a T score half way between 50 and the third lowest T score. On the Thought Problems scale of the profile, for example, the second lowest T score would have been 59 if we based it directly on the midpoint percentile. However, by assigning this T score to a point half way between 50 and the third lowest T score, we assigned the second lowest score a $T = 58$, thus reducing the gap slightly between the lowest and second lowest T score.

Highest *T* Scores

Most children in the normative samples obtained scores that were well below the maximum possible on each syndrome scale. It was therefore impossible to base *T* scores on percentiles at the high end of the syndrome scales. On the *Aggressive Behavior* scale shown in Figure 3-1, for example, the maximum possible score is 40, but 98% of the normative sample of 4- to 11-year-old girls obtained scores below 21. Furthermore, most of the scores from 21 to 40 were not obtained by any children in the normative sample. Basing *T* scores on percentiles above the 98th percentile would thus not really reflect differences among scores obtained by children in the normative sample. We therefore based *T* scores on percentiles only up to a *T* score of 70, which approximates the 97.7th percentile (Abramowitz & Stegun, 1968).

For the highest scores on the syndrome scales, we assigned *T* scores from 71 to 100 in as many increments as there were remaining raw scores on the scale. For example, on the *Aggressive Behavior* scale for girls 4-11, the raw score of 20 was assigned a *T* score of 70. Because there are 20 items on the scale, the maximum possible score is 40 (i.e., if a girl received a score of 2 on all 20 items, her raw scale score would be 40). There are 30 intervals from 71 to 100, but only 20 possible raw scores from 21 through 40. To assign *T* scores to the 20 raw scores, we divided 30 by 20. Because $30/20 = 1.5$, *T* scores were assigned to raw scores in intervals of 1.5. Thus, a raw score of 21 was assigned a *T* score of $70 + 1.5 = 71.5$, rounded off to 72. A raw score of 22 was assigned a *T* score of $71.5 + 1.5 = 73$, and so on.

Because of the skewed raw score distributions, truncation of low scores at $T = 50$, and assignment of high *T* scores in equal intervals, the mean *T* scores of the syndrome scales are above 50 and their standard deviations are below 10, although this is not true of the Internalizing, Externalizing, and total problem scores. The T scores of the syndrome scales do not conform to the mean of 50 and standard deviation of 10 expected when normal distributions are transformed directly into T scores. The means and standard deviations also differ between normative and clinical samples, of course. Table 3-4 presents the means, standard deviations, and standard errors for the normative samples. Appendix B presents the corresponding data for all CBCL scales in demographically matched referred and nonreferred samples of each sex at ages 4-11 and 12-18.

ASSIGNING NORMALIZED T SCORES TO TOTAL PROBLEM SCORES

We based normalized T scores on midpoint percentiles of the total problem score in the same way as described for the syndrome scales, with the following two differences:

1. The total number of problem items is much greater than the number of items on any syndrome scale, and at least some problems are reported for most children. Consequently, very few children in our normative samples obtained extremely low total problem scores. It was therefore unnecessary to set a minimum T score at which to group low raw scores as we did for the syndrome scales. Instead, we based normalized T scores directly on percentiles of the distribution of total problem scores obtained by our normative samples, up to the 97.7th percentile ($T = 70$).

2. No child in either our normative or clinical samples obtained a total problem score approaching the maximum possible of 236. If we assigned T scores above 70 by dividing all the top raw scores into the

Table 3-4
Problem Scale Scores for CBCL Normative Samples

Scale	Boys 4-11	Boys 12-18	Girls 4-11	Girls 12-18
N =	581	564	619	604
Withdrawn				
Raw Score				
Mean	1.8	2.4	2.0	2.6
SD	1.9	2.2	2.0	2.4
SE[a]	.1	.1	.1	.1
T score				
Mean	54.0	54.0	54.0	53.9
SD	5.6	6.2	5.7	6.0
SE[a]	.2	.3	.2	.2
Somatic Complaints				
Raw Score				
Mean	.8	1.0	1.0	1.4
SD	1.3	1.5	1.6	2.0
SE[a]	.1	.1	.1	.1
T score				
Mean	53.8	54.0	53.9	53.9
SD	5.8	5.8	5.7	6.0
SE[a]	.2	.2	.2	.2
Anxious/Depressed				
Raw Score				
Mean	3.1	3.2	3.4	3.7
SD	3.1	3.3	3.3	3.8
SE[a]	.1	.1	.1	.2
T score				
Mean	54.0	54.2	54.0	54.1
SD	5.9	6.1	5.7	6.1
SE[a]	.2	.3	.2	.2
Social Problems				
Raw Score				
Mean	2.0	1.6	1.9	1.7
SD	1.9	1.8	1.7	2.0
SE[a]	.1	.1	.1	.1
T score				
Mean	53.9	53.8	54.0	53.9
SD	5.6	5.9	5.9	5.8
SE[a]	.2	.2	.2	.2

Table 3-4 (Continued)

Scale	Boys 4-11	Boys 12-18	Girls 4-11	Girls 12-18
Thought Problems				
Raw Score				
Mean	.5	.5	.5	.6
SD	.9	1.0	1.0	1.1
SE[a]	.0	.0	.0	.0
T score				
Mean	53.4	53.3	53.2	53.4
SD	5.5	5.6	5.7	5.8
SE[a]	.2	.2	.2	.2
Attention Problems				
Raw Score				
Mean	3.3	3.3	2.5	2.6
SD	2.8	3.1	2.5	2.9
SE[a]	.1	.1	.1	.1
T score				
Mean	54.0	54.0	54.0	54.0
SD	5.8	5.9	5.9	5.9
SE[a]	.2	.2	.2	.2
Delinquent Behavior				
Raw Score				
Mean	1.6	1.9	1.2	1.4
SD	1.7	2.5	1.4	1.9
SE[a]	.1	.1	.1	.1
T score				
Mean	53.8	53.9	53.8	54.0
SD	5.7	5.9	5.7	5.8
SE[a]	.2	.2	.2	.2
Aggressive Behavior				
Raw Score				
Mean	8.2	6.8	7.0	5.7
SD	5.8	5.7	5.2	5.2
SE[a]	.2	.2	.2	.2
T score				
Mean	54.1	54.1	54.0	54.1
SD	6.0	6.2	5.8	6.3
SE[a]	.3	.3	.2	.3

Table 3-4 (Continued)

Scale	Boys 4-11	Boys 12-18	Girls 4-11	Girls 12-18
Sex Problems (ages 4-11)				
Raw Score				
Mean	.1	---	.2	---
SD	.5	---	.5	---
SE[a]	.0	---	.0	---
T score				
Mean	51.6	---	52.0	---
SD	5.0	---	5.4	---
SE[a]	.2	---	.2	---
Internalizing				
Raw Score				
Mean	5.6	6.4	6.3	7.5
SD	4.7	5.5	5.5	6.6
SE[a]	.2	.2	.2	.3
T score				
Mean	50.2	50.3	50.0	50.0
SD	9.6	9.8	9.7	10.0
SE[a]	.4	.4	.4	.4
Externalizing				
Raw Score				
Mean	9.8	8.7	8.2	7.1
SD	7.1	7.6	6.1	6.6
SE[a]	.3	.3	.2	.3
T score				
Mean	50.0	50.1	50.0	50.2
SD	9.9	9.8	9.6	9.8
SE[a]	.4	.4	.4	.4
Total Problems				
Raw Score				
Mean	24.3	22.5	23.1	22.0
SD	15.6	17.0	15.5	17.7
SE[a]	.6	.7	.6	.7
T score				
Mean	50.1	50.0	50.1	50.0
SD	9.9	10.0	9.9	10.2
SE[a]	.4	.4	.4	.4

[a]SE = standard error of the mean

30 intervals from 71 to 100, we would have compressed scores actually obtained by our clinical samples into a narrow range of T scores. We would also have assigned raw scores above those actually obtained to a broad range of T scores. For example, the highest total score obtained in our sample of clinically referred 4- to 11-year-old girls was 161. If we had assigned T scores in equal intervals from 70 to 100, only 17 T scores would have been allocated to the range of 99 raw scores above $T = 70$ actually found in our clinical sample, whereas 13 T scores would have been allocated to the 75 raw scores above those actually found.

To enable the upper T scores to reflect differences among the raw scores that are most likely to occur, we assigned a T score of 89 for each sex/age group to the mean of the five highest raw scores found in the clinical sample on which the principal components analyses were performed. (In contrast to the use of the single highest score in the pre-1991 profiles, we used the mean of the five highest scores to reduce the effect of single extreme outliers.) The raw scores ranging from $T = 70$ to the mean of the five highest scores were then assigned T scores in equal intervals from 71 through 89. The raw scores above the mean of the five highest were assigned T scores in equal intervals from 90 through 100. The T score assigned to each raw total problem score is displayed in a box to the right of the hand-scored profile and is printed out by the computer-scoring program.

NORMAL, BORDERLINE,
AND CLINICAL RANGES

Syndrome Scales

As shown in Figure 3-1, broken lines are printed across the profile at the T scores of 67 and 70. These represent a borderline clinical range in which scores are not so clearly in the clinical range as those that are above $T = 70$. This borderline range is analogous to the one shown in Figure 2-1 for the competence scales and was chosen to provide efficient discrimination between demographically matched referred and nonreferred samples (described in Chapter 6), while minimizing the number of "false positives," i.e., normal children who score in the clinical range. If maximum discrimination is sought between deviant and nondeviant children without regard to the increase in false positives, cutpoints below $T = 67$ on the syndrome scales may improve discrimination in some samples.

Just as with the competence scales, there is no well-validated criterion for categorically distinguishing between children who are "normal" and those who are "abnormal" with respect to each syndrome. Because children are continually changing and because all assessment procedures are subject to errors of measurement and other limitations, no single score precisely indicates a child's status. Instead, a child's score on a syndrome scale should be interpreted as an approximation of the child's status as seen by a particular informant at the time the informant completes the CBCL.

The test-retest reliability of parents' ratings is high (Chapter 5) and the standard error of measurement is small (Appendix B). This means that, on the average, the range of scores represented by a particular score is relatively narrow. Nevertheless, in deciding whether a child is clinically deviant on a particular syndrome, it is important to remember that each score is just one point on a continuum of quantitative variation. It is especially important to be aware of such variation when a score is at the low end of the clinical range. When a syndrome score is on or between the broken lines, it should be described as "borderline clinical."

If a specific categorical cutpoint is desired for statistical purposes, the T score of 67 can be used to represent the bottom of the clinical range. As shown in Chapter 6, T scores of 67 significantly discriminated between referred and nonreferred children on the eight cross-informant syndromes scored from the CBCL. Furthermore, there were significant differences between the proportions of referred and nonreferred children scoring in the normal, borderline, and clinical ranges. These findings support the cutpoint of $T = 67$ and the tripartite division into the normal, borderline, and clinical ranges. However, other cutpoints and borderline ranges might be chosen for particular research objectives with particular samples.

Total Problem Score

To test the discriminative efficiency of various cutpoints, we used a Relative Operating Characteristics (ROC) type of analysis (Swets & Pickett, 1982). We did this by comparing the distributions of total problem scores in demographically matched referred and nonreferred children, separately for each sex in each of the two age ranges. (The matched samples are described in Chapter 6.) For each sex/age group, we identified a range of scores where the differences between the cumulative percents of referred and nonreferred children were greatest. That is, we computed the difference between the cumulative percent of referred children who obtained all scores up to a particular score and the cumulative percent of nonreferred children who obtained all scores up to that same score. The score at which the nonreferred children exceeded the referred children by the greatest percent represented the most efficient cutpoint, in terms of minimizing the percent of nonreferred children who scored above the cutpoint ("false positives"), *plus* the percent of referred children who scored *below* the cutpoint ("false negatives").

The cutpoints for both sexes and all age ranges on the CBCL, YSR, and TRF were compared to determine whether a similar cutpoint and borderline range could provide efficient discrimination for all of them.   Scores in the normative samples ranging from about the 82nd to the 90th percentile were found to provide the most efficient discrimination for most sex/age groups on all three instruments. *T* scores of 60 to 63, which span these percentiles, were therefore chosen to demarcate the borderline clinical range.

For categorical discrimination between deviant and nondeviant groups, $T = 60$ serves as the bottom of the clinical range.   However, by designating a borderline clinical range, we emphasize that *T* scores from 60 to 63 are less clearly deviant than scores above it. Furthermore, cutpoints other than $T = 60$ may be more effective for particular purposes in particular samples.

SUMMARY

Beside describing children in terms of specific items, the CBCL is designed to identify syndromes of problems. To identify syndromes, we performed principal components/varimax analyses of the CBCL problem items scored for clinically referred children, separately for each sex at ages 4-5, 6-11, and 12-18.   Two sets of analyses were performed for each sex/age group. In one set of analyses, all but the very low prevalence problem items were included. In the second set, only the 89 items common to the CBCL, YSR, and TRF were included.

Syndromes identified in multiple sex/age groups were compared to identify items that were common to a syndrome across sex/age groups. These items were used to construct a *core syndrome* of items to be scored on the 1991 CBCL profile. The version of the core syndrome derived from the 89 common items was compared with analogous core syndromes derived from the YSR and TRF. Items that were found in the analogous core syndrome from at least two of the three instruments were used to form a *cross-informant syndrome construct*.

The following eight cross-informant syndromes are displayed on the 1991 CBCL profile: *Withdrawn, Somatic Complaints, Anxious/Depressed, Social Problems, Thought Problems, Attention Problems, Delinquent Behavior,* and *Aggressive Behavior*. An additional syndrome, designated as *Sex Problems*, can also be scored from the CBCL but does not have counterparts on the YSR or TRF.

Profiles for hand scoring and computer scoring the CBCL display scores for every problem item, as well as raw scores and T scores for the syndrome scales, Internalizing, Externalizing, and total problem score. Normal, borderline, and clinical ranges are also designated for the scale scores.

Chapter 4
Internalizing and Externalizing Groupings of Syndromes

As shown in Figure 3-1, the syndrome scales designated as *Withdrawn, Somatic Complaints*, and *Anxious/Depressed* are grouped under the heading *Internalizing*. The syndrome scales designated as *Delinquent Behavior* and *Aggressive Behavior* are grouped under the heading *Externalizing*. These groupings of syndromes reflect a distinction that has been detected in numerous multivariate analyses of children's behavioral/emotional problems. The two groups of problems have been variously called Personality Problem versus Conduct Problem (Peterson, 1961), Internalizing versus Externalizing (Achenbach, 1966), Inhibition versus Aggression (Miller, 1967), and Overcontrolled versus Undercontrolled (Achenbach & Edelbrock, 1978).

In the pre-1991 profiles, we identified two broad groupings of syndromes that we designated as Internalizing and Externalizing, consistent with the terminology used since the initial multivariate study in this research program (Achenbach, 1966). The pre-1991 groupings were identified by performing second-order principal components analyses of the syndrome scales for each sex/age group on the CBCL, YSR, and TRF. Each group's Internalizing and Externalizing scores were based on their respective set of syndromes. Because the syndrome scales and the items of these scales varied somewhat from one sex/age group and instrument to another, the composition of the Internalizing and Externalizing scores was not uniform.

1991 INTERNALIZING AND EXTERNALIZING GROUPINGS

To increase the consistency between the different sex/age groups on the CBCL, YSR, and TRF and between these instruments, we derived the 1991 Internalizing and Externalizing groupings as follows:

1. Using the clinical samples from which our syndrome scales were derived, we computed correlations between the raw scores on the syndrome scales separately for each sex/age group on the CBCL, YSR, and TRF. Items that appear on more than one scale were scored only on the scale for which they had the highest loading.

2. We performed principal factor analyses of the correlations among the scale scores separately for each sex/age group. Principal factor analyses are like principal components analyses except that estimates of communality among the variables are used instead of 1.0 in the principal diagonal. Our choice of factor analysis here was based on new evidence for the superiority of factor analysis in applications to small numbers of variables, such as our eight syndrome scales (Snook & Gorsuch, 1989). Squared multiple correlations among syndrome scale scores were used in the principal diagonal.

3. The two largest factors in each solution were rotated to the varimax criterion. Both rotated factors had eigenvalues >1.0 in all groups.

4. Averaged across all groups on all three instruments, the loadings of the syndrome scales yielded the following rank order of syndromes on the Internaliz-

ing factors (mean loadings are in parentheses): 1. Withdrawn (.784); 2. Somatic Complaints (.690); 3. Anxious/Depressed (.650). The rank order of syndromes on the Externalizing factors was: 1. Aggressive Behavior (.791); 2. Delinquent Behavior (.778).

5. The Internalizing score for each profile is the sum of items on the three Internalizing scales of that profile. The Externalizing score is the sum of items on the two Externalizing scales of that profile. No item is counted twice within either the Internalizing score or the Externalizing score, and no item is included in both an Internalizing and Externalizing scale.

6. Because the composition of some syndrome scales differs among the profiles, there are small differences among the CBCL, YSR, and TRF versions of the Internalizing and Externalizing scores.

Although the Attention Problems scale had moderately high loadings on the various versions of the Externalizing factor, its mean loading of .618 was enough lower than the mean loading of .791 for the Aggressive scale and .778 for the Delinquent scale that it was deemed inappropriate to include with the Externalizing grouping. The Attention Problems scale is therefore displayed in the middle section of the profiles with the Social Problems and Thought Problems scales, neither of which had consistently high loadings on the Internalizing or Externalizing factors.

Starting on the left side of the profile, the Internalizing scales are listed from left to right in descending order of their rank on the Internalizing factors (Withdrawal, Somatic Complaints, Anxious/Depressed). On the right side of the profile, the two Externalizing scales are listed from left to right in ascending order of their rank on the Externalizing factors, i. e., Delinquent Behavior, followed by Aggressive Behavior, which is the rightmost scale.

ASSIGNMENT OF INTERNALIZING AND EXTERNALIZING T SCORES

To provide norm referenced scores, we summed the scores obtained on the Internalizing and Externalizing items by the normative samples of each sex/age group on each instrument. The one item that appears on more than one Internalizing scale was counted only once in the Internalizing score. No items of the Delinquent or Aggressive Behavior scales are included on any other syndrome scale.

Percentiles were computed according to the procedure described in Chapter 3. Normalized T scores were assigned in the same manner as described in Chapter 3 for the total problem scores. That is, the T scores were based directly on percentiles up to the 97.7th percentile ($T = 70$). The raw scores ranging from $T = 70$ to the mean of the five highest scores in our clinical samples were then assigned T scores in equal intervals from 71 through 89. The raw scores above the mean of the five highest in our clinical samples were assigned T scores in equal intervals from 90 through 100. Just as with the total problem score, the clinical cutpoint was established at $T = 60$, with the borderline clinical range including T scores of 60 through 63.

To assess a child's problems in terms of the Internalizing and Externalizing groupings, the hand-scored profiles provide guidelines for summing the Internalizing and Externalizing scale scores. Appendix A provides detailed scoring instructions. To the right of the profile, a table is provided for determining the T score equivalent of each Internalizing and Externalizing raw score (see Appendix A for instructions). The computer-scoring programs automatically compute raw scores and T scores for Internalizing and Externalizing.

RELATIONS BETWEEN INTERNALIZING AND EXTERNALIZING SCORES

The Internalizing and Externalizing groupings reflect empirical associations among subsets of scales that involve contrasting kinds of problems. These problems are not mutually exclusive, however, because some individuals may have both kinds of problems. In many samples of children, positive correlations are found between Internalizing and Externalizing scores. Across our normative samples of each sex/age group on each instrument, the mean correlation between Internalizing and Externalizing was .52, computed by Fisher's z transformation. This reflects the fact that children who have very high problem scores in one of the two areas also tend to have at least above-average problem scores in the other area as well. Conversely, children who have very low scores in one area also tend to have relatively low scores in the other area.

Appendix C lists the correlations between CBCL Internalizing and Externalizing scores for demographically matched referred and nonreferred samples of each sex in each age range. The mean Pearson r between CBCL Internalizing and Externalizing scores was .54 for the referred samples and .59 for the nonreferred samples, computed by z transformation.

Despite the positive association between Internalizing and Externalizing scores found in our samples as a whole, some children's problems are primarily Internalizing, whereas other children's problems are primarily Externalizing. This is analogous to the relation between Verbal IQ and Performance IQ on the Wechsler intelligence tests: In most samples of children, there is a positive correlation between the Wechsler Verbal IQ and Performance IQ (e.g., Wechsler, 1989). Nevertheless, some children have much higher Verbal than Performance scores or vice versa. Children who have much higher Verbal than Performance scores may differ in other important ways from children who have much higher Performance than Verbal scores. Similarly, children who have much higher Internalizing scores than Externalizing scores may differ in other important ways from those who show the opposite pattern. Numerous studies have in fact shown significant differences between children classified as having primarily Internalizing versus primarily Externalizing problems (e.g., Achenbach, 1966; Achenbach & Lewis, 1971; Katz, Zigler, & Zalk, 1975; McConaughy, Achenbach, & Gent, 1988; Weintraub, 1973).

Distinguishing Between Internalizing and Externalizing Patterns

Users of the profiles may wish to distinguish between children whose reported problems are primarily from the Internalizing grouping and those whose problems are primarily from the Externalizing grouping. Such distinctions may be clinically useful for choosing approaches to intervention and for identifying groups of clients with similar problems for purposes such as group therapy, parent training groups, and assignment to residential units. Such distinctions may also be useful for testing hypotheses about differences in etiology, responsiveness to particular treatments, and long-term outcomes.

The specific criteria for distinguishing between children having primarily Internalizing versus Externalizing problems should be based on the user's aims and the size and nature of the available sample. The criteria chosen for distinguishing between Internalizing and Externalizing patterns will affect the proportion of a sample that can be classified, the homogeneity of the resulting groups, and the associations that may be found between the Internalizing-Externalizing classification and other variables. Very stringent criteria, for example, will severely limit the proportion of children classified as manifesting Internalizing versus Externalizing patterns. But stringent criteria will also yield relatively extreme groups who are likely to differ more on other variables than would less extreme Internalizing and Externalizing groups.

The trade-offs between stringency of criteria, proportion of children classified, and degree of association with other variables must be weighed by users of the profiles when choosing criteria for their own purposes. As a general guideline, we suggest that children not be classified as Internalizing or Externalizing unless (a) their total problem score exceeds the clinical cutoff on at least one of the three instruments, and (b) the difference between their Internalizing and Externalizing T score is at least 10 points on one instrument or at least 5 points on two instruments. The larger the difference is between T scores and the more consistent the difference is between two or more instruments, the more distinctive the Internalizing and Externalizing groups will be.

SUMMARY

Internalizing and Externalizing groupings of behavioral/emotional problems were identified by performing second-order factor analyses of the eight 1991 syndrome scales scored separately from each instrument for each sex/age group. The largest two rotated factors in all analyses reflected a distinction between problems of withdrawal, somatic complaints, and anxiety/depression, on the one hand, and delinquent and aggressive behavior, on the other.

On all 1991 profiles, the Internalizing grouping is operationally defined as the sum of scores on the problem items of the Withdrawal, Somatic Complaints, and Anxious/Depressed scales. The Externalizing grouping is defined as the sum of scores on the problem items of the Delinquent and Aggressive Behavior scales.

The eight scales of the profiles are arranged in order starting with the three Internalizing scales on the left, followed by three scales that did not have consistently high loadings on either the Internalizing or Externalizing factors (Social Problems, Thought Problems, Attention Problems), and ending with the two Externalizing scales on the right. T scores were assigned to the Internalizing and Externalizing scores in the same way as was done for the total problem scores.

The relations between Internalizing and Externalizing scores is analogous to the relation between verbal and performance IQ scores on intelligence tests. Although Internalizing and Externalizing scores represent contrasting kinds of problems, they are not mutually exclusive. Across groups of children, Internalizing scores typically correlate positively with Externalizing scores, because children who have very high scores in one area tend to have at least above-average scores in the other area as well. Nevertheless, children who have much higher Internalizing than Externalizing scores may differ in important ways from children who show the reverse pattern. Guidelines were provided for distinguishing between children whose problems are primarily in the Internalizing area and those whose problems are primarily in the Externalizing area.

Chapter 5
Reliability, Interparent Agreement, and Stability

Reliability refers to agreement between repeated assessments of phenomena when the phenomena themselves remain constant. When instruments are administered by interviewers, it is important to know the degree to which different interviewers obtain similar results, i.e., the degree of *inter-interviewer reliability*. When rating instruments such as the CBCL are self-administered, it is important to know the degree to which the same informants provide the same scores over periods when the subjects' behavior is not expected to change, i.e., the degree of *test-retest reliability*. This chapter first presents data on inter-interviewer reliability with respect to our procedures for obtaining data on general population samples in home interview surveys. It then presents the test-retest reliability obtained when parents independently completed CBCLs at a mean interval of 7 days.

Beside reliability, it is also helpful to know the degree of agreement between scores from mothers and fathers and the degree of stability in scores over periods long enough that the subjects' behavior may change significantly. Interparent agreement and long-term stability are not expected to be as high as inter-interviewer or test-retest reliability, because reliability involves agreement between assessments of the *same* phenomena. Ratings by mothers and fathers, on the other hand, are based on somewhat different samples of their children's behavior. Analogously, the same informants rerating children's behavior over long periods are likely to see different behavior at different periods. Findings for interparent agreement and long-term stability are therefore presented separately from findings for reliability.

An additional property of scales is their *internal consistency*. This refers to the correlation between half of a scale's items and the other half of its items. Although internal consistency is sometimes referred to as "split-half reliability," it cannot tell us the degree to which a scale will produce the same results over different occasions when the target phenomena are expected to remain constant. Furthermore, scales with relatively low internal consistency may be more *valid* than scales with very high internal consistency. For example, if a scale consists of 20 repetitions of exactly the same item, it should produce very high internal consistency, because respondents should repeatedly score the same item the same way on a particular occasion. However, such a scale would usually be less valid than a scale that uses 20 different items to assess the same phenomenon. Because each of the 20 different items is likely to tap different aspects of the target phenomenon and to be subject to different errors of measurement, the 20 different items are likely to provide better measurement despite lower internal consistency than a scale that repeats the same item 20 times.

Our syndrome scales were derived from principal components analyses of the correlations among items. The composition of the scales is therefore based on internal consistency among certain subsets of items. Measures of the internal consistency of these scales are thus redundant. Nevertheless, because some users may wish to know the degree of internal consistency of our scales, Cronbach's (1951) *alpha* is displayed for each scale in Appendix B. *Alpha* represents the mean of the correlations between all possible sets of half the items comprising a scale. *Alpha* tends to be directly related to the length of the scale, because half the items of a short scale provide a less stable measure than half the items of a long scale.

RELIABILITY OF ITEM SCORES

To assess the reliability of CBCL item scores, we computed the intraclass correlation coefficient (ICC) from one-way analyses of variance (Bartko, 1976). Used in this way, the ICC reflects the proportion of total variance in item scores that is associated with differences between the items themselves, after the variance due to a specific source of unreliability has been subtracted.

The ICC can be affected both by differences in the *rank ordering* of the correlated scores and differences in their *magnitude*. The Pearson correlation, by contrast, mainly reflects differences in *rank ordering*. Pearson correlations can therefore be large even when two sets of correlated scores differ markedly in magnitude. For example, if Rater A scores every subject 10 points lower than Rater B, their ratings can nevertheless have a Pearson correlation of 1.00. This reflects the identical rank ordering of subjects by both raters, despite the numerical differences in the magnitudes of the scores they assign each subject.

On the other hand, *tests of differences* between the *magnitudes* of two sets of scores can obscure differences between the rank orders of the scores. For example, a *t* test of the difference between scores assigned by Rater C and Rater D might show no significant differences, suggesting good agreement. Yet, the Pearson correlation between their ratings may be .00, reflecting no agreement between their *ranking* of subjects.

Agreement in rank ordering is especially important for some purposes, whereas agreement in the magnitude of scores is important for other purposes. As reported later, we have assessed both kinds of agreement in scale scores.

However, the range of scores for individual items is small (3 points for all problem items and most competence items). Neither correlation coefficients that reflect similarities of rank order nor tests of differences between scores therefore seem as appropriate as the ICC, which reflects both aspects of variance. Because the ICC is applicable to both types of item reliability that we assessed, plus interparent agreement, it also offers a common scale for comparing the relative amount of unreliability contributed by each source of variance.

Inter-Interviewer Reliability of Item Scores

Although the CBCL is designed to be self-administered, there are situations in which an interviewer administers it. To assess the effect of interviewer differences, we compared the results obtained by three interviewers who participated in the home interview survey that provided our pre-1991 normative data on nonreferred children (Achenbach & Edelbrock, 1981). Rather than having each interviewer administer the CBCL to the same parents — which would have confounded test-retest and inter-interviewer reliability — we compared the data obtained by each interviewer on 241 children who were matched for age, sex, ethnicity, and SES to 241 children whose parents were interviewed by each of the other two interviewers.

We thus compared scores obtained by three interviewers on 241 matched triads of children, for a total sample of 723 children. The overall ICC was .927 for the 20 competence items and .959 for the 118 specific problem items (both $p < .001$). This indicates very high inter-interviewer reliability in scores obtained for each item relative to scores obtained for each other item.

Test-Retest Reliability of Item Scores

Test-retest item reliabilities were computed from CBCLs obtained by a single interviewer who visited mothers of 72 nonreferred 4- to 16-year-olds at a 1-week interval. Ratings of nonreferred children were used to assess test-retest reliability, because their scores would be less susceptible to regression toward the mean than the scores of referred children. The overall ICC was .996 for the 20 competence items and .952 for the 118 specific problem items (both $p < .001$). This indicates very high test-retest reliability in scores obtained for each item relative to scores obtained for each other item.

TEST-RETEST RELIABILITY
OF SCALE SCORES

To assess reliability in both the rank ordering and magnitude of scale scores, we computed test-retest rs and t tests of differences between mothers' ratings of 80 nonreferred 4- to 16-year-olds at a mean interval of 7 days (72 subjects were the same as those for whom ICCs were computed for test-retest reliabilities, plus 8 subjects who were added later). Table 5-1 shows the results for boys and girls separately, as well as the mean of their rs. All test-retest rs were significant at $p < .01$. The mean of the rs for all competence scales was .87, while the mean of the rs for all problem scales was .89. All rs were in the .80s and .90s, except the Activities scale (rs .60 to .78), the Withdrawn scale for boys ($r = .75$), and the Thought Problems scale for girls ($r = .63$).

None of the competence scales showed significant changes in mean scores over the 7-day interval. However, there were significant ($p < .05$) declines in scores on the problem scales that are marked with superscript a in Table

Table 5-1
One-Week Test-Retest Reliabilities

Scale		Boys	Girls	Mean r
	N =	39	41	80
Activities		.78	.60	.70
Social		.88	.95	.92
School		.95	.89	.92
Total Competence		.90	.82	.87
	Mean r	.89	.85	.87
Withdrawn		.75[ab]	.87	.82
Somatic Complaints		.97	.92[ab]	.95
Anxious/Depressed		.87[ab]	.85[a]	.86
Social Problems		.87	.86	.87
Thought Problems		.92	.63	.82
Attention Problems		.88[a]	.92	.90
Delinquent Behavior		.87	.85	.86
Aggressive Behavior		.91	.91[a]	.91
Sex Problems[c]		.85	.80	.83
Internalizing		.90[ab]	.87[a]	.89
Externalizing		.91	.95[ab]	.93
Total Problems		.92[ab]	.94[a]	.93
	Mean r	.90	.88	.89

Note. All Pearson *rs* were significant at $p < .001$.
[a]Time 1 > Time 2, $p < .05$ by *t* test.
[b]When corrected for the number of comparisons, Time 1/Time 2 difference was not significant.
[c]Scored only for 24 boys and 29 girls aged 4-11.

5-1. Six of the 11 significant declines would be expected by chance in the 32 comparisons that were made, using a $p <.01$ protection level (Sakoda, Cohen, & Beall, 1954). Superscript b indicates the differences that were most likely to be significant by chance, because they yielded the smallest t values.

The tendency for problem scores to decline over brief test-retest intervals is called a "practice effect" (Milich, Roberts, Loney, & Caputo, 1980), and it has been found in many rating scales (e.g., Evans, 1975; Miller, Hampe, Barrett, & Noble, 1972). It has also been found in structured psychiatric interviews of children (Edelbrock, Costello, Dulcan, Kalas, & Conover, 1985) and adults (Robins, 1985). The declines in CBCL problem scores were small, accounting for a mean of 2% of variance in scale scores, which is at the low end of Cohen's (1988) criteria of 1 to 5.9% for small effect sizes in t tests. Viewed another way, the mean decrease in problem scale scores was 10.7% from their Time 1 to Time 2 mean scores.

As reported later in the chapter, problem scores do not typically decline significantly for nonreferred children over longer periods, such as one and two years. Because assessment decisions are unlikely to be based on readministrations of rating forms over very brief periods, the small declines in problem scores are unlikely to be of much practical significance. To evaluate a child's score relative to the CBCL norms, the child's initial CBCL ratings should be used, as was done in obtaining the normative data. If later reassessments are done to evaluate the effects of interventions on CBCL scores or other measures, it is always advisable to have control groups that did not receive the intervention being evaluated.

If individual children are reassessed, it is advisable to allow at least 2 months between assessments, both to minimize possible "practice effects" and to allow time for behavioral changes to occur and become apparent to raters.

If reassessment intervals shorter than 6 months are used, raters should be instructed to use the same rating period at each interval, rather than the standard 6-month period specified at the top of page 3 of the CBCL/4-18. For example, if children are to be reassessed over a 3-month interval, instructing raters to use a 3-month base period for both their initial and reassessment ratings will avoid allowing differences in lengths of the rating periods to contribute to differences between the initial and reassessment scores. Differences in rating periods such as 3 versus 6 months are not likely to produce large differences in scale scores. Nevertheless, the standard 6-month rating period may pick up a few more reports of low frequency but important and memorable behaviors, such as suicide attempts, running away from home, and firesetting.

INTERPARENT AGREEMENT

Correlations Between Scale Scores

Table 5-2 lists Pearson correlations between raw scale scores from CBCLs completed by parents of American children from clinical and general population samples, plus an Australian general population sample participating in a longitudinal study (Sawyer, 1990). Among the competence scales, the highest interparent correlation was on the School scale for all four groups, where the mean $r = .87$ showed very good agreement between parents. The lowest interparent correlation for competence scales was on the Activities scale for all four groups, with a mean $r = .59$, which also indicated a large degree of association according to Cohen's (1988) criteria. The rs for the competence scales did not differ much in relation to the sex and age of the children, with mean rs ranging from .74 to .76 for the four sex/age groups.

Table 5-2

Interparent Agreement on Scale Scores

Scale	Boys		Girls		Mean r	Odds Ratios[b]
	4-11	12-18	4-11	12-18		
N^a =	182	156	141	120		599
Activities	.62	.53	.59	.62	.59	15.8
Social	.77	.73	.72	.71	.73	23.9
School	.88	.91	.85	.85	.87	116.5
Total Competence	.80	.79	.76	.79	.79	20.4
Mean r	.78	.77	.74	.76		
Withdrawn	.73	.68	.59	.61	.66	11.6
Somatic Complaints	.46	.55	.63	.43	.52	11.5
Anxious/Depressed	.69	.70	.56	.66	.66	15.7
Social Problems	.77	.80	.71	.78	.77	21.3
Thought Problems	.71	.45	.44	.26	.48	10.4
Attention Problems	.80	.78	.82	.75	.79	23.5
Delinquent Behavior	.78	.79	.76	.81	.78	40.2
Aggressive Behavior	.86	.77	.66	.77	.77	28.0
Sex Problems	.54	---	.50	---	.52	14.9
Internalizing	.71	.70	.57	.66	.66	12.0
Externalizing	.86	.79	.70	.81	.80	38.6
Total Problems	.82	.77	.69	.74	.76	25.9
Mean r	.75	.72	.65	.69		

Note. Correlations are Pearson rs between raw scores from CBCLs filled out by parents of American children in clinical and general population samples (N = 213), plus an Australian general population sample participating in a longitudinal study (N = 386; Sawyer, 1990). Seven of the 64 comparisons showed higher mother than father scores by t test at p <.05, but this was fewer than the eight expected by chance, using a .01 protection level (Sakoda, et al., 1954). All rs were significant at p <.01.

[a]Lack of data on some competence items (e.g., for subjects not attending school) reduced sample sizes for competence scales to as low as N = 153, 111, 117, and 87 for the four sex/age groups.

[b]Odds ratios indicate the odds that children would be scored in the clinical range by fathers if they had been scored in the clinical range by mothers, relative to the odds for children who were scored in the normal range by mothers. Confidence intervals showed that all odds ratios were significant at p <.01.

On the problem scales, the highest mean rs across sex/age groups were for Social Problems ($r = .77$), Attention Problems (.79), Delinquent Behavior (.78), Aggressive Behavior (.79), Externalizing (.80), and total problems (.76). The lowest mean rs were for Somatic Complaints ($r = .52$), Thought Problems (.48), and Sex Problems (.52), which all comprise relatively uncommon items. The mean rs for the four sex/age groups ranged from .65 for girls 4-11 to .75 for boys 4-11. All of these exceeded the mean $r = .59$ found for interparent agreement in meta-analyses of many studies (Achenbach et al., 1987).

Magnitude of Scale Scores

The mean scale scores showed nominally significant differences between mothers' and fathers' ratings in 7 of the 64 comparisons at $p < .05$ by t tests. These differences are not marked in Table 5-2, because they are fewer than the 8 out of 64 $p < .05$ differences expected by chance (using a .01 protection level; Sakoda et al., 1954). All differences reflected higher scores in mothers' ratings, including the Somatic Complaints scale for three sex/age groups, Internalizing for both age groups of girls, and Activities and Anxious/Depressed scales each for one group of girls. Although mothers may have a tendency to score their daughters slightly higher in certain areas, the overall tendency did not exceed chance expectations even with the high statistical power afforded by our large samples.

**Odds Ratios for Scores in the
Normal versus Clinical Range**

The rightmost column of Table 5-2 displays relative risk odds ratios (Fleiss, 1981) indicating the degree of agreement between parents in scoring their children in the normal versus clinical range. Because odds ratios are nonparametric statistics based on 2 x 2 tables, children of both sexes and all ages were combined. The odds ratios in Table 5-2 indicate the elevation in odds that children would be scored in the clinical range by their fathers if they had been scored in the clinical range by their mothers, as compared to the odds for children who had not been scored in the clinical range by their mothers. Thus, for example, the odds ratio of 40.2 for Delinquent Behavior in Table 5-2 means that children scored in the clinical range by their mothers were 40.2 times more likely to be scored in the clinical range by their fathers than were children who had not been scored in the clinical range by their mothers. The interparent agreement in classifying children in the normal versus clinical range was exceptionally high for the School scale, as indicated by an odds ratio of 116.5. Confidence intervals showed that all the odds ratios were significantly greater than 1.0, at $p <.01$, demonstrating good agreement between ratings by mothers and fathers in classifying their children in the normal versus clinical range.

LONG-TERM STABILITY OF SCALE SCORES

Table 5-3 displays Pearson correlations between CBCL scale scores for children who were participating in a longitudinal study that included low birthweight and normal birthweight subjects (Achenbach, Phares, Howell, Rauh, & Nurcombe, 1990). Mothers completed the CBCL annually. The correlations are displayed separately for two 1-year intervals (ages 6 to 7 and 7 to 8), as well as for the 2-year interval from age 6 to 8.

As can be seen from Table 5-3, all stability correlations were significant at $p <.01$ over 1- and 2-year periods, except the Sex Problems scale over the 1-year period from age 7 to 8. Averaged across all problem scales, the mean stabilities were large and very similar for both 1-year

Table 5-3
Stability of Scale Scores over 1 and 2 years

| Scale | Age: | 1 year | | 2 years |
		6 vs 7	7 vs 8	6 vs 8
	N =	76	65	70
Activities		.53	.58	.46
Social		.60	.59	.68
School		.63	.72	.51
Total Competence		.67	.59	.56
	Mean r	.61	.63	.56
Withdrawn		.79	.75	.59
Somatic Complaints		.54	.61	.52
Anxious/Depressed		.68	.73	.67
Social Problems		.63	.72	.71
Thought Problems		.49	.68	.60
Attention Problems		.71	.77	.75
Delinquent Behavior		.76	.65	.69
Aggressive Behavior		.84	.87	.87
Sex Problems		.41	(.20)	.39
Internalizing		.75	.82	.70
Externalizing		.87	.86	.86
Total Problems		.84	.86	.85
	Mean r	.72	.74	.71

Note. All rs were significant (*p* <.01) except the one in parentheses. Mean rs were computed by z transformation. Ns were as low as 66, 56, and 60, respectively, for Total Competence because some subjects lacked complete competence data. The nominally significant differences between means did not exceed the number expected by chance.

periods and the 2-year period. Mean rs ranged from .71 to .74, all reflecting large degrees of association, according to Cohen's (1988) criteria for correlations. The highest correlations were found for the Aggressive Behavior, Externalizing, and total problem scores, which ranged from .84 to .87.

The mean stabilities were somewhat lower for the competence scales, ranging from .56 for the 2-year period to .63 for age 7 to 8, but all mean rs for the competence scales were also large according to Cohen's criteria. Only 5 of the 48 comparisons of mean scores showed differences significant at $p < .05$ by t test. Because this is fewer than the 7 expected by chance (Sakoda et al., 1954), they are not indicated in Table 5-3. The overall picture thus indicates considerable stability in mothers' ratings of their children over 1- and 2-year periods. Although two-thirds of the children had been low birthweight (but not organically damaged) infants, their mean problem scores were in the normal range and few had received mental health services.

Among children receiving mental health services, long-term stability coefficients have generally been lower, and significant decreases have been found in problem scores while increases have been found in competence scores (e.g., Achenbach & Edelbrock, 1983, pp. 48-49). Furthermore, experimental studies have shown that certain interventions can reduce CBCL problem scores significantly more than do other interventions or no intervention (Kazdin, Esveldt-Dawson, French, & Unis, 1987). The relatively high long-term stability found in our longitudinal sample thus does not mean that parents' CBCL ratings are insensitive to the effects of interventions with deviant children.

SUMMARY

The inter-interviewer and test-retest reliabilities of the CBCL item scores were supported by intra-class correlations in the .90s for the mean item scores obtained by different interviewers and for reports by parents on two occasions 7 days apart. The test-retest reliability of CBCL scale scores was supported by a mean test-retest $r = .87$ for the competence scales and .89 for the problem scales over a 7-day period. The commonly found tendency for problem scores to decline over brief rating intervals was evident in the CBCL scale scores, but it accounted for a mean of only 2% of the variance in the scores.

Over 1- and 2-year periods, changes in mean scores did not exceed chance expectations. The mean rs over 1-year periods were .62 for competence scales and .75 for problem scales. Over a 2-year period, the mean r was .56 for competence scales and .71 for problem scales.

Good interparent agreement was indicated by mean rs for competence scales ranging from .74 to .76 for the four sex/age groups and mean rs for the problem scales ranging from .65 to .75. Differences in the size of scale scores obtained from mothers and fathers did not exceed chance expectations. Odds ratios showed highly significant agreement between mothers' and fathers' ratings in classifying children as being in the normal versus clinical range on all CBCL scales.

Chapter 6
Validity

The concept of validity pertains to the accuracy with which a procedure measures what it is supposed to measure. Like reliability, validity has multiple facets.

CONTENT VALIDITY

The most elementary form of validity is content validity —i.e., whether a measure's content includes what it is intended to measure. Chapter 1 presented our procedures for assembling CBCL items that tap a broad range of competencies and problems of clinical concern to parents and mental health workers. As documented in Chapter 7, clinically referred children obtained significantly lower scores than demographically similar nonreferred children on nearly all the competence items and higher scores on nearly all the problem items. One competence item (II. Number of nonsports activities) and two problem items (2. Allergy and 4. Asthma) did not show significant differences between referred and nonreferred children on either the CBCL or YSR. Consequently, these items are omitted from the 1991 competence and problem scale scores. The significant associations with referral status for the remaining items indicate that they indeed relate to the independently established mental health concerns that led to referral. However, prospective users should judge whether the content of the CBCL is appropriate for their particular purposes.

CONSTRUCT VALIDITY

Construct validity is perhaps the most discussed but also the most elusive form of validity. For variables that lack a standard operational criterion, construct validity involves a "nomological network" of interrelated procedures intended to reflect the hypothesized variables in different ways (Cronbach & Meehl, 1955). It was the lack of satisfactory constructs and operational definitions for childhood disorders that prompted us to develop the CBCL in order to assess parents' perceptions of their children's competencies and problems. A key index of the validity of the resulting measures is their ability to identify children whose problems arouse enough concern to warrant referral for professional help. This will be discussed in the section on criterion-related validity.

The total problem score can be viewed as representing a general dimension of problems analogous to the construct of general ability represented by total scores on intelligence tests. Similarly, the syndrome scales can be viewed as subgroupings of problems somewhat analogous to the subtests included in many general ability tests, such as the WISC-R. However, most ability subtests consist of items chosen to redundantly measure the hypothetical construct of a specific ability. Our syndromes, by contrast, were empirically derived from covariation among items selected to be nonredundant. Furthermore, the eight cross-informant syndromes were constructed from the common elements of syndromes identified in YSR and TRF ratings, as well as in CBCL ratings.

A key aim of the empirically derived syndromes is to provide common foci for practical applications, research, and training based on sets of problems that have been found to co-occur. In addition, the syndromes can guide inferences about relations between childhood disorders and other variables and can be used to group children in order to test differences in etiology, prognosis, response to treatment, and outcomes. Diverse practical and research applications are discussed in Chapters 9 and 10. The *Bibliography of Published Studies Using the Child Behavior Checklist and Related Materials* (Achenbach & Brown, 1991) lists numerous studies that report findings on relations between CBCL syndrome scales and other variables. The correlates of the syndromes identified through research contribute to construct validity in the sense of advancing the nomological network of which the syndromes are a part.

Correlations with Conners and Quay-Peterson Scales

Another approach to construct validity is by testing associations with assessment procedures that may measure similar constructs. Our empirically derived syndromes were intended to provide a basis for developing better constructs of childhood disorders rather than to operationalize pre-existing constructs. Insofar as other instruments have been used to derive syndromes in multivariate analyses, we can test associations between them and the CBCL scored for the same children, even though the CBCL and the other instruments were not deliberately designed to assess the same items or constructs. Table 6-1 displays correlations between CBCL scale scores and scores from the closest counterpart scales of the Conners (1973) *Parent Question-naire*, while Table 6-2 displays correlations between the CBCL and the Quay-Peterson (1983) *Revised Behavior Problem Checklist*. The data were obtained by having parents of 60 clinically referred 6- to 11-year-olds fill out the three instruments in sequences that were counterbalanced across the sample. The children were being seen in 60 outpatient settings distributed widely across the United States and Canada. CBCL scales that lack counterparts in the Conners or Quay-Peterson instruments are not listed.

Table 6-1
Pearson Correlations Between CBCL Problem
Scales and Connors Parent Questionnaire

Connors (1973) Parent Questionnaire

CBCL	Psycho-somatic	Anxiety	Impuls.-Hyper.	Anti-social	Conduct Problem	Total Problems
Somatic Complaints	.70					
Anxious/ Depressed		.67				
Attention Problems			.59			
Delinquent Behavior				.77	.72	
Aggressive Behavior					.86	
Internalizing	.56	.62				
Externalizing				.67	.86	
Total Problems						.82

Note. Correlations are between CBCL and Conners scales that are most similar in content. N = 42 boys and 18 girls aged 6-11 seen in 60 outpatient settings throughout the United States and Canada. All *rs* were significant at $p < .0001$.

As shown in Table 6-1, the correlations between the CBCL and Conners syndrome scales ranged from .59 for CBCL Attention Problems with Conners Impulsive-Hyperactive, to .86 for CBCL Aggressive Behavior with Conners Conduct Problem. The CBCL and Conners total problem scores correlated .82. Table 6-1 also shows correlations of the CBCL Internalizing and Externalizing scores with Conners scales that correspond to CBCL syndromes belonging to one or the other of the two broad groupings. These correlations were substantial, ranging from .56 to .86, but were generally lower than the correlations of the same Conners scales with their corresponding CBCL syndrome scales.

Table 6-2

Pearson Correlations Between CBCL Problem Scales and Quay-Peterson Revised Behavior Problem Checklist

CBCL	Quay-Peterson (1983) Revised Behavior Problem Checklist						
	Anxiety-Withdr.	Psychotic	Attention Probs	Motor Excess	Socialized Aggress	Conduct Disorder	Total Probs
Withdrawn	.66						
Anxious/ Depressed	.78						
Thought Problems		.64					
Attention Problems			.77	.66			
Delinquent Behavior					.59	.73	
Aggressive Behavior						.88	
Internalizing	.72						
Externalizing					.52	.88	
Total Problems							.81

Note. Correlations are between CBCL and Quay-peterson scales that are most similar in content. $N = 42$ boys and 18 girls aged 6-11 seen in 60 outpatient settings throughout the United States and Canada. All rs were significant at $p < .0001$.

Table 6-2 reveals a similar picture with respect to the Quay-Peterson. The correlations between syndrome scales ranged from .59 for CBCL Delinquent Behavior with Quay-

Peterson Socialized Aggressive, to .88 for CBCL Aggressive Behavior with Quay-Peterson Conduct Disorder. The total problem scores correlated .81, while the correlations of CBCL Internalizing and Externalizing scores with corresponding Quay-Peterson scales ranged from .52 to .88.

Although the item pools, instructions to respondents, response scales, derivation samples, and statistical procedures differed among the three instruments, the correlations in Tables 6-1 and 6-2 indicate that they are tapping several similar constructs. All three instruments clearly tap constructs corresponding to the CBCL Anxious/Depressed, Attention Problems, Delinquent Behavior, and Aggressive Behavior syndromes. The Conners also taps a construct corresponding to the CBCL Somatic Complaints syndrome, while the Quay-Peterson taps additional constructs corresponding to the CBCL Withdrawn and Thought Problems syndromes. Although neither the Conners nor Quay-Peterson had clear counterparts of the CBCL Social Problems syndrome, a clear counterpart of this syndrome was found in the ACQ Behavior Checklist that was developed collaboratively by Achenbach, Conners, and Quay (see Achenbach, Conners, Quay, Verhulst, & Howell, 1989).

The correlations of the CBCL total problem score with those on the Conners *Parent Questionnaire* ($r = .82$) and the Quay-Peterson *Revised Behavior Problem Checklist* ($r = .81$) were as high as are found between full-scale scores on intelligence tests. Similarly, the correlations between our syndrome scales and their counterparts on the Conners and Quay-Peterson instruments were as high as those typically found between different scales designed to test the same abilities (e.g., Wechsler, 1989). Other studies have also shown substantial correlations of the CBCL with the Conners (Achenbach & Edelbrock, 1978; Weissman, Orvashel, & Padian, 1980) and with the Werry-Weiss-Peters Activity Scale (Mash & Johnston, 1983).

CRITERION RELATED VALIDITY

As discussed in the preceding section, the lack of well-validated taxonomic and diagnostic constructs for childhood disorders was a primary reason for developing the CBCL. Although the American Psychiatric Association's (1980, 1987) *Diagnostic and Statistical Manual* (DSM) serves as an official administrative classification, its categories of childhood disorders have not been based on direct assessment of children, and the reliability of DSM childhood diagnoses has been mediocre (e.g., American Psychiatric Association, 1980; Mezzich, Mezzich, & Coffman, 1985). Furthermore, both the descriptive features to be assessed and the diagnostic categories of the DSM underwent major changes from DSM-III to DSM-III-R and are changing again in DSM-IV. The changes prevent precise calibration between diagnoses made with one edition of the DSM and diagnoses made with other editions.

Studies have shown significant relations between DSM diagnoses and pre-1991 CBCL, TRF, and YSR syndrome scores (Edelbrock & Costello, 1988; Edelbrock, Costello, & Kessler, 1984; Weinstein, Noam, Grimes, Stone, & Schwab-Stone, 1990). These findings indicate some degree of convergence between the empirically derived syndromes and the DSM approach. It is to be hoped that there will be further research on relations between the two approaches and further convergence. However, because the DSM cannot be properly regarded as a criterion for the empirically derived scales and there is no other recognized external criterion that is specific to our scales, we analyzed the degree to which each scale discriminated between criterion groups consisting of children referred for mental health services and demographically matched nonreferred children.

Referral status is not an infallible criterion of children's need for help. Some children in our referred samples may have been referred because of custody disputes, parents' desire for help with their own problems, or excessive concern about behavior that is in the normal range. On the other hand, some children in our nonreferred samples may have been candidates for imminent referral. If we were able to exclude *(a)* referred children who should not have been referred and *(b)* nonreferred children who should have been referred, this could increase the differences between the scores of our referred and nonreferred samples. Furthermore, the criterion of referral is not specific to any one of our scales. Although some children may have problems mainly of the sort included on one of our syndrome scales, other referred children may not be deviant on that scale at all but have problems in other areas.

Because the criterion of referral is fallible and referred children may be deviant in ways very different from what is represented by a particular scale, our findings may underestimate the associations between our scales and deviance specific to the area tapped by a particular scale. Nevertheless, because of the lack of other well-established validity criteria, clinical referral seemed an ecologically more valid criterion than other criteria that can be applied to large representative samples (Achenbach & Edelbrock, 1981, have reviewed alternative criteria).

By comparing demographically matched referred and nonreferred samples, we prevented possible demographic differences in scores from being confounded with referral status. In addition to referral status (coded 0 versus 1), we included age, ethnicity, and SES as independent variables in multiple regression analyses where CBCL scale scores were the dependent variables. In the regression analysis of each scale, we computed the percent of total variance accounted for by each independent variable after variables accounting for more variance were partialled out. In this way, we could identify the statistical significance and magnitude of any demographic differences, as well as differences between the scale scores obtained by referred versus nonreferred children.

Samples Analyzed

To form demographically matched samples, we drew subjects from our clinical sample (described in Chapter 3) who could be matched to subjects of the same age and sex from our normative sample (described in Chapter 2). The subjects were precisely matched for sex and age and were matched as closely as possible for who completed the CBCL (mother, father, other), ethnicity, and SES scored on Hollingshead's (1975) 9-step scale for parental occupation. For the nonreferred sample, 82% of CBCLs were completed by mothers, 15% by fathers, and 3% by other informants, compared to 81%, 11%, and 9%, respectively, for the referred sample. Mean SES was 5.5 (SD = 2.2) for the nonreferred sample, compared to 5.2 (SD = 2.3) for the referred sample. Ethnicity was 74% white, 16% black, and 10% mixed or other for the nonreferred sample, compared to 83% white, 14% black, and 3% mixed or other for the referred sample.

Multiple regressions were performed for all competence and problem scores separately for each sex at ages 4-11 and 12-18. (Competence scales were not scored for ages 4-5.) Table 6-3 displays the N for each sample and the percent of variance in each scale that was accounted for by significant ($p < .01$) associations with referral status, age within the age range analyzed, SES, and ethnicity, which was analyzed via dummy variables coded as white = 1, nonwhite = 0 and black = 1, nonblack = 0. There were not enough subjects of any one other ethnic group to warrant entry as a separate independent variable. To take account of possible chance effects occurring in such a large number of analyses, we have marked (superscript f) the number of nominally significant effects that could have arisen by chance in the analyses of each independent variable within each sex/age group. In view of our large Ns, we used a .01 alpha level and a .01 protection level for determining the number of significant findings apt to occur by chance (Sakoda et al., 1954). The effects marked with superscript f are the nominally significant effects that had the smallest F values, which are assumed to be the effects most likely to be significant by chance.

The effect size for each variable is represented by the semipartial r^2 obtained after partialling out any other independent variables that accounted for more variance in the scale score. According to Cohen's (1988) criteria for effect sizes when other independent variables are partialled out, regression coefficients accounting for 2 to 13% of variance in the dependent variable are considered small; coefficients accounting for 13 to 26% of variance are medium; and effects accounting for >26% of variance are large.

Referral Status Differences Between Scale Scores

As shown in Table 6-3, all competence scales were scored higher and all problem scales were scored lower for nonreferred than referred children at $p < .01$. The differences between referred and nonreferred children were consistently large across all four sex/age groups on the Attention Problems scale, where referral status accounted for 26 to 32% of variance, and on the total problem score, where referral status accounted for 29 to 32% of variance. The School scale and total competence score both showed large effects of referral status in three of the four sex/age groups, with effect sizes ranging from 31 to 37% of variance in the School scale and 26 to 35% of variance in the total competence score for the three groups. Large effects of referral status were also found on the Social scale for boys at ages

Table 6-3
Percent of Variance Accounted for by Significant ($p < .01$) Effects of Referral Status, Age, SES, and Ethnicity in Scale Scores for Matched Referred and Nonreferred Samples

Scale[a]	1,164 Boys Aged 4-11				1,238 Girls Aged 4-11			
	Ref Stat[b]	Age[c]	SES[d]	White[e]	Ref Stat[b]	Age[c]	SES[d]	White[e]
Activities	3[f]	2[O]	<1[f]	--	5[f]	4[O]	<1[f]	--
Social	18	1[O]	--	<1[Wf]	16	1[O]	4	<1[Wf]
School	37	<1[Yf]	<1	--	31	--	1	--
Total Competence	26	1[O]	<1[f]	2[Wf]	24	3[O]	4	2[N]
Withdrawn	16	<1[O]	--	--	18	<1[Of]	--	--
Somatic Complaints	7	1[O]	--	--	7	3[O]	--	--
Anxious/Depressed	21	2[O]	<1	--	23	3[O]	--	--
Social Problems	24	--	<1	--	25	<1[Of]	<1	--
Thought Problems	16	--	--	--	15	--	--	--
Attention Problems	31	1[O]	<1	--	30	<1[O]	<1[f]	--
Delinquent Behavior	21	1[O]	<1	--	16	--	--	<1[Nf]
Aggressive Behavior	24	--	<1	--	20	--	--	--
Sex Problems	5[f]	<1[Yf]	--	--	5[f]	--	--	--
Internalizing	23	2[O]	<1	--	23	3[O]	--	--
Externalizing	26	--	<1	--	21	--	--	--
Total Problems	32	--	<1	--	30	--	--	--

Scale	900 Boys Aged 12-18					918 Girls Aged 12-18				
Activities	6[f]	1[Y]	<1[f]	--	1[Wf]	7[f]	1[Yf]	2	<1[f]?	1[Wf]
Social	30	--	<1	--	--[Wf]	20	--	2	--	1[Wf]
School	31	--	--	--	<1[Wf]	25	--	--	--	--
Total Competence	35	--	<1[f]	--	<1[W]	26	--	2	--	1[W]
Withdrawn	19	--	--	--	--	22	--	--	<1[f]	--
Somatic Complaints	7[f]	--	--	--	--	10[f]	--	--	--	--
Anxious/Depressed	20	--	--	--	--	22	--	--	--	--
Social Problems	19	2[Y]	--	--	--	12	--	--	--	--
Thought Problems	16	--	--	--	--	15	--	--	--	--
Attention Problems	32	--	--	--	--	26	--	--	<1[f]	--
Delinquent Behavior	25	--	--	--	--	24	--	--	1	--
Aggressive Behavior	20	3[Y]	--	--	--	20	--	--	<1	--
Internalizing	21	--	--	--	--	24	--	--	--	--
Externalizing	25	<1[Yf]	--	--	--	24	--	--	1	--
Total Problems	31	<1[Yf]	--	--	--	29	--	--	<1	--

Note. Analyses were multiple regressions of raw scale scores on referral status, age, SES, white vs. nonwhite, and black vs. nonblack. The percent of variance accounted for by each independent variable is represented by the semipartial r^2 for that variable after partialling out the effects of variables accounting for more variance. [a]Competence scales exclude 246 boys and 298 girls aged 4-5. [b]All competence scores were higher and problem scores were lower for nonreferred than referred. [c]O=older scored higher; Y=younger scored higher. [d]All significant SES effects reflected higher competence and lower problem scores for upper than lower SES. [e]W=whites scored higher; N=nonwhite scored higher. The number of significant effects for black vs. nonblack did not exceed chance expectations. [f]Not significant when corrected for number of analyses.

12-18 (30% of variance) and the Externalizing scale for boys at ages 4-11 (26% of variance).

The consistency with which the Attention Problems scale showed large effects is especially important in light of findings that this syndrome was among the best predictors of signs of disturbance from 1986 to 1989 in the national general population sample from which many of our non-referred subjects were drawn (McConaughy, Stanger, & Achenbach, 1991; Stanger, McConaughy, & Achenbach, 1991). On the basis of its strong concurrent association with referral and its strong 3-year predictive power, the Attention Problems scale thus appears to be an especially good indicator of need for help.

At the other extreme, the only scales that consistently showed small effects of referral status across all four sex/age groups were Activities, with effect sizes ranging from 3 to 7% of variance, and Somatic Complaints, with effects ranging from 7 to 10% of variance. The Sex Problems syndrome, which is scored only for ages 4-11, also showed small effects of 5% for both sexes. Because the Sex Problems syndrome was found only in CBCL ratings of 4-to 11-year-olds and consists of low frequency items, it is not displayed on the profile. It should be viewed as providing supplementary data about a particular class of problems rather than as a strong indicator of need for professional help. Similarly, the Activities and Somatic Complaints scales are apt to be more useful as descriptions of particular areas of functioning than as strong indicators of need for professional help.

The only other difference between referred and non-referred children that fell within Cohen's criteria for small effects was the 12% effect of referral status on the Social Problems scale for 12- to 18-year-old girls. All other differences between referred and nonreferred children accounted for >15% of variance in scale scores.

Demographic Differences Between Scale Scores

Because the number of significant effects of black versus nonblack ethnicity did not exceed the two expected by chance for any sex/age group, these are not displayed in Table 6-3. All of the significant effects of age, SES, and white versus nonwhite ethnicity fell either at the very low end of the 2 to 13% range defined by Cohen as small or below this range. Age effects ran in both directions, with some reflecting higher scores among younger children and some higher scores among older children. The exact shape of the age effects can be seen in Figure 6-1, which shows the mean raw scale scores obtained by referred and non-referred children of each sex from 4 to 18 years of age. The significant SES effects all reflected higher competence scores and lower problem scores for upper than lower SES children. The few effects of white versus nonwhite ethnicity ran in both directions, with some scores being higher for whites and some for nonwhites.

CLASSIFICATION OF CHILDREN ACCORDING TO CLINICAL CUTPOINTS

The regression analyses reported in the previous section showed that all quantitative scale scores significantly discriminated between referred and nonreferred children after partialling out the effects of demographic variables. Beside the quantitative scores, each scale has cutpoints for distinguishing categorically between the normal and clinical range. The choice of cutpoints for the different scales was discussed in Chapters 2, 3, and 4.

For some clinical and research purposes, users may wish to distinguish between children who are in the normal versus clinical range according to the cutpoints. Because categorical distinctions are usually least reliable for individ-

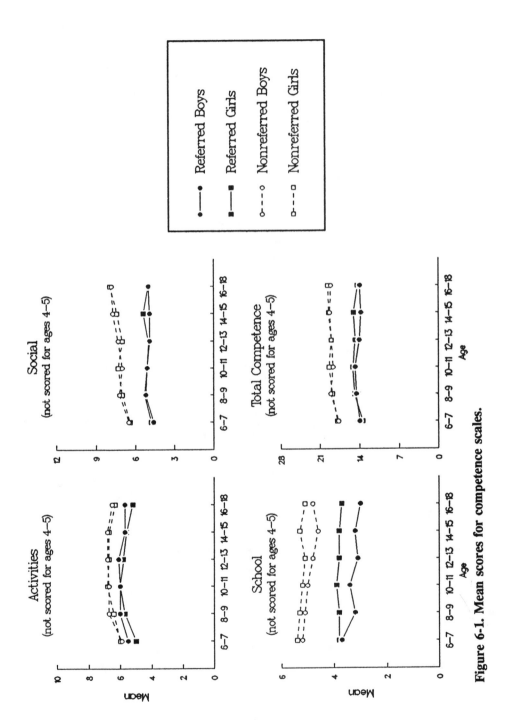

Figure 6-1. Mean scores for competence scales.

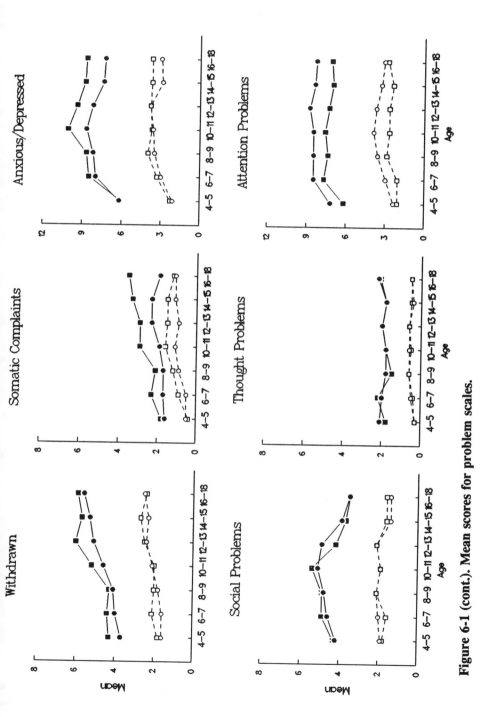

Figure 6-1 (cont.). Mean scores for problem scales.

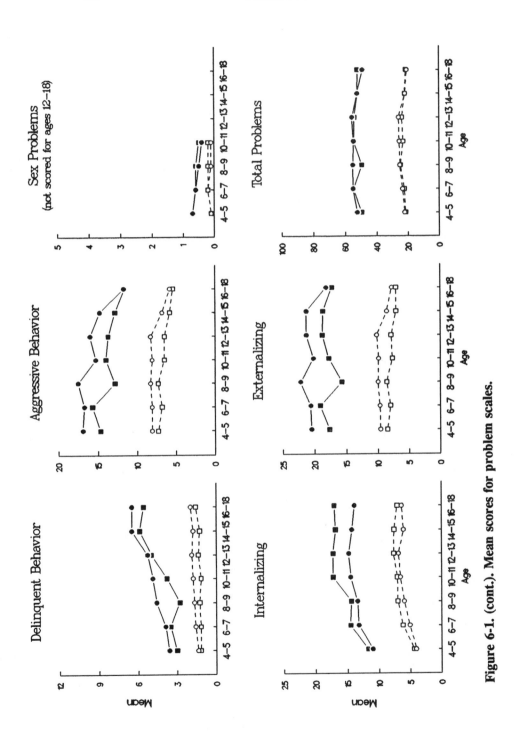

Figure 6-1. (cont.). Mean scores for problem scales.

uals who score close to the border of a category, we have identified a borderline clinical range for each scale. The addition of a borderline category often yields stronger associations between clinical status and classification of children according to their scale scores. This was demonstrated by phi correlations computed in our matched samples for the association between clinical status and scores trichotomized into the normal, borderline clinical, and clinical ranges versus phi correlations for scores dichtomized into the normal and clinical range (including borderline clinical scores). In virtually all comparisons on all scales for each sex/age group, the inclusion of the borderline range yielded higher phi correlations than did the dichotomous classification into the normal versus clinical range. Inclusion of the borderline category also yielded higher phi correlations for agreement between scores obtained from pairs of informants, including mother versus father, parent versus teacher, parent versus youth, and teacher versus youth (Achenbach, 1991a).

Despite the greater statistical power generally afforded by continuous quantitative scores and even by inclusion of a borderline range, users may wish to distinguish categorically between the normal and clinical range. The following sections report findings that indicate the degree to which classification of CBCL scale scores as normal versus clinical distinguish between demographically matched referred versus nonreferred children.

Odds Ratios

One approach to analyzing associations between categorical classifications is by computing *relative risk odds ratios* (Fleiss, 1981), which are used in epidemiological research. The odds ratio indicates the odds of having a particular condition (usually a disorder) among people who have a particular risk factor, relative to the odds of having the condition among people who lack that risk factor. The comparison between outcome rates for those who do and do not have the risk factor is expressed as the ratio of the odds of having the outcome if the risk factor is present, to the odds of having the outcome if the risk factor is absent. For example, a study of relations between smoking and lung cancer may yield a relative risk odds ratio of 5.5. This means that people who smoke have 5.5 times greater odds of developing lung cancer than people who do not smoke.

We applied odds ratio analyses to the relations between CBCL scores and referral status as follows: For each CBCL scale, we first classified children from our matched referred and nonreferred samples according to whether they scored in the normal range or in the clinical range (including the borderline clinical range). Being in the clinical range was thus equivalent to a "risk factor" in epidemiological research. We then computed the odds that children who were in the clinical range on a particular scale were from the referred sample, relative to the odds for children who were not in the clinical range. (Because referred children were already referred at the time they were rated on the CBCL, we could also have made referral status the "risk factor" and CBCL scores the "outcome variable." However, because we used odds ratios to indicate the strength of the contemporaneous association between CBCL scores and referral status, rather than a predictive relation between a risk factor and a later outcome, the choice of the risk factor was not important and did not affect the obtained odds ratios.)

The relative risk odds ratio is a nonparametric statistic computed from a 2 x 2 table. We therefore included both sexes and all ages in the same analysis to provide a summary odds ratio across all subjects. The statistical significance of the odds ratio is evaluated by computing confidence intervals.

Table 6-4 summarizes the odds ratios for relations between scale scores in the clinical range and referral status. Table 6-4 also shows the percent of referred and nonreferred children who scored in the clinical range according to the cutpoints on the scales. Confidence intervals showed that all the odds ratios were significantly greater than 1.0, while chi squares showed that the differences between referred and nonreferred children scoring in the clinical range were significant in all comparisons. Nine of the odds ratios were greater than 10, indicating that the odds of being in the referred group were more than 10 time higher for children whose scale scores were in the clinical range than for children whose scale scores were in the normal range. The largest odds ratios were for Attention Problems (odds ratio = 13.7), the School scale (13.6), and deviance on either one or both of the total competence and total problem scores versus deviance on neither score (11.0).

Combined Competence and Problem Scores

Each competence and syndrome scale reflects deviance in a particular area that may characterize only a small proportion of referred children. The total competence and total problem scores, on the other hand, tap the full range of functioning assessed by the CBCL. The less extreme cutpoints for these scores automatically classify larger percents of both the referred and nonreferred samples as being in the clinical range than do the more extreme cutpoints of the specific competence and syndrome scales. As Table 6-4 shows, 61% of referred children scored in the clinical range on the total competence score and 68% on the total problem score. This compares with 16% of the nonreferred children scoring in the clinical range on the total competence score and 18% on the total problem score.

Table 6-4
Odds Ratios and Percent of Referred and
Nonreferred Samples Scoring in the Clinical Range

Scale	Odds ratio	Percent in Clinical Range	
		Referred	Nonreferred
Activities (ages 6-18)	2.4	10	4
Social (ages 6-18)	7.6	28	5
School (ages 6-18)	13.6	40	4
Total Competence (ages 6-18)	8.0	61	16
Withdrawn	8.3	30	5
Somatic Complaints	3.9	20	6
Anxious/Depressed	10.1	34	5
Social Problems	10.9	34	5
Thought Problems	8.5	28	4
Attention Problems	13.7	43	5
Delinquent Behavior	10.5	40	6
Aggressive Behavior	10.2	36	5
Sex Problems (ages 4-11)	5.4	14	3
Internalizing	7.0	60	18
Externalizing	7.2	60	17
Total Problems	10.2	68	18
≥1 Syndrome in Clinical Range	10.8	75	22
Int and/or Ext in Clinical Range	8.5	76	27
Total Comp and/or Probs in Clinical Range	11.0	82	30

Note. Total N = 2,110 referred and 2,110 demographically-matched nonreferred, except Competence (N = 3,716) and Sex Problems (N = 2,402). In all analyses, the proportion of referred scoring in the clinical range was significantly greater than the proportion of nonreferred at $p < .01$ according to confidence intervals for odds ratios and chi squares for 2 x 2 tables.

When the cutpoints for the total competence and problem scores were combined by classifying children as clinical if they were deviant on either or both scores, 82% of the referred sample and 30% of the nonreferred sample were classified as clinical, as shown in Table 6-4.

The combination of the total competence and problem scores can be used to create a borderline range that takes account of both measures. This can be done by classifying children into the following four categories: *(a)* normal range on both the total competence and total problem scores; *(b)* clinical range on the competence score but normal on the problem score; *(c)* normal on the competence score but clinical on the problem score; and *(d)* clinical on both scores. When category *a* was defined as normal, categories *b* and *c* as borderline, and category *d* as clinical, 17.7% of the referred children were classified as normal (i.e., they were "false negatives"), while 4.2% of the nonreferred children were classified as clinical (i.e., they were "false positives"). (These percents were obtained by computing the percents of false negatives and false positives separately for each of the four sex/age groups and then taking their unweighted mean.)

Combining the false negatives obtained in the referred samples with the false positives obtained in the nonreferred samples produced an overall misclassification rate of 10.9%, with 29.8% classified as borderline. The borderline group could be reduced to 12.7% by combining category *c* (deviant only on the total problem score) with category *d* (deviant on both the competence and problem scores). However, this increased the false positive rate to 17.4%, for an overall misclassification rate of 17.5%.

Because it is seldom warranted to make a definitive clinical versus nonclinical judgment on the basis of any single procedure, it is prudent to allow a borderline group. Thus, the combination of total competence and total problem scores can yield a very good overall misclassification rate of 10.9% (17.7% false negatives and 4.2% false positives) as judged by our criterion of referral status, if a 29.8% borderline group is allowed. This borderline group can be reduced to 12.7% by including only children who are in the normal range on the total problem score but deviant on the total competence score, yielding an overall misclassification rate of 17.5%.

Discriminant Analyses

The foregoing sections dealt with the use of unweighted combinations of total competence and problem scores to discriminate between children who were referred for help with behavioral/emotional problems versus children who were not referred. It is possible that weighted combinations of total scores, scales, or items might produce better discrimination. To test this possibility, we performed discriminant analyses in which the criterion groups were the demographically matched referred and nonreferred children, analyzed separately for each sex at ages 6-11 and 12-18 (4-5-year-olds were omitted, because they are not scored on the 1991 competence scales). Sample sizes ranged from 740 to 857.

The following three sets of discriminant analyses were performed for each sex/age group: *(a)* the total competence and problem scores were used as predictors; *(b)* the three competence scales and all the syndrome scales (including Sex Problems for 6-11-year-olds) were used as candidate predictors from which significant predictors were selected; *(c)* all the competence and problem items were used as candidate predictors from which significant predictors were selected.

Discriminant analyses selectively weight predictors to maximize their collective associations with the particular criterion groups being analyzed. The weighting process makes use of characteristics of the sample that may differ from other samples. To avoid overestimating the accuracy of the classification obtained by discriminant analyses, it is therefore necessary to correct for the "shrinkage" in associations that would occur when discriminant weights derived in one sample are applied in a new sample. To correct for shrinkage, we employed a "jackknife" procedure whereby the discriminant function for each sample is computed multiple times with a different subject held out of the sample each time (SAS Institute, 1988). The discriminant function is then cross-validated multiple times by testing the accuracy of its prediction for each of the "hold-out" subjects. Finally, the percentage of correct predictions is computed across all the hold-out subjects. It is these cross-validated predictions that we will present.

Total Competence and Problem Scores. In all four sex/age groups, the percent of nonreferred children obtaining weighted combinations of scores in the clinical range was about half the percent of referred children obtaining weighted combinations of scores in the normal range. Averaged across the four sex/age groups, 14.1% of nonreferred children were classified as clinical (false positives), whereas 27.0% of referred children were classified as normal (false negatives). The mean misclassification rate of 20.6% was somewhat better than the mean misclassification rate of 23.6% obtained by classifying children as normal if both their (unweighted) total competence and problem scores were in the normal range and as clinical if one or both scores were in the clinical range. However, it was not as good as the 10.9% misclassification rate obtained by allowing 29.8% borderline cases who were normal on one score but not the other.

Scale Scores. When the three competence scales and all the syndrome scales were tested as candidate predictors, from four to six scales were retained as making significant

(p <.05) independent contributions. Of the competence scales, both the School and Social scales were significant predictors in all four sex/age groups. Of the syndrome scales, the Anxious/Depressed syndrome was a significant predictor in all four groups, while the Attention Problems and Delinquent Behavior syndromes were significant predictors in three groups. The Aggressive Behavior, Social Problems, and Withdrawn syndromes were significant predictors in one group each. The false positive rate was 12.1% and false negative rate was 23.2%, for a total misclassification rate of 17.7%, which was better than the 20.6% obtained with the weighted combination of total competence and problem scores.

Item Scores. When all competence and problem items were tested as candidate predictors, from 17 to 19 problem items and from 7 to 9 competence items were retained as significant (p <.05) predictors. Among the competence items, the open-ended item for reporting school problems was the strongest predictor in all four sex/age groups, while *Gets along with others* and *Academic performance* were among the three strongest predictors in three of the four sex/age groups.

Among the problem items, Item *103. Unhappy, sad, or depressed* was among the three strongest predictors for all four sex/age groups. (As reported in Chapter 7, the exceptionally good discriminative power of this item was also evident in ANCOVAs that combined all ages and both sexes.) Item *61. Poor school work* was among the three strongest predictors for all groups except 12-18-year-old girls, while Item *43. Lying or cheating* was among the three strongest predictors for 12-18-year-olds of both sexes.

Averaged across the four sex/age groups, misclassifications included 8.4% false positives and 21.8% false negatives, for a total misclassification rate of 15.1%. Although this is a relatively low misclassification rate, it was obtained

Table 6-5
Probability of Total Competence T Score
Being from Referred Sample

Total T Score	Boys 4-11	Boys 12-18	Girls 4-11	Girls 12-18
N^a =	788	726	836	772
0 - 24	.93	.94	1.00	1.00
25 - 28	.91	.90	.88	.85
29 - 32	.87	.92	.81	.87
33 - 36	.81	.83	.75	.83
37 - 40[b]	.65	.69	.74	.66
41 - 44	.58	.46	.60	.56
45 - 48	.38	.43	.41	.42
49 - 52	.28	.31	.32	.32
53 - 56	.20	.07	.25	.23
57 - 60	.23	.09	.09	.16
61 - 64	.17	.00	.09	.19
65 - 80	.00	.07	.20	.11

Note. Samples were demographically matched referred and nonreferred children, excluding ages 4-5 for whom competence scales are not scored.
[a]Ns are smaller than for total problem scores because ages 4-5 and children not attending school were excluded.
[b]T scores $\leq$ 40 are in the clinical range.

by using different weighted combinations of numerous items for each sex/age group. If optimal discrimination is sought between deviant and nondeviant children, it still seems preferable to use a criterion of the unweighted total competence and problem scores being in the normal versus clinical range, with children who are deviant on only one of the scores being classified as borderline.

Table 6-6
Probability of Total Problem T Score
Being from Referred Sample

Total T Score	Boys 4-11	Boys 12-18	Girls 4-11	Girls 12-18
$N =$	1,164	900	1,238	918
0 - 35	.12	.08	.15	.17
36 - 39	.12	.03	.19	.24
40 - 43	.19	.09	.18	.11
44 - 47	.20	.18	.23	.19
48 - 51	.22	.21	.27	.22
52 - 55	.38	.35	.33	.34
56 - 59	.46	.54	.40	.49
60[a]- 63	.48	.63	.57	.59
64 - 67	.74	.77	.76	.78
68 - 71	.87	.83	.85	.82
72 - 75	.94	.92	.92	.93
76 - 100	.99	.95	1.00	.95

Note. Samples were demographically matched referred and nonreferred children.
[a]T scores ≥ 60 are in the clinical range.

PROBABILITY OF PARTICULAR TOTAL SCORES BEING FROM THE REFERRED VERSUS NONREFERRED SAMPLES

To provide a further picture of relations between particular scores and referral status, Tables 6-5 and 6-6 display the probability of particular total competence and problem T scores being from our referred samples. The probabilities were determined by tabulating the proportion of children from our matched referred and nonreferred samples who had scores within each of the intervals shown. T scores were used to provide a uniform metric across all four sex/age groups. Because T scores for the total competence and problem scores were not truncated, they are highly correlated with the raw scores.

As can be seen from Table 6-5, the probability that a competence score was from the referred sample *decreased* steadily as the magnitude of competence scores increased. Once a probability of .50 was reached, all the succeeding scores had probabilities <.50. Conversely, in Table 6-6, the probability that a total problem score was from the referred sample *increased* steadily with the magnitude of the scores. Once a probability of .50 was reached, all the succeeding scores had probabilities >.50. Users can refer to Tables 6-5 and 6-6 to estimate the likelihood that particular competence and problem scores represent deviance severe enough to warrant concern.

SUMMARY

This chapter presented several kinds of evidence for the validity of CBCL scores. *Content validity* is supported by the ability of nearly all CBCL items to discriminate significantly between demographically matched referred and nonreferred children (documented by analyses presented in Chapter 7). *Construct validity* is supported by numerous correlates of CBCL scales, including significant associations with analogous scales on the Conners (1973) *Parent Questionnaire* and the Quay-Peterson (1983) *Revised Behavior Problem Checklist*. *Criterion-related validity* is supported by the ability of the CBCL's quantitative scale scores to discriminate between referred and nonreferred children after demographic effects were partialled out.

Clinical cutpoints on the scale scores were also shown to discriminate significantly between demographically matched referred and nonreferred children.

Several procedures were presented for discriminating between children like those in our referred versus non-referred samples. One of the most effective ways to optimize discrimination is by classifying children as normal if their total competence and problem scores are both in the normal range and as deviant if both these scores are in the clinical range. Children who are in the normal range on one score and in the clinical range on the other are then classified as borderline between the two groups that are more clearly classifiable. Findings from discriminant analyses indicated the individual items and scales that contribute the most discriminative power when taken together with all other items or scales.

Chapter 7
Item Scores

Beside being the basis for the CBCL profile scales, the CBCL items provide scores for specific competencies and problems, as reported by parents. To determine which items discriminated significantly between children referred for mental health services and nonreferred children, we performed analyses of covariance (ANCOVA) on the item scores obtained by the demographically matched samples described in Chapter 6. The ANCOVA design was 2 (referral status) x 2 (sex) x 7 (ages 4-5, 6-7, 8-9, 10-11, 12-13, 14-15, 16-18). The number of subjects per cell ranged from 118 for 16-18-year-old girls to 185 for 12-13 year-old girls, with a mean of 149 children per cell. The total N was 4,220, with equal numbers of demographically matched referred and nonreferred children. SES was covaried using the 9-step Hollingshead (1975) scores for parental occupation. Ethnicity was covaried by creating a dummy variable scored 1 for white versus 0 for nonwhite and a second dummy variable scored 1 for black versus 0 for nonblack. There were not enough subjects of any one other ethnic group to warrant creating an additional dummy variable for another ethnic group.

COMPETENCE SCORES

As reported in Chapter 6, the competence scales were included in the regression analyses of scale scores, but they were also included in the ANCOVAs reported here to provide direct comparison with findings for the item scores.

111

The competence scales and items were scored as they are scored on the CBCL profile. For example, on Item *I. Please list the sports your child most likes to take part in*, a *0* is scored if the parent indicates either no sport or one sport. A *1* is scored if the parent lists two sports, and a *2* is scored if the parent lists three sports. Similar scores are assigned to the items for nonsports hobbies, games, and activities, number of organizations, and number of jobs and chores. Appendix A provides the scoring rules for all the competence items.

Initial 2 x 2 x 7 ANCOVAs yielded numerous age x referral status interactions. Least significant difference contrasts revealed that many of these interactions were due to smaller differences between the referred and nonreferred samples at ages 4-5 than at older ages. In fact, the differences between referred and nonreferred 4-5-year-olds were small enough that there seemed to be insufficient justification for including their competence scores in scales or analyses with those for older children. We therefore performed new 2 x 2 x 6 ANCOVAs of the competence scores without the 4-5-year-olds, and these ages are omitted from the 1991 competence scales.

Table 7-1 displays the ANCOVA results in terms of the percent of variance accounted for by each effect that was significant at $p < .01$. According to Cohen's (1988) criteria for the magnitude of effects in ANCOVA, effects accounting for 1 to 5.9% of variance are considered small, effects accounting for 5.9 to 13.8% of variance are medium, and effects accounting for $\geq 13.8\%$ of variance are large. Because the effect of each independent variable and covariate was tested for each of the 16 competence items, 3 scales, and total competence score, we have indicated with superscript *h* the 2 out of 20 effects that were most likely to be significant by chance, because they had the smallest *F* values (Sakoda et al., 1954).

Table 7-1

Percent of Variance Accounted for by Significant

(p < .01) Effects of Referral Status and

Demographic Variables on Competence Scores

Item	Ref Status[a]	Sex[b]	Age[c]	Interactions[d]			SES[e]	Covariates	
				RxS	RxA	SxA		White[f]	Black[g]
I. A.Number of sports	<1[h]	2[M]	3[Y]	—	—	—	<1	—	<1[N]
B.Sports part/skill	2	<1[M]	<1[NL]	—	—	—	<1[h]	<1	—
II. A.Number of activ	—	<1[Fh]	5[Y]	—	—	—	1	<1	—
B.Activ part/skill	2	—	—	—	—	—	<1	<1	—
III. A.Number of organ	3	—	1[O]	—	<1[h]	<1[h]	2	<1	—
B.Partic in organ	6	—	<1[O]	—	<1[h]	—	1	<1	—
IV. A.Number of jobs	1[h]	—	2[O]	—	—	—	—	—	—
B.Job performance	6	<1[Fh]	2[O]	—	—	—	—	—	—
V. 1.Number of friends	9	—	<1[O]	—	—	—	—	<1[Nh]	<1[Bh]
2.Contacts with fr	2	<1[M]	—	<1[h]	—	—	—	<1	<1[B]
VI. A.Gets along	21	—	<1[Oh]	—	—	—	<1	—	—
B.Work/play alone	8	—	—	<1[h]	—	<1[h]	<1[h]	<1	—
VII. 1.Mean acad perf	19	2[F]	<1[Y]	<1[h]	—	—	<1	<1	—
2.(No) Spec class	10	<1[F]	<1[NL]	<1	—	—	<1	—	—
3.(No) Repeat grade	3	2[F]	2[Y]	—	—	—	—	<1[h]	—
4.(No) Acad prob	29	<1[F]	<1[Yh]	—	—	—	<1	—	—

Table 7-1 (Continued)

Item	Ref Status[a]	Sex[b]	Age[c]	Interactions[d] RxS	RxA	SxA	Covariates SES[e]	White[f]	Black[g]
Activities scale	5	<1[M]	2[NL]	--	--	--	<1	<1	--
Social scale	21	--	1[O]	--	<1	--	1	<1	<1[Nh]
School scale	29	2[F]	<1[Y]	<1	--	<1	<1	--	--
Total competence	26	--	<1[O]	--	--	--	1	<1	--

Note. $N = 3,716$ demographically matched referred and nonreferred 6- to 18-year-olds (4-5-year-olds are omitted). Items are designated with summary labels for their content. Effects of 3-way interactions are omitted because they did not exceed chance expectations.

[a]All scores were higher for nonreferred than referred.

[b]F = females scored higher; M = males scored higher.

[c]NL = nonlinear effect of age; O = older scored higher; Y = younger scored higher.

[d]R x S = referral status x sex; R x A = referral status x age; S x A = sex x age.

[e]All significant effects indicated higher scores for upper SES.

[f]Except Item V.1. (superscripted N), all significant effects indicated higher scores for whites.

[g]B = higher scores for blacks; N = higher scores for nonblacks.

[h]Not significant when corrected for number of analyses.

Referral Status Differences in Competence Scores

As Table 7-1 shows, all scales and items except *II.A. Number of nonsports activities* yielded significantly lower scores for referred than nonreferred children at p <.01. Because the mean scores for number of nonsports activities were 1.1 for both the referred and nonreferred samples, it was deleted from the 1991 Activities and total competence scores, as discussed in Chapter 2.

Differences between referred and nonreferred children had large effects on the reports of school problems and total School scale, with referral status accounting for 29% of the variance in both of them. Differences between referred and nonreferred children also had large effects on the total competence score (26% of variance), the mean of scores for getting along with siblings, other children and parents (21%), the Social scale (21%), and the mean of scores for performance in academic subjects (19%). Referral status had medium effects in 4 comparisons, small effects in 8, and accounted for <1% of variance in the remaining comparison, which concerned the number of sports.

There was one significant 3-way interaction, which accounted for <1% of variance. Because it did not exceed the two significant effects expected by chance, this interaction is not displayed in Table 7-1. Three significant interactions of referral status x sex, referral status x age, and sex x age all accounted for <1% of variance, as indicated in Table 7-1. In all comparisons among the cells involved in these interactions, referred children obtained lower scores than nonreferred children, although the magnitude of the differences varied somewhat by age and sex. The relations between age, sex, and referral status can be seen for each item in Figure 7-1, where the data points correspond to the cells of the 2 x 2 x 6 ANCOVAs. (Similar figures for the scale scores were presented in Chapter 6.)

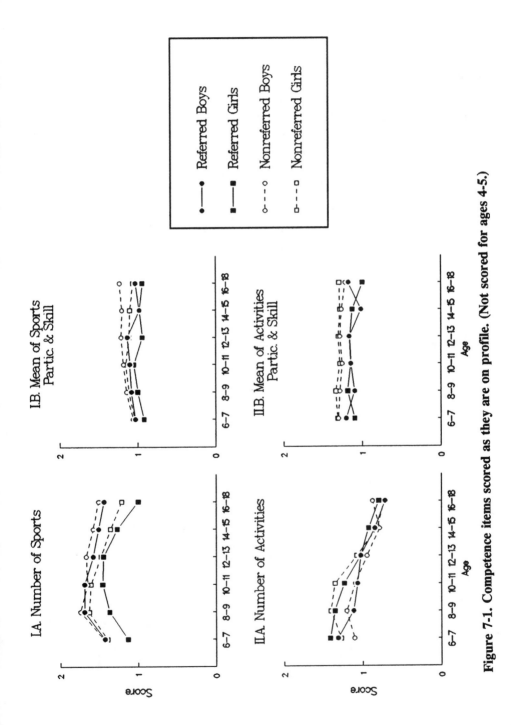

Figure 7-1. Competence items scored as they are on profile. (Not scored for ages 4-5.)

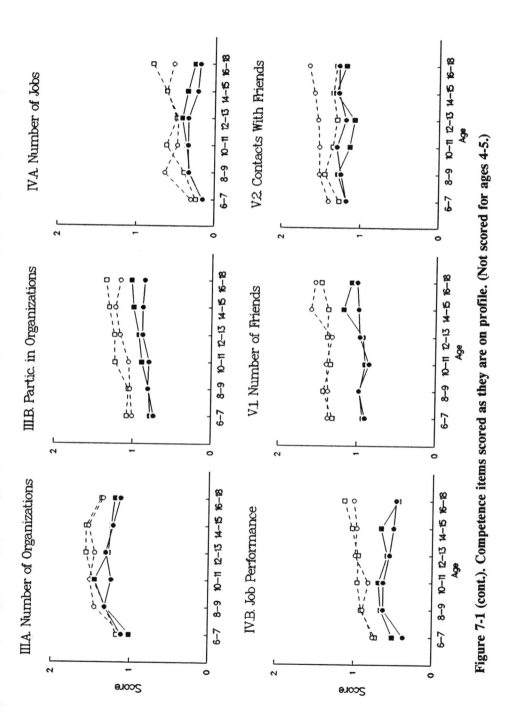

Figure 7-1 (cont.). Competence items scored as they are on profile. (Not scored for ages 4-5.)

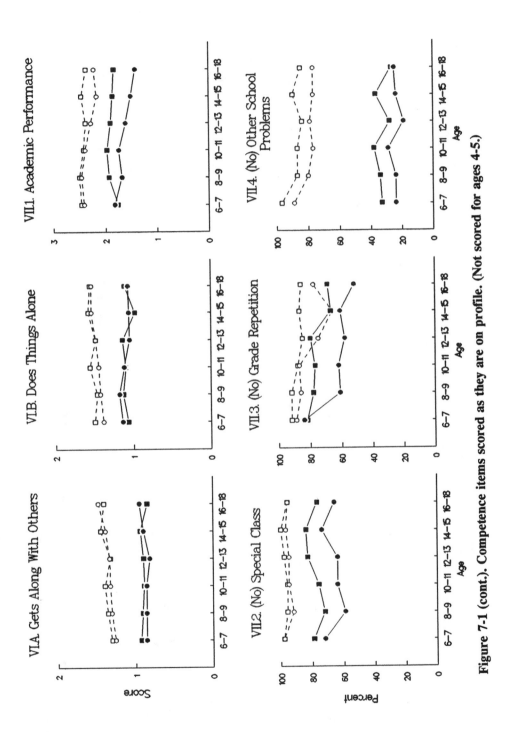

Figure 7-1 (cont.). Competence items scored as they are on profile. (Not scored for ages 4-5.)

Demographic Differences in Competence Scores

Table 7-1 displays the significant main effects of sex and age, plus the significant effects of the SES, white-nonwhite, and black-nonblack covariates. Boys scored significantly higher in three comparisons, while girls scored significantly higher in seven. The largest sex differences accounted for 2% of the variance on three school related items, where girls scored higher, and on the number of sports, where boys scored higher. There was no significant sex difference in the total competence score.

Younger children scored higher in six comparisons, older children in eight comparisons, and there were nonlinear effects of age in three. The largest age effect was in number of nonsports activities, where the tendency for younger children to obtain higher scores accounted for 5% of variance. There was a small tendency for older children to obtain higher total competence scores, accounting for <1% of variance.

All 14 SES effects reflected the tendency of upper SES parents to score their children higher than did lower SES parents. The largest SES effect accounted for 2% of the variance in number of organizations. The tendency for upper SES children to obtain higher total competence scores accounted for 1% of the variance.

Among the 12 effects of the white-nonwhite covariate, 11 indicated higher scores for whites, while nonwhites obtained higher scores for number of close friends. Of the four effects of the black-nonblack covariate, two indicated higher scores for blacks on number of friends and frequency of contacts with friends, whereas nonblacks obtained higher scores for number of sports and the Social scale. All the effects of ethnicity accounted for <1% of the variance.

PROBLEM ITEM SCORES

The 0-1-2 scores on the problem items were analyzed for the 4,220 matched referred and nonreferred children using the same 2 (referral status) x 2 (sex) x 7 (age level) ANCOVA design as was initially used for the competence items, before deleting 4- and 5-year-olds from the final competence item analyses. SES, white versus nonwhite, and black versus nonblack were the covariates, as they were in the ANCOVAs of competence items. Table 7-2 displays the ANCOVA results in terms of the percent of variance that was accounted for by each effect that was significant at p <.01. To take account of findings that might be significant by chance, we have indicated with superscript f the 5 out of 120 tests of each variable that were most likely to be significant by chance, because they had the smallest F values (Sakoda et al., 1954).

Referral Status Differences in Problem Scores

As Table 7-2 shows, referred children were scored significantly (p <.01) higher on all problem items except Items 2, 4, 75, 83, and 99. Because Items *2. Allergy* and *4. Asthma* failed to discriminate significantly between referred and nonreferred samples on the YSR as well as on the CBCL, these items are omitted from the total problem score on the 1991 profiles, although their scores are displayed separately at the bottom of the profiles. (*Allergy* and *Asthma* do not appear on the TRF.) Of the other three items, both Item *75. Shy or timid* and *83. Stores up things he/she doesn't need* discriminated between referred and nonreferred children on the CBCL at p <.02. Item *99. Too concerned about neatness or cleanliness* was scored nonsignificantly higher for referred than nonreferred children on the CBCL but the differences between referred

Table 7-2
Percent of Variance Accounted for by Significant ($p < .01$) Effects of Referral Status and Demographic Variables on Problem Scores

Item	Ref Status[a]	Sex[b]	Age[c]	Interactions[d] RxS	RxA	SxA	Cov. SES[e]
1. Acts too young	11	$<1^M$	--	--	--	--	--
2. Allergy	--	--	$<1^O$	--	--	--	--
3. Argues a lot	8	--	1^{NL}	--	--	--	<1
4. Asthma	--	--	--	--	--	--	--
5. Acts like opposite sex	<1	1^F	$<1^{Yf}$	--	--	--	--
6. BM outside toilet	1	--	2^Y	--	<1	--	--
7. Brags	2	2^M	$<1^{NL}$	--	--	<1	--
8. Can't concentrate	17	2^M	$<1^Y$	--	--	--	<1
9. Can't get mind off thoughts	10	--	$<1^O$	--	--	--	--
10. Can't sit still	8	2^M	2^Y	<1	--	--	<1
11. Too dependent	5	$<1^F$	5^Y	--	<1	--	<1
12. Lonely	5	1^F	$<1^{NL}$	--	--	<1	--
13. Confused	12	--	$<1^O$	--	--	--	--
14. Cries a lot	7	1^F	5^Y	<1	<1	--	--
15. Cruel to animals	4	$<1^M$	$<1^Y$	--	--	--	--
16. Mean to others	10	$<1^M$	--	--	--	--	$<1^f$
17. Daydreams	5	--	2^O	--	--	--	--
18. Harms self	4	--	$<1^O$	--	<1	<1	--
19. Demands attention	12	--	5^Y	--	--	--	--
20. Destroys own things	10	2^M	2^Y	<1	--	--	<1
21. Destroys others' things	9	2^M	2^Y	<1	--	--	<1
22. Disobeys at home	15	$<1^{Mf}$	1^Y	--	--	--	$<1^f$
23. Disobeys at school	15	2^M	$<1^{NL}$	--	--	--	<1
24. Doesn't eat well	1	$<1^F$	1^Y	--	--	--	--
25. Doesn't get along	16	--	1^Y	--	$<1^f$	--	<1
26. Lacks guilt	11	$<1^M$	--	--	--	--	<1
27. Jealous	7	$<1^F$	2^Y	--	--	--	<1
28. Eats nonfood	<1	--	$<1^Y$	--	<1	--	--
29. Fears	<1	$<1^F$	2^Y	--	$<1^f$	--	--
30. Fears school	5	--	--	--	--	--	$<1^f$
31. Fears impulses	3	--	$<1^{NL}$	--	--	--	--
32. Needs to be perfect	<1	$<1^F$	2^O	--	--	--	--
33. Feels unloved	9	$<1^F$	1^{NL}	--	<1	--	--

Table 7-2 (Continued)

Item	Ref Status[a]	Sex[b]	Age[c]	Interactions[d] RxS	RxA	SxA	Cov. SES[e]
34. Feels persecuted	10	<1^M	2^O	<1^f	<1	--	--
35. Feels worthless	16	--	3°	--	1	--	--
36. Accident-prone	3	--	1^Y	--	<1^f	--	--
37. Fighting	11	<1^M	<1^Y	<1	--	<1^f	<1
38. Is teased	6	<1^M	2^{NL}	<1^f	<1	--	<1
39. Hangs around kids who get in trouble	8	<1^M	4°	--	2	<1^f	<1
40. Hears things	2	--	--	--	--	--	--
41. Acts without thinking	13	<1^M	--	<1^f	--	--	--
42. Would rather be alone	1	--	3°	--	--	--	--
43. Lying, cheating	14	<1^M	--	--	<1	--	<1
44. Bites fingernails	2	<1^F	1^O	--	--	--	--
45. Nervous	17	--	<1^O	--	--	--	<1
46. Nervous movements	7	<1^M	<1^{NLf}	--	--	--	--
47. Nightmares	3	<1^F	4^Y	--	--	--	<1
48. Not liked	12	--	1^{NL}	--	<1	--	--
49. Constipated	1	<1^F	--	--	--	--	--
50. Fearful, anxious	10	--	--	--	--	--	<1^f
51. Dizzy	2	<1^F	3°	--	<1	--	--
52. Feels too guilty	6	--	<1^O	--	--	--	<1
53. Eats too much	1	<1^F	2^O	--	--	--	<1
54. Overtired	4	--	2^O	--	--	--	--
55. Overweight	<1^f	<1^F	2^O	<1^f	--	--	--
56a. Aches, pains	3	<1^F	<1^O	--	--	--	--
56b. Headaches	3	<1^F	3°	<1	--	--	--
56c. Nausea, feels sick	2	<1^F	<1^O	--	--	--	<1
56d. Eye problems	1	--	<1^O	--	--	--	--
56e. Skin problems	2	<1^F	<1^O	--	--	--	--
56f. Stomachaches	3	2^{Ff}	<1^{NL}	--	--	<1	--
56g. Vomiting	2	--	--	--	--	<1^f	--
56h. Other physical problem	<1	--	--	--	--	--	--
57. Attacks people	8	<1^M	1^Y	<1	--	--	--
58. Picking	3	<1^{Mf}	3^Y	--	--	--	--
59. Plays with sex parts in public	1	<1^M	2^Y	--	1	--	--

Table 7-2 (Continued)

Item	Ref Status[a]	Sex[b]	Age[c]	RxS	RxA	SxA	Cov. SES[e]
60. Plays with sex parts too much	2	--	2^Y	--	2	--	--
61. Poor school work	16	1^M	6°	--	1	$<1^f$	--
62. Clumsy	7	--	$<1^Y$	--	<1	--	--
63. Prefers older kids	2	$<1^M$	$<1^Y$	--	--	--	<1
64. Prefers younger kids	4	--	1^Y	--	--	--	<1
65. Refuses to talk	9	--	1^O	--	--	--	--
66. Repeats actions	7	--	--	--	--	--	--
67. Runs away from home	5	--	2^O	$<1^f$	2	--	--
68. Screams a lot	7	$<1^F$	2^Y	--	--	--	<1
69. Secretive	10	--	6°	--	<1	--	<1
70. Sees things	1	--	--	--	--	--	--
71. Self-conscious	1	$<1^{Ff}$	2^O	--	--	--	<1
72. Sets fires	2	1^M	--	<1	--	--	--
73. Sex problems	3	--	2^O	--	<1	--	--
74. Shows off	3	5^M	2^Y	--	--	<1	--
75. Shy	--	$<1^F$	$<1^{Yf}$	--	--	--	--
76. Sleeps little	3	--	$<1^Y$	--	<1	--	--
77. Sleeps much	2	--	2^O	--	<1	--	--
78. Smears BM	$<1^f$	--	$<1^Y$	--	$<1^f$	--	--
79. Speech problem	4	$<1^M$	3^Y	--	<1	--	--
80. Stares blankly	6	--	--	--	--	--	--
81. Steals at home	9	--	$<1^O$	--	<1	--	--
82. Steals outside home	7	$<1^M$	--	<1	--	--	--
83. Stores up unneeded things	--	$<1^{Ff}$	$<1^{NL}$	--	--	--	--
84. Strange behavior	7	--	--	--	--	--	--
85. Strange thoughts	4	--	--	--	--	--	--
86. Stubborn	10	--	--	--	--	--	--
87. Moody	14	$<1^F$	$<1^O$	--	--	--	--
88. Sulks a lot	10	$<1^F$	$<1^{NLf}$	<1	--	--	<1
89. Suspicious	6	--	1^O	--	<1	--	<1
90. Swearing	9	2^M	3°	<1	<1	--	--
91. Suicidal thoughts	5	--	$<1^O$	--	<1	<1	--
92. Talks, walks in sleep	$<1^f$	--	$<1^Y$	--	--	--	--
93. Talks too much	$<1^f$	--	3^Y	--	--	--	<1

Table 7-2 (Continued)

Item	Ref Status[a]	Sex[b]	Age[c]	Interactions[d] RxS	RxA	SxA	Cov. SES[e]
94. Teases a lot	2	3^M	$<1^{NL}$	--	<1	<1	<1
95. Hot temper	10	$<1^M$	$<1^Y$	--	--	--	--
96. Thinks about sex	2	--	2^O	--	$<1^f$	<1	<1
97. Threatens people	8	$<1^M$	--	<1	--	--	$<1^f$
98. Thumbsucking	$<1^f$	$<1^F$	4^Y	--	--	--	--
99. Concerned with neat, clean	--	$<1^F$	--	--	--	--	<1
100. Trouble sleeping	6	--	--	--	--	--	--
101. Truancy	4	--	8°	--	4	--	<1
102. Lacks energy	4	$<1^F$	3°	--	<1	--	--
103. Unhappy, sad, depressed	20	$<1^F$	2^O	<1	<1	--	--
104. Loud	7	$<1^M$	$<1^Y$	--	--	<1	<1
105. Alcohol, drugs	3	--	11°	--	6	<1	<1
106. Vandalism	3	$<1^M$	$<1^O$	<1	<1	--	--
107. Wets during day	2	--	5^Y	--	2	--	--
108. Wets bed	2	--	7^Y	--	<1	--	--
109. Whining	2	$<1^F$	12^Y	--	<1	--	--
110. Wishes to be opposite sex	1	--	--	--	--	--	--
111. Withdrawn	10	--	$<1^{Of}$	--	--	--	--
112. Worries	6	$<1^F$	2^O	--	--	--	--
113. Other problems	11	--	--	--	--	$<1^f$	--
Total Problems	29	--	--	--	--	--	<1

Note. $N = 4{,}220$ demographically-matched referred and nonreferred 4- to 18-year-olds. Items are designated with summary labels for their content. Effects of 3-way interactions and the white-nonwhite and black-nonblack covariates are omitted because they were minimal, as discussed in the text.

[a]All scores were higher for referred than nonreferred. Differences on items 75 and 83 were significant at $p < .02$.

[b]F = females scored higher; M = males scored higher.

[c]NL = nonlinear effect of age; O = older scored higher; Y = younger scored higher.

[d]RxS = referral status x sex; RxA = referral status x age; SxA = sex x age.

[e]All significant effects indicated higher scores for lower SES.

[f]Not significant when corrected for number of analyses.

and nonreferred samples were highly significant on the YSR and TRF (both p <.0001). To maintain comparability among the three instruments, Item 99 is retained for the total problem score on all three.

Differences between referred and nonreferred children had a very large effect on the total problem score, accounting for 29% of the variance. These differences were quite consistent across all groups, as there were no significant effects of sex, age, interactions, or the covariates of white-nonwhite or black-nonblack ethnicity. An SES effect accounting for <1% of variance reflected a tendency for lower SES parents to report slightly more problems than upper SES parents. However, this SES effect was dwarfed by the overall differences between referred and nonreferred children across all groups.

Item *103. Unhappy, sad, or depressed* was the item showing the largest difference between referred and non-referred children, as indicated by the 20% of variance accounted for by referral status. This item also showed the largest difference between referred children and our 1976 general population sample of nonreferred children (Achenbach & Edelbrock, 1981). Despite the elapse of 13 years between the previous and current samples, the change from a regional to a national sample, and the upward extension to age 18, parents' endorsements of this item thus remained an especially powerful sign of clinical deviance. Referral status also accounted for more variance in Item 103 than in any other item in the 1991 YSR analyses and it showed one of the largest effects of referral status in the 1991 TRF analyses (Achenbach, 1991b, 1991c).

Although many other items are also important in their own right and in their contributions to scale scores, these findings indicate that parent-, self-, and teacher-reports of depressed affect should receive high priority in judging whether a child is likely to need special help and in the evaluation of outcomes. This does not necessarily mean that all children for whom Item 103 is reported should be diagnosed as having depressive disorders. On the contrary, depressed affect may be evident for many different reasons. Some children who manifest depressed affect may not be deviant with respect to other aspects of a depressive pattern, such as those encompassed by the CBCL Anxious/ Depressed syndrome. Some children who *are* deviant with respect to the syndrome, on the other hand, may also be deviant in other areas, indicating that their problems should not be interpreted in terms of depression alone. Still other children may manifest depressed affect only in certain contexts. It is therefore important to consider reports of depressed affect in relation to multiple sources of data on multiple aspects of children's functioning, rather than simply equating it with a depressive disorder.

As Table 7-2 shows, there was a very small tendency for girls to score higher than boys on Item 103 and for there to be an interaction between referral status and sex (both effects accounted for <1% of variance). The interaction reflected a tendency for the sex difference to be greater among referred than nonreferred children. There was also a significant linear trend (accounting for 2% of variance) for older children to score higher than younger children on Item 103, and a very small interaction effect (<1% of variance) reflecting a larger age trend for referred than nonreferred children. A small tendency for nonblacks to score higher than blacks (<1% of variance) could be considered chance, because it was among the five smallest significant effects for the black versus nonblack covariate. The small associations of demographic variables with Item 103 thus did not affect its overall strength as a discriminator between referred and nonreferred 4- to 18-year-olds of both sexes and different SES and ethnic groups.

The following items also showed large differences (≥13.8% of variance) between referred and nonreferred children: *8. Can't concentrate, can't pay attention for long*

(17% of variance); *22. Disobedient at home* (15%); *23. Disobedient at school* (15%); *25. Doesn't get along with other kids* (16%); *35. Feels worthless or inferior* (16%); *43. Lying or cheating* (14%); *45. Nervous, highstrung, or tense* (17%); and *61. Poor school work* (16%). As Table 7-2 shows, all demographic effects associated with these items were far smaller than the percent of variance accounted for by referral status. Of the significant ($p < .01$) effects of referral status on the other items, 44 were medium, 52 were small, and 10 accounted for <1% of variance.

To provide a detailed picture of the prevalence rate for each problem item, Figure 7-2 displays the percent of children for whom each problem was reported (i.e., was scored 1 or 2). The data points correspond to the cells of the ANCOVAs, with children grouped according to referral status, sex, and age. Appendix D presents the actual percent of referred and nonreferred children who received scores of 1 and 2, plus the mean item scores for children grouped by ages 4-11 and 12-18 to correspond with the age intervals used on the CBCL/4-18 profile. (A figure displaying the mean total problem scores was presented in Chapter 6.)

Demographic Differences in Problem Scores

Table 7-2 displays significant main effects of sex and age, interactions of these variables with referral status and with each other, and effects of the SES covariate. The white-nonwhite and black-nonblack covariates and 3-way interactions are not displayed, because the few that were significant all accounted for <1% of variance. Only two effects of the white-nonwhite covariate and 3-way interactions reached $p < .01$, which is fewer than the five expected by chance (Sakoda et al., 1954). The black-nonblack covariate showed higher scores on Item *4. Asthma* for blacks and higher scores for nonblacks on 12 items. Excluding the five items likely to be significant by chance,

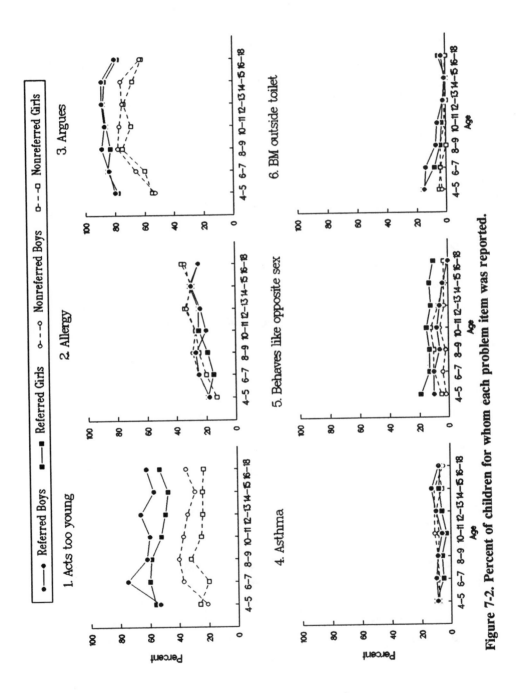

Figure 7-2. Percent of children for whom each problem item was reported.

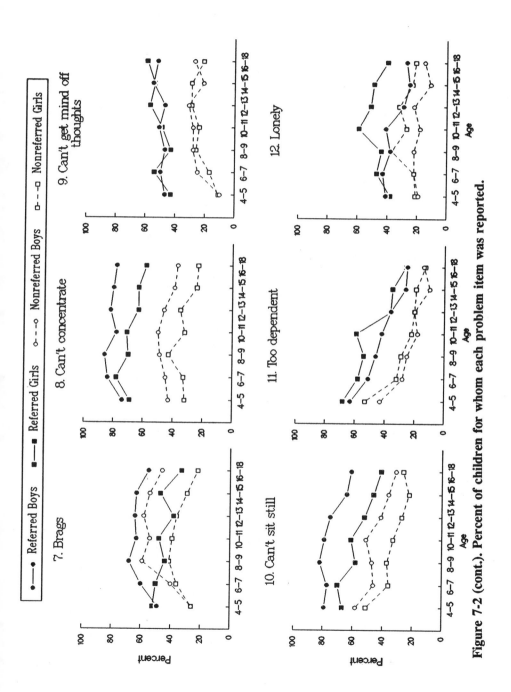

Figure 7-2 (cont.). Percent of children for whom each problem item was reported.

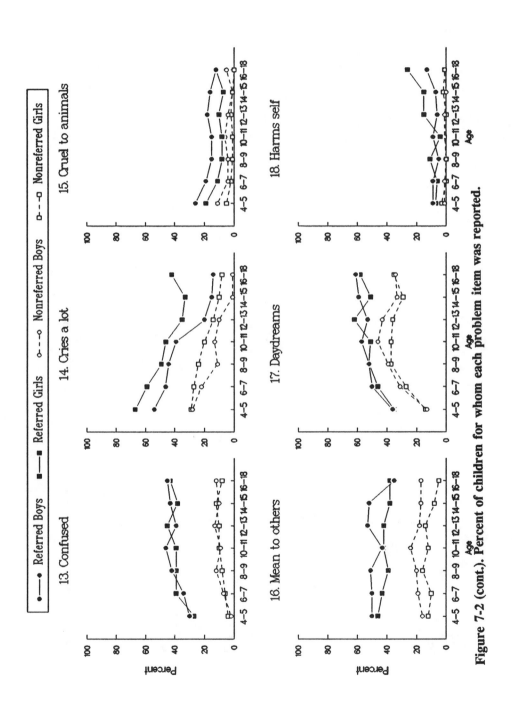

Figure 7-2 (cont). Percent of children for whom each problem item was reported.

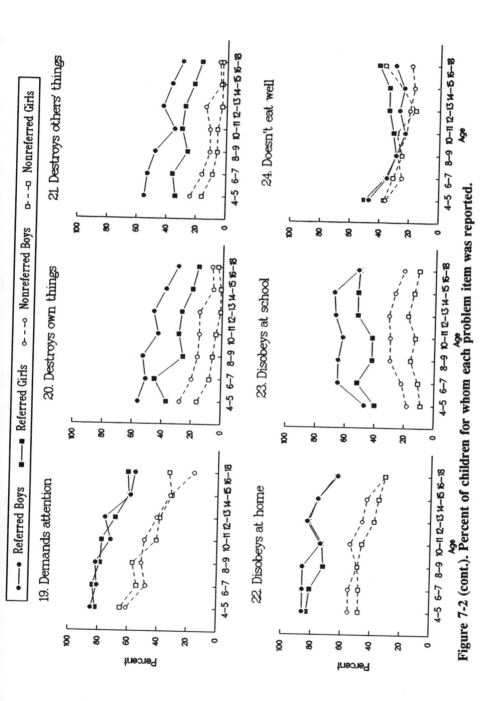

Figure 7-2 (cont). Percent of children for whom each problem item was reported.

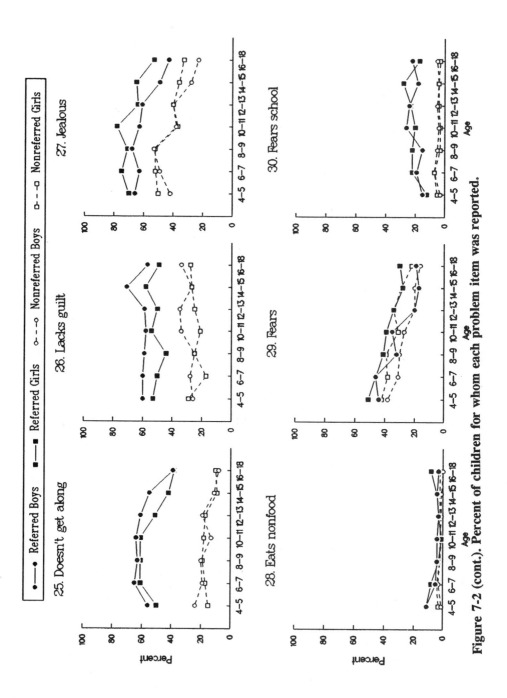

Figure 7-2 (cont.). Percent of children for whom each problem item was reported.

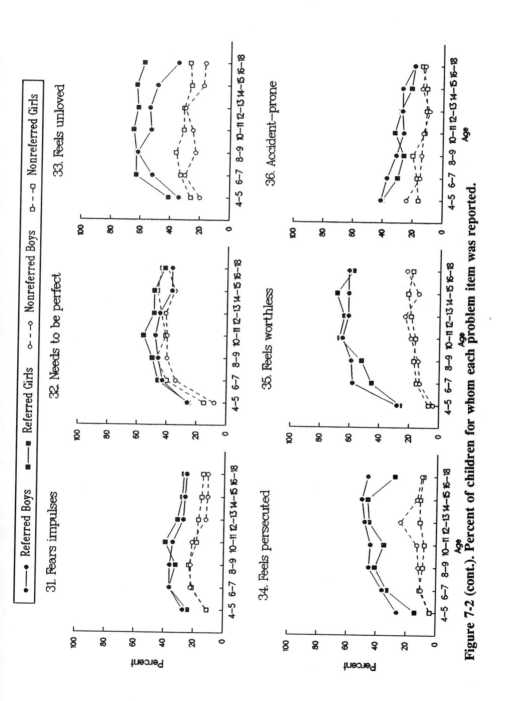

Figure 7-2 (cont.). Percent of children for whom each problem item was reported.

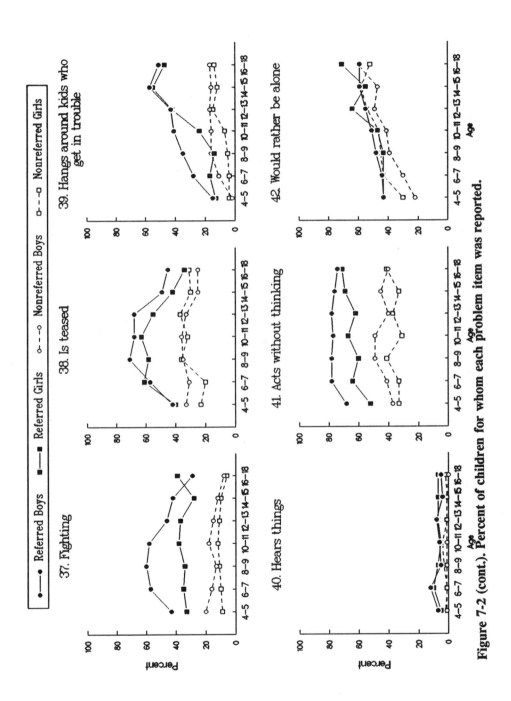

Figure 7-2 (cont.). Percent of children for whom each problem item was reported.

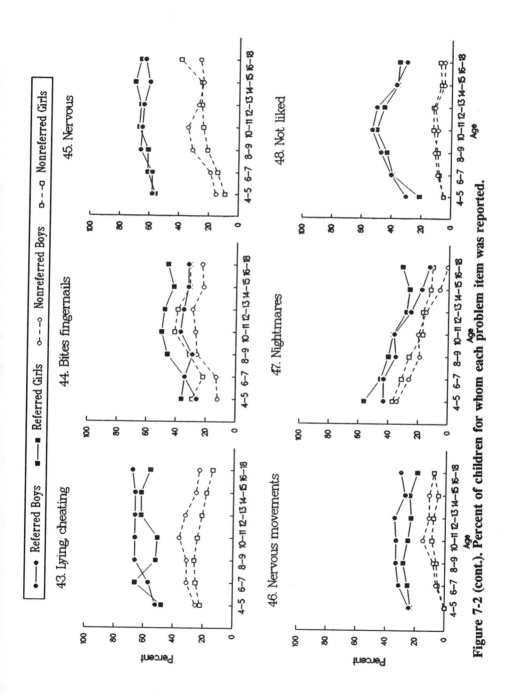

Figure 7-2 (cont.). Percent of children for whom each problem item was reported.

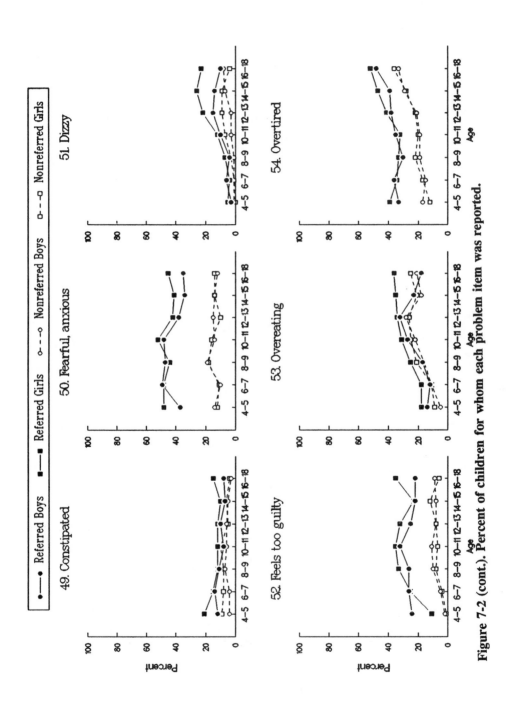

Figure 7-2 (cont). Percent of children for whom each problem item was reported.

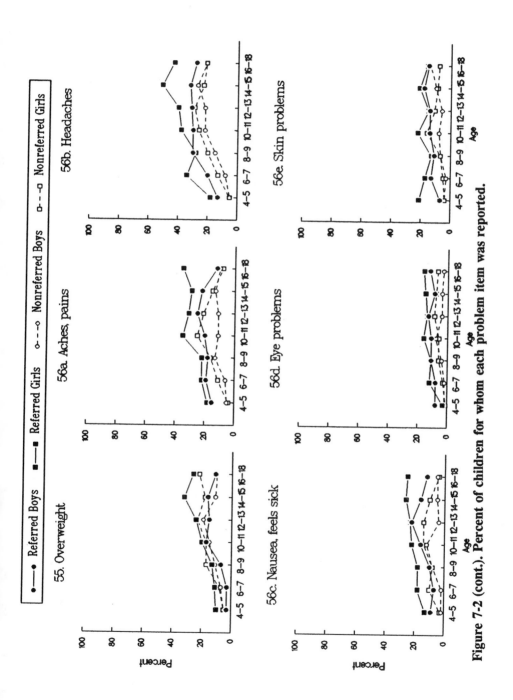

Figure 7-2 (cont.). Percent of children for whom each problem item was reported.

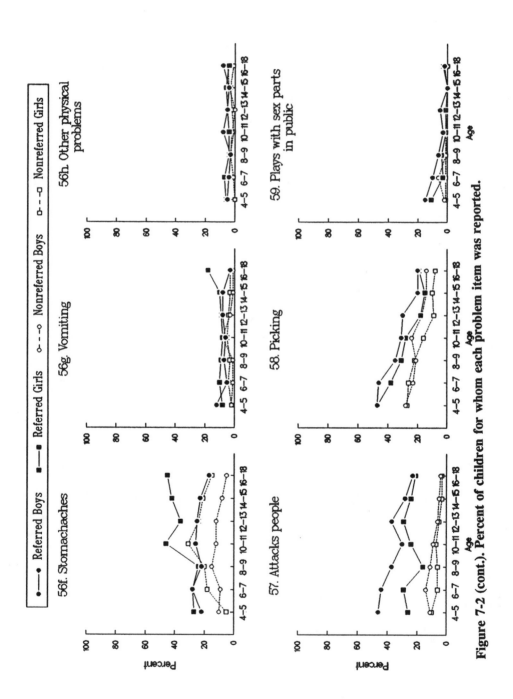

Figure 7-2 (cont.). Percent of children for whom each problem item was reported.

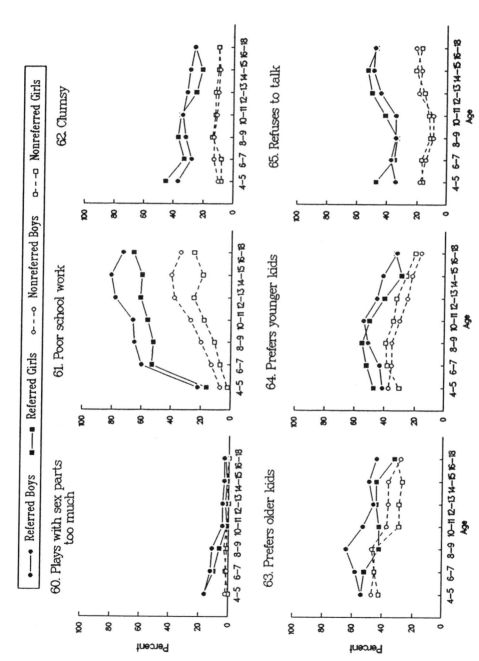

Figure 7-2 (cont). Percent of children for whom each problem item was reported.

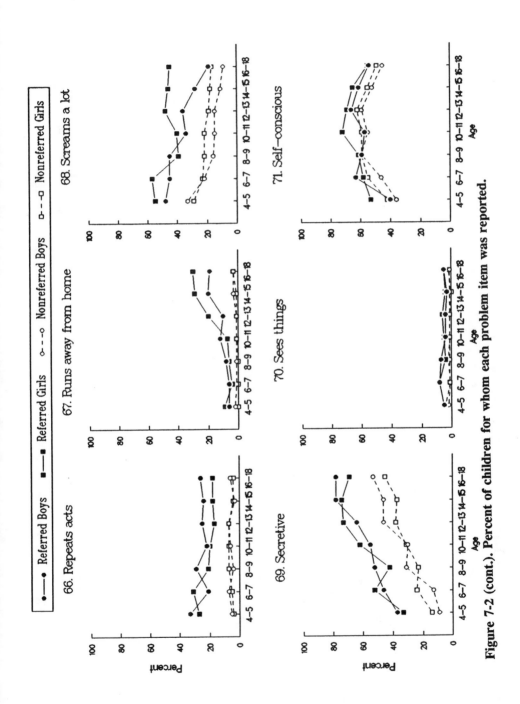

Figure 7-2 (cont.). Percent of children for whom each problem item was reported.

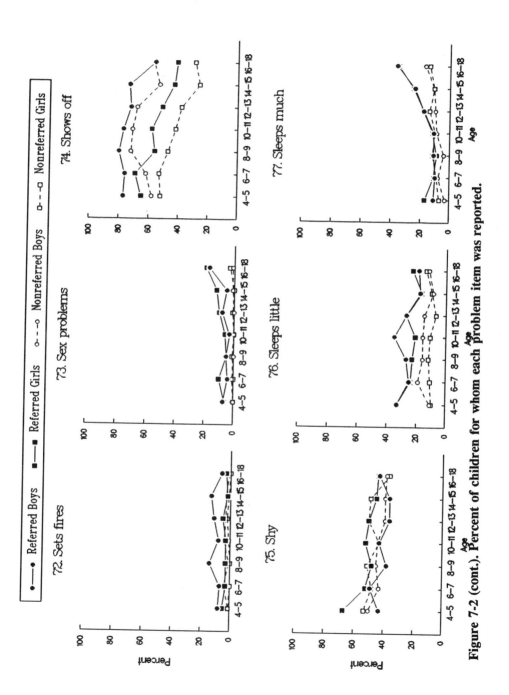

Figure 7-2 (cont.). Percent of children for whom each problem item was reported.

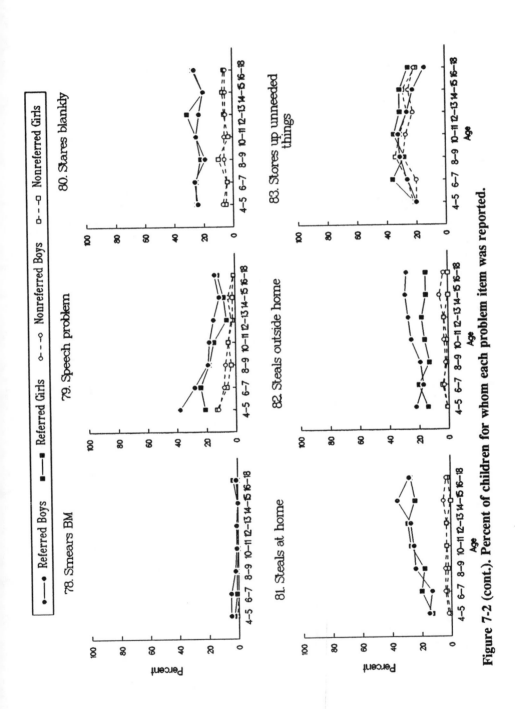

Figure 7-2 (cont.). Percent of children for whom each problem item was reported.

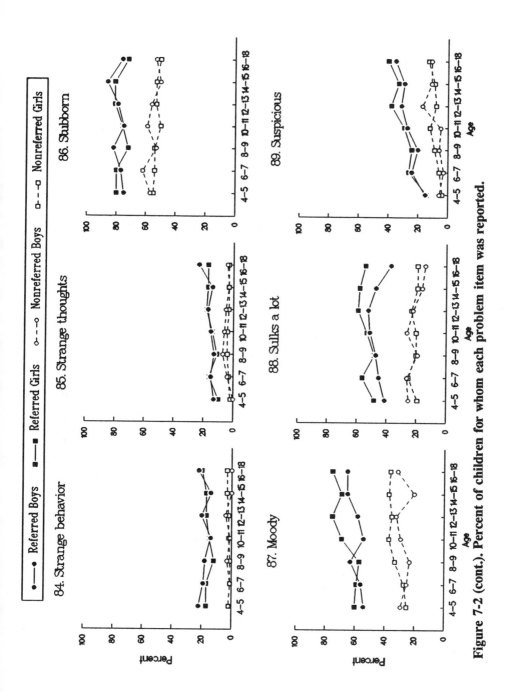

Figure 7-2 (cont.). Percent of children for whom each problem item was reported.

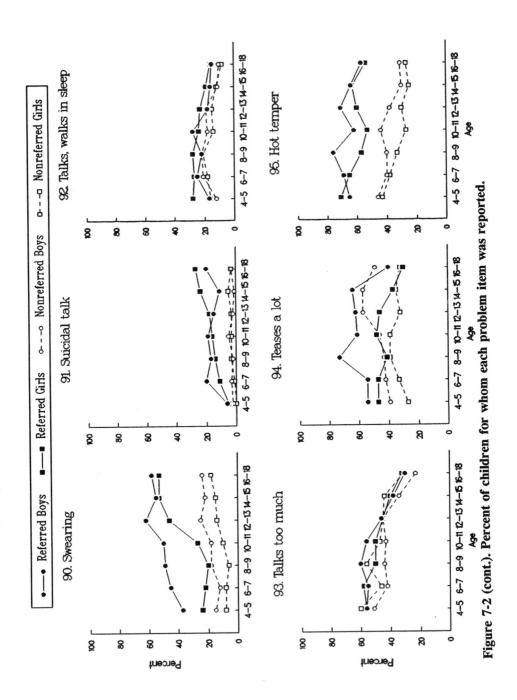

Figure 7-2 (cont.). Percent of children for whom each problem item was reported.

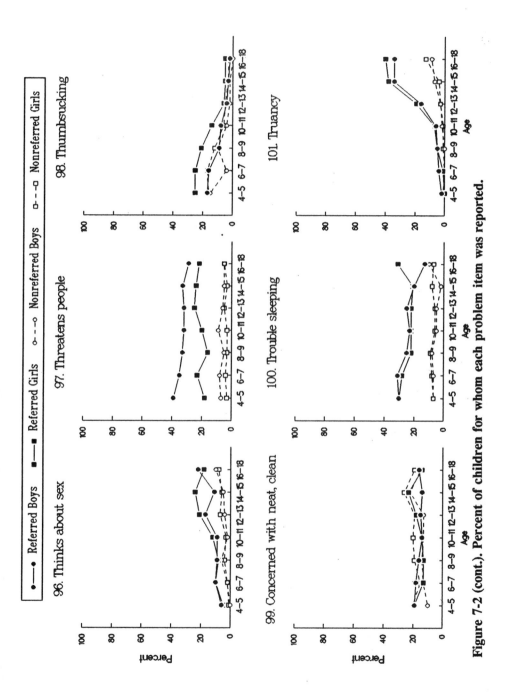

Figure 7-2 (cont.). Percent of children for whom each problem item was reported.

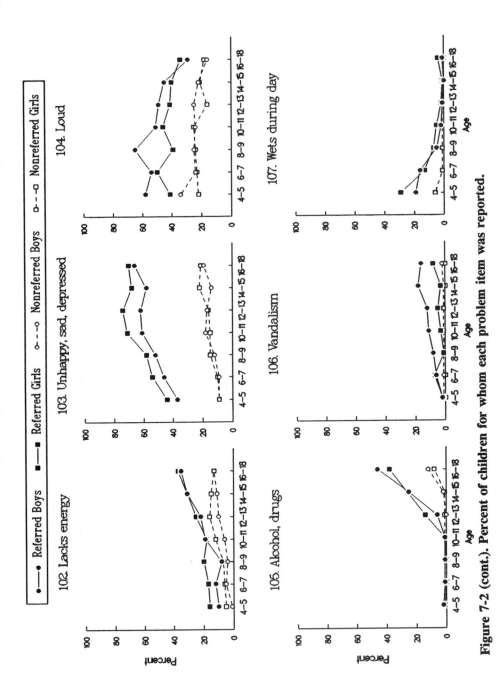

Figure 7-2 (cont.). Percent of children for whom each problem item was reported.

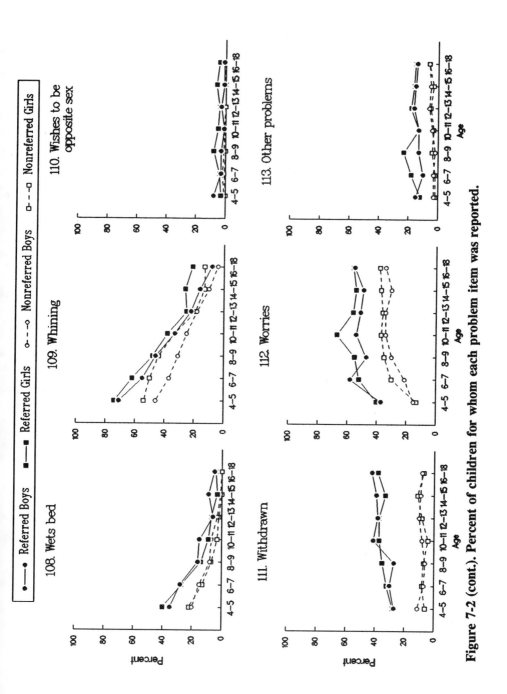

Figure 7-2 (cont.). Percent of children for whom each problem item was reported.

the seven showing higher scores for nonblacks were:
14. Cries a lot; *33. Feels or complains that no one loves
him/her*; *35. Feels worthless or inferior*; *54. Overtired*;
68. Screams a lot; *91. Talks about killing self*; and
109. Whining. Items 14, 33, 35, and 109 also yielded
higher scores for nonblacks than blacks in the Achenbach
and Edelbrock (1981) analyses. These items evidently
reflect persisting ethnic differences, but they are of tiny
magnitude, all accounting for <1% of variance.

There were significant sex effects on 65 items, 32 of
which were scored higher for girls and 33 for boys. No sex
differences exceeded Cohen's criteria for small effects. The
largest accounted for 5% of the variance in Item *74. Showing off or clowning*, where boys scored higher. The item
showing the largest effect of higher scores for girls was
56f. Stomachaches or cramps, where the sex difference
accounted for 2% of variance. Of the 17 Internalizing
items that showed significant sex differences, 16 were
scored higher for girls. Of the 24 Externalizing items that
showed significant sex differences, 21 were scored higher
for boys ($\chi^2 = 26.66$, $p < .001$). This highly significant
tendency for girls to be scored higher on Internalizing items
and boys on Externalizing items is consistent with findings
across numerous cultures (Achenbach, Bird, Canino, Phares,
Gould, & Rubio-Stipec, 1990; Achenbach, Hensley, Phares,
& Grayson, 1990).

Linear age effects reflected significantly higher scores
for older children on 42 items and for younger children on
40 items. An additional 13 items showed nonlinear age
effects, as indicated by the superscript *NL* in Table 7-2.
The shapes of these nonlinear age effects can be seen from
the graphs of the item scores in Figure 7-2. The largest age
effects accounted for 12% of the variance in Item *109.
Whining*, where younger children scored higher, and 11%
in item *105. Uses alcohol or drugs for nonmedical purposes*, where older children scored higher. The only other age

differences that exceeded Cohen's criteria for small effects were on Item *101. Truancy, skips school*, where higher scores among older children accounted for 8% of the variance, and *108. Wets the bed*, where higher scores among younger children accounted for 7% of the variance. Of the 23 Internalizing items showing significant age differences, 21 were scored higher for older children. Of the 21 Externalizing items showing significant differences, 13 were scored higher for younger children ($\chi^2 = 13.29$, $p < .001$). There was thus a strong tendency for Internalizing problems to be more common among older children, while Externalizing problems were more common among younger children.

All of the 19 significant interactions between referral status and sex and the 15 significant interactions between sex and age accounted for <1% of variance. Among the 41 interactions between age and referral status, none exceeded Cohen's criteria for small effects. The largest accounted for 5.5% (rounded to 6% in Table 7-2) of variance on Item *105. Uses alcohol or drugs for nonmedical purposes* and 4% of variance on Item *101. Truancy, skips school*. Both of these reflected the fact that referred children's scores exceeded nonreferred children's scores more at older than younger ages.

All 38 significant SES effects on problem items reflected higher scores for lower than upper SES children, although none of the effects accounted for as much as 1% of the variance. A significantly larger proportion of Externalizing than Internalizing items were scored higher by lower SES parents ($\chi^2 = 7.87$, $p < .02$).

SUMMARY

This chapter reported ANCOVAs of scores obtained by matched referred and nonreferred children on the CBCL competence items and scales, problem items, and total problem score. Because referred and nonreferred 4-5-year-olds were not found to differ much on the competence items, they were omitted from the final ANCOVAs of the competence items and scales. Referred children scored significantly ($p < .01$) lower than nonreferred children on all the competence items and scales, except for number of nonsports activities, which is now omitted from the Activities and total competence scales. Demographic differences in competence scores were quite small. The most consistent demographic effect was for upper SES parents to score their children somewhat higher than lower SES parents, but SES effects were much smaller than the effects of referral status in most comparisons.

Nearly all problem items were scored significantly ($p < .01$) higher for referred than nonreferred children. Because Items *2. Allergy* and *4. Asthma* did not discriminate significantly between referred and nonreferred children on the CBCL or the YSR, they are no longer counted in the total problem score.

Differences between referred and nonreferred children accounted for 29% of the variance in total problem scores. These differences were quite consistent across all groups, as there were no significant effects of sex, age, interactions, or ethnicity on the total problem scores. An SES effect accounting for <1% of the variance in the total problem score and in 38 individual items reflected the tendency for lower SES parents to report slightly more problems than upper SES parents. The item showing the largest difference between referred and nonreferred children was *103. Unhappy, sad, or depressed*, which was also among the best discriminators between referred and nonreferred samples on the YSR and TRF.

Chapter 8
Relations Between Pre-1991 and 1991 CBCL Scales

This chapter summarizes differences between the pre-1991 and 1991 CBCL scales, the scales having counterparts in the two editions, and correlations between the counterpart scales.

Beside the differences in the scales themselves, an innovation applied to all the 1991 scales is the designation of a borderline range adjoining the clinical cutpoint. The purpose is to emphasize that all scores are subject to variation and that a clinical cutpoint does not mark a definitive boundary between the normal and abnormal. For purposes of statistical analysis, a specific cutpoint is specified for each scale, but clinical evaluations of individual children whose scores are among the 4 T scores of the borderline range should emphasize that they are in the borderline clinical range.

Additional innovations include the following:

1. Normalized T scores were based on the midpoints between percentiles of the raw score distributions.

2. All syndrome scales were truncated at $T = 50$, rather than 55 to 59 as on the pre-1991 scales.

3. Gaps of more than 5 points between $T = 50$ and the next higher T score were limited by using the mean of $T = 50$ and the third highest T score.

4. $T = 89$ was assigned to the mean of the five highest raw scores obtained by our clinical samples on the Internalizing, Externalizing, and total problem scores, rather than to the highest scores, as were used to establish $T = 89$ on the pre-1991 scales.

5. Items 2. *Allergy* and 4. *Asthma* are omitted from the total problem score.

6. On the hand-scored profiles, scale scores for the two age groups of boys are listed side-by-side, as are scores for the two age groups of girls. Users should be careful to select the column of scores designated for the age of the child being scored.

7. Internalizing and Externalizing scores can be computed from scale scores on the hand-scored profile without having to enter each Internalizing and Externalizing item's score.

CONSTRUCTION OF SCALES

Syndrome Scales

The pre-1991 profiles were developed separately for each sex/age group on the CBCL. Furthermore, the CBCL scales were developed separately from the YSR and TRF scales. Although the pre-1991 CBCL norms for the different sex/age groups were drawn from a single general population sample and the competence scales were similar for all sex/age groups, the syndrome scales were developed separately for each group whether or not similar patterns were found for other groups or on the other instruments.

As the use of the instruments spread and research advanced, closer integration of syndrome scales across sex/age groups and sources of data became more important. For clinical or research reassessment of children as they grow older, for example, it is advantageous to have continuity of scales, while still providing appropriate age norms. For research that involves both sexes, it is helpful to be able to compare them on similar scales. And the limited agreement among informants argues strongly for coordinating multisource data around similar foci.

As outlined in Chapter 3, the 1991 CBCL syndrome scales were constructed by deriving *core syndromes* of items that were common to most of the sex/age groups. Furthermore, the core syndromes derived from the CBCL, YSR, and TRF were compared to identify items common to each core syndrome in at least two of the three instruments. The items that were common to a core syndrome in at least two of the three instruments were used to define a *cross-informant syndrome construct.* The items defining the construct represent an hypothetical variable that may underlie the varying manifestations reportable by parents, youths, and teachers. By including on the syndrome scales the items that were specific to the core syndrome derived from a particular type of informant, we retained those aspects of a syndrome that may be evident only to that type of informant. We thus retained variations in problem behavior that may differentiate between the manifestations of particular syndromes in different contexts while advancing the coordination of multiple data sources and highlighting elements of disorders that may be consistent across contexts.

To capture syndromes that may be reportable by only one kind of informant, and/or for particular sex/age groups, we retained the *Sex Problems* syndrome that was found in the CBCL analyses for both sexes at ages 4 to 5 and 6 to 11. The Sex Problems items are routinely scored on the CBCL and contribute to the total problem score, as do other CBCL problem items. However, because the Sex Problems syndrome did not have counterparts in CBCL ratings of adolescents, nor in the YSR or TRF, it is provided as an optional scale. Because the Sex Problems scale had counterparts in the pre-1991 profiles, it is included in the comparisons reported later in this chapter.

A syndrome designated as *Cruel* was included in the pre-1991 profiles for 6-11- and 12-16-year-old girls. Some evidence for a similar syndrome was found in our components analyses of girls for the 1991 profile. It was not very consistent between analyses for 4-5-, 6-11-, and 12-18-year-old girls, however, and most of its items were also on the Aggressive syndrome. It was therefore not retained as a syndrome on the profile. The items were different enough from the pre-1991 Cruel syndrome that *Destructive* seemed a more appropriate title. However, for users wishing to assess girls in terms of this syndrome, Table 8-1 lists the items and the *T* scores for girls 4-11 and 12-18.

Syndrome Scale Names. The 1991 Withdrawn, Somatic Complaints, Delinquent Behavior, Aggressive Behavior, and Sex Problems syndromes have names quite similar to those on the pre-1991 profile. The 1991 Anxious/Depressed syndrome is the counterpart of the pre-1991 CBCL, YSR, and TRF Depressed syndrome for most sex/age groups, the CBCL Anxious-Obsessive syndrome for girls 12-16, and the TRF Anxious syndrome. This syndrome includes items indicative of both anxiety and depression. Some children who score high on the syndrome scale may primarily have anxiety problems that would qualify for a DSM anxiety disorder diagnosis. Other children who score high on the scale may primarily have depressive problems that would qualify for a depressive disorder diagnosis.

Although it is possible to discriminate between feelings of anxiety and feelings of depression, our analyses indicate that these kinds of problems are closely intertwined in

Table 8-1
Items and *T* Scores of the 1991
Destructive Syndrome for Girls

		T Score	
Items	*Raw Score*	*4-11*	*12-18*
15. Cruel to animals	0	50	50
16. Bullies	1	56	58
18. Harms self	2	62	65
20. Destroys own things	3	65	68
21. Destroys others' things	4	68	69
37. Fights	5	70	70
57. Attacks people	6	72	72
82. Steals outside home	7	74	74
91. Talks about suicide	8	76	76
97. Threatens	9	78	78
	10	80	80
	11	82	82
	12	84	84
	13	86	86
	14	88	88
	15	90	90
	16	92	92
	17	94	94
	18	96	96
	19	98	98
	20	100	100

Note. Versions of this syndrome were found in the components analyses of all items for girls 4-5 and 12-18 and the common items for girls 6-11.

children. Many other studies of childhood disorders have also found close associations between problems of anxiety and depression (e.g., Bernstein & Garfinkel, 1986; Cole, 1987; Saylor et al., 1984; Strauss, Last, Hersen, & Kazdin, 1988; Treiber & Mabe, 1987).

The 1991 Social Problems syndrome is a counterpart of the pre-1991 TRF and YSR Unpopular syndrome. On the CBCL, the pre-1991 syndrome that was designated as Social Withdrawal for boys 6-11 and Hostile Withdrawal for boys 12-16 comprised a similar set of items. These were the CBCL syndromes that were used in comparisons with the ACQ Behavior Checklist and the Dutch CBCL to identify the syndrome that was called Socially Inept (Achenbach et al., 1989). (The pre-1991 counterparts of the 1991 Withdrawn syndrome on the CBCL were the Social Withdrawal and the Depressed Withdrawal syndromes for girls and the Uncommunicative syndrome for boys.)

The 1991 syndrome designated as Thought Problems is a rough counterpart to the pre-1991 Schizoid scale for girls and the Obsessive-Compulsive scale for boys. It comprises low prevalence problems that were found in a variety of patterns in the pre-1991 analyses. Partly because of the low prevalence of the problems and partly because the problems may lead to a variety of other problem behaviors that vary by sex, age, and context, some of the features that justified the Schizoid label are not consistent enough to be detectable across sex, age, and informant. The items that were consistent enough generally concern problems of thought.

The 1991 Attention Problems syndrome is a counterpart of the pre-1991 CBCL Hyperactive syndrome and the pre-1991 TRF Inattentive and Nervous-Overactive syndromes. The title reflects the tendency for the attention problem items, such as *8. Can't concentrate, can't pay attention for long*, to have the highest loadings in most versions of the syndrome.

Internalizing and Externalizing

Like the syndrome scales, the pre-1991 Internalizing and Externalizing groupings were constructed separately for each sex/age group on each instrument. Although there were general similarities among the various versions of the Internalizing and Externalizing groupings, the precise compositions differed because of variations in the syndromes on which they were based. Furthermore, several items were scored on more than one syndrome within the Internalizing or Externalizing grouping, and some items were even scored in both groupings.

For the 1991 profiles, uniform Internalizing and Externalizing groupings were established by averaging the loadings obtained for each of the eight syndromes in separate second-order factor analyses of each sex/age group scored on the CBCL, YSR, and TRF. The three syndromes having the highest mean loadings on the second-order Internalizing factor and the two syndromes having the highest mean loadings on the second-order Externalizing factor were used to define the Internalizing and Externalizing groupings across all sex/age groups on the 1991 CBCL, YSR, and TRF profiles.

Like the cross-informant syndromes, the 1991 Internalizing and Externalizing groupings are quite uniform, although there are also some variations reflecting the items of certain syndromes that are specific to one instrument. Unlike the pre-1991 versions, no items are scored on both Internalizing and Externalizing syndromes, and only one item—*103. Unhappy, sad, or depressed*—is scored on two syndromes (Withdrawn and Anxious/Depressed) within one grouping. However, this item counts only once toward the Internalizing score.

Total Problem Score

The 1991 total problem score differs from the pre-1991 version only with respect to the omission of Items *2. Allergy* and *4. Asthma*, which did not discriminate significantly between referred and nonreferred children. Because these problems may nevertheless be important in clinical evaluations of individual children, they are retained on the CBCL and their scores are displayed separately on the profile.

STATISTICAL RELATIONS BETWEEN PRE-1991 AND 1991 SCALES

Table 8-2 shows Pearson correlations between the raw scores of the pre-1991 and 1991 counterpart scales scored for our 1991 matched referred and nonreferred samples combined. Correlations computed separately for the referred and nonreferred samples did not differ much from those shown in Table 8-2 for the combined samples.

As Table 8-2 shows, most correlations were in the .90s, indicating that particular subjects would have very similar rank orders in the distributions of scores on the corresponding pre-1991 and 1991 scales. Correlational analyses and analyses involving the relative magnitude of scores within particular distributions would thus produce similar results using the corresponding pre-1991 and 1991 scales. However, t tests showed significant differences between the absolute magnitude of scores obtained by the same subjects on most of the pre-1991 and 1991 versions of the scales. The significant differences between scale scores reflect the differences between the pre-1991 and 1991 scales in the number and the content of their items. A particular scale score on a pre-1991 scale is thus not necessarily equivalent to the same score on the 1991 counterpart of the scale.

Table 8-2
Pearson Correlations Between Raw Scores
for 1991 and Pre-1991 Counterpart Scales

		Boys		Girls	
		4-11	12-18	4-11	12-18
Competence[a]	N =	1,164	900	1,238	918
Activities		.93	.94	.95	.94
Total Competence		.98	.98	.99	.98
Problems					
Withdrawn[b]		.90	.95	.98	.97
Somatic Complaints		.92	.90	.92	.95
Anxious/Depressed[c]		.99	---	.97	.96
Social Problems[d]		.86	.86	---	---
Thought Problems[e]		.81	.83	.86	.81
Attention Problems[f]		.95	.92	.95	.88
Delinquent Behavior		.91	.93	.92	.94
Aggressive Behavior		.99	.97	.98	.98
Sex Problems[g]		---	---	.48	---
Internalizing		.96	.94	.97	.98
Externalizing		.97	.98	.96	.99
Total Problems		1.00	1.00	1.00	1.00

Note. Correlations were computed in the matched referred and nonreferred samples combined, all $p < .00001$. Pre-1991 scales were the closest age 6-11 and 12-16 counterparts of the 1991 scales, as indicated in footnotes b-g below for scales differing in pre-1991 names.

[a]Competence scales omit ages 4-5. Social and school scales are not shown because scoring is identical in 1991 and pre-1991 versions.

[b]Pre-1991 scales were Uncommunicative for boys 6-11 and 12-16, Social Withdrawal for girls 6-11, and Depressed Withdrawal for girls 12-16.

[c]Pre-1991 scales were Depressed for both sexes 6-11, no counterpart for boys 12-16, Anxious-Obsessive for girls 12-16.

[d]Pre-1991 scales were Social Withdrawal for boys 6-11, Hostile Withdrawal for boys 12-16, and no counterparts for girls.

[e]Pre-1991 scales were Obsessive-Compulsive for boys 6-11 and 12-16, Schizoid-Obsessive for girls 6-11, and Schizoid for girls 12-16.

[f]Pre-1991 scales were Hyperactive for all groups except Immature-Hyperactive for girls 12-16.

[g]Pre-1991 Sex Problems scale was scored only for boys 4-5 and girls 6-11.

The relatively low correlation of .48 between the pre-1991 and 1991 versions of the Sex Problems scale indicates a considerably weaker correspondence between scores on the two versions of this scale than on the other scales. The low correlation may be partly due to the low prevalence rates of the Sex Problems items. If so, the pre-1991 and 1991 versions of the Sex Problems scale might correlate higher in samples having many of these problems.

SUMMARY

This chapter summarized differences between the pre-1991 and 1991 CBCL scales, the scales having counterparts in the two editions, and correlations between the counterpart scales.

Innovations in the 1991 scales include: Derivation of cross-informant syndrome scales that are common to both sexes and different ages scored on the CBCL, YSR, and TRF; provision of a borderline clinical range on each scale; normalized T scores based on midpoint percentiles; syndrome scales truncated at $T = 50$; deletion of Items *2. Allergy* and *4. Asthma* from the total problem scores; easier hand scoring of Internalizing and Externalizing.

The *Sex Problems* and *Destructive* syndromes that are specific to the CBCL were described. T scores were provided for the Destructive syndrome, which is scored only for girls.

Correlations between most pre-1991 scales and their 1991 counterpart scales were in the .90s, indicating great similarity in the rank ordering of children on the counterpart scales. The only correlation below .81 was for the Sex Problems scale, where the correlation of .48 may be due partly to the low prevalence of the scale's items.

The mean scores obtained on most of the pre-1991 scales differed significantly from those obtained on the

1991 scales, owing to differences in the number and content of particular items. A particular score on a pre-1991 scale is thus not necessarily equivalent to the same score on the 1991 counterpart of the scale. Nevertheless, the very high correlations between most pre-1991 scales and their 1991 counterparts indicate that correlational analyses and other analyses involving the relative magnitude of scores within particular distributions would produce similar results on the pre-1991 and 1991 scales.

Chapter 9
Practical Applications
of the CBCL and Profile

This chapter addresses applications of the CBCL to making *practical decisions* about *particular* cases, groups, programs, policies, etc. Practical applications can be contrasted with *research applications*, discussed in Chapter 10, which aim to establish *principles* that are *generalizable* and *testable*. Designed for both practical and research applications, the CBCL is intended to utilize the fruits of research to improve practical assessment and to enrich research by linking it to practical assessment procedures.

The standardized descriptions of children's functioning obtained with the CBCL provide a common language for practitioners and researchers who have contact with parents in diverse contexts. The CBCL is also a key component of multiaxial assessment, for which practical applications are detailed in the *Integrative Guide for the 1991 CBCL/4-18, YSR, and TRF Profiles* (Achenbach, 1991a).

In presenting practical applications, we do not offer clinical "interpretations." Although such interpretations are often sought from assessment instruments, we believe that the meaning and utility of assessment data depend on the situation in which they are to be used. In evaluating children, the skilled practitioner applies knowledge and procedures developed on other cases to obtain a clear picture of the individual case. Our assessment procedures obtain descriptive data in a standardized fashion, aggregated into empirically based scales and normed on large representative samples. These procedures aid the practitioner in identifying specific features of the child as seen by particular informants and compared with normative samples of peers. The profiles show the areas in which the child is in the normal, borderline, or clinical range. The procedures presented in the *Integrative Guide* (Achenbach, 1991a) enable the practitioner to systematically compare data from multiple sources. Hundreds of published studies have reported correlates of the profile scales (Achenbach & Brown, 1991).

Our standardized assessment procedures and their numerous correlates can bring a great deal of accumulated knowledge to bear on the individual case. However, we feel that it would be wrong to provide "canned" interpretations as if they could be mechanically applied to each case. Our procedures can greatly improve the assessment and documentation of children's functioning. Yet, the unique features of each case limit the accuracy with which any procedure can extrapolate clinical interpretations of behavioral/emotional problems to specific cases. Canned interpretations should not be allowed to substitute for the detailed study of the individual case. It is the practitioner who must integrate standardized assessment data with unique information to attain a comprehensive understanding of the case. The essence of clinical creativity is to synthesize diverse procedures and data into an optimal solution for each case.

Responsible practice requires practitioners to test their judgment against various kinds of evidence. The profiles facilitate this process by enabling practitioners to compare informants' descriptions with what similar informants report about normative samples of peers, as well as with the practitioners' own impressions. The profiles also make it possible to compare descriptions of children at different points in time, such as at intake into a service, after an intervention, and at follow-up. In the following sections, we provide illustrations and guidelines for using the CBCL in conjunction with the typical procedures of various settings.

APPLICATIONS IN MENTAL HEALTH CONTEXTS

The CBCL can be used in virtually all mental health settings for children where parents or parent surrogates are available as informants. These settings include private practices, outpatient clinics, acute care hospitals, group homes, and residential centers. The CBCL can be most useful if it is routinely obtained at intake for all cases. Routine use of the CBCL provides standardized documentation of presenting problems and competencies for purposes of case records, accumulating experience with the CBCL in the particular setting, and providing a baseline from which to assess change. Figure 9-1 illustrates a typical sequence where the parent is the first informant.

Intake and Evaluation

A key application of the CBCL is in the intake and evaluation of children referred for mental health services. The CBCL is designed to be self-explanatory for parents with reading skills as low as the fifth grade level. Because most parents involved in a referral expect to report on their child's behavior, the CBCL is a natural part of the intake routine. If intake materials are sent to parents before their first appointment, the CBCL can be enclosed to be filled out at home and returned by mail or brought to the first appointment.

If intake materials are not routinely mailed in advance, parents can be asked to come about 20 minutes before their first interview to fill out the CBCL in the waiting room. It is helpful for parents to have access to someone who can

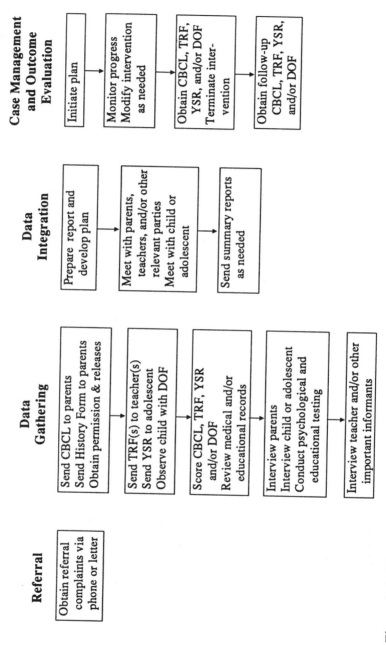

Figure 9-1. Illustrative sequence of empirically-based assessment where the parent is the first informant.

answer questions about the CBCL, such as a receptionist or intake worker who is familiar with the CBCL. However, answers to parents' questions about filling out the CBCL should focus only on the meaning of the items, with examples of relevant behaviors where necessary. The person answering the questions should *not* try to probe the parent's personality or encourage the parent to make inferences about the child's psychodynamics, but should merely help the parent fill out the CBCL to describe the child's behavior as the parent sees it.

If a parent cannot read or has other problems in filling out the CBCL, it is helpful to give the parent a copy of the CBCL while an interviewer reads each item from a second copy and enters the responses. However, the focus should always be on the parent's *description* of the child's behavior, rather than on either the parent's or the child's psychodynamics.

Having Both Parents Fill Out CBCLs

Whenever feasible, it is valuable to have both parents independently fill out CBCLs. If both parents are not available, it is also useful to have CBCLs filled out by one parent and another adult who knows the child well, such as a grandparent, or by parent surrogates if no parent is available. The purpose can be explained in words such as the following:

"We would like each of you to fill out this form to describe your child's behavior. Parents sometimes differ somewhat in the way they see their children, so don't worry if your spouse does not report exactly the same behavior as you do. Just fill it out to describe the way *you* see your child."

The specific behaviors reported and the profiles scored from both CBCLs can then be compared to reveal areas of agreement and disagreement. Small semantic disagreements are not uncommon. For example, one parent may score item *37. Gets in many fights* for approximately the same behavior as another parent scores item *57. Physically attacks people.* However, most such semantic differences do not result in different scale scores on the profile, because the items are closely enough related to be scored on the same scales. The cross-informant computer program (Achenbach, 1991a) facilitates comparisons between CBCL reports by mothers and fathers, but comparisons can also be made by using hand-scored profiles completed for each parent's CBCL.

Furthermore, interparent agreement data (Chapter 5) show that mothers' CBCLs do not yield significantly higher or lower scores than fathers' CBCLs on most scales of the profile. Consequently, when major disagreements *do* occur between a particular mother and father, they are clinically informative and should be explored to answer questions such as the following:

1. Do a parent's own problems or biases toward the child make that parent a poor informant?

2. Does lack of contact with the child make one parent a poor informant?

3. Does one parent evoke particular problem behaviors from the child?

4. Is one parent absent when the problems occur?

5. Do differences in values cause one parent to judge particular behavior more harshly than the other parent?

6. Is one parent less tolerant of difficult behavior than the other parent?

7. Is one parent prone to deny problems for reasons of social desirability?

Disagreements between parents' CBCL responses can be explored in interviews with the parents. The reasons for the disagreements are often important in formulating plans for interventions. In some cases, for example, the goal may be to change one parent's perceptions of the child or behavior toward the child, rather than to change the child's behavior. In such cases, reassessment with the CBCL after the intervention can show whether a parent's perceptions have indeed changed.

Clinical Example. As an example, Figure 9-2 shows profiles of 13-year-old Donald hand-scored from CBCLs filled out by his mother and father. (Our cross-informant computer program would print the profiles from both parents and would display side-by-side their scores on corresponding items and scale scores, as well as YSR and TRF scores, if available.) Even though Donald's parents did not give exactly the same scores on every item, their total scores were quite similar on all scales except the Aggressive Behavior scale. On the Aggressive scale, the mother reported problems that earned a total raw score of 25, which is in the clinical range. The father, by contrast, reported problems that earned a total raw score of 16, which falls at about the 93rd percentile of the normal range.

Examination of scores for each item of the Aggressive scale reveals that both parents agreed on certain problems, but the mother scored them 2, whereas the father scored them 1. On only one item, *97. Threatens people,* did the mother score a 2 where the father scored a 0. There was thus fairly good agreement on the presence of aggressive behaviors, but the father saw them as less intense than the mother. When this discrepancy was pursued in interviews with the parents, they agreed that it was because most of

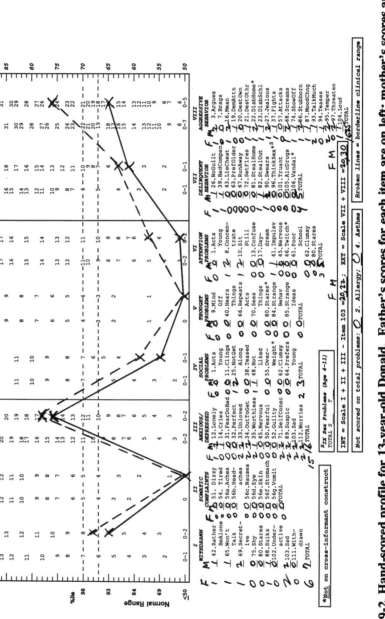

Figure 9-2. Hand-scored profile for 13-year-old Donald. Father's scores for each item are on left; mother's scores are on right. Solid line is profile scored from father's responses; broken line is profile scored from mother's responses.

the aggressive behaviors occurred in interactions between mother and son. The father was aware of them, but was not present when the most intense aggression took place in the course of mother-son battles. It was during these battles that the son often threatened his mother, leading the mother to score *97. Threatens people* as 2, whereas the father had been unaware of this particular behavior.

Although the mother's picture of her son was somewhat more negative than the father's, the behavior of both the mother and son seemed to need changing, rather than just the mother's perceptions of her son. The high scores on the Anxious/Depressed scale obtained from both parents' CBCLs also indicated that depressive feelings were of concern in their own right. It would be especially important to determine whether the aggression toward mother led to depressive feelings or vice versa, or whether problems in both areas were byproducts of something else. A low score on the Social scale of the competence portion of the profile (not shown) suggests that a lack of positive social involvement with others was another facet of Donald's problems. Strengthening social involvement outside the home might be one avenue to improving Donald's feelings about himself and relieving conflict with his mother.

Clinical Interviewing

When the practitioner first interviews a parent, it is helpful to have the completed CBCL (and, if possible, the scored profile) as a take-off point for interviewing. Parents may spontaneously wish to discuss some of their responses. The practitioner may wish to ask for clarification of certain items that the parent reports, especially such items as *9. Can't get mind off certain thoughts, obsessions; 40. Hears sounds or voices that aren't there; 70. Sees things that aren't there; 84. Strange behavior;* and *85. Strange ideas.*

After obtaining clarification of the parent's responses, the practitioner can use the items of greatest concern and the profile scales showing the most deviance as foci for interviewing about the history and context of the problems. The competence portion of the profile can also be used to identify a child's current strengths and needs for improvement.

As other data become available, such as the YSR, TRF, DOF, psychological and laboratory tests, etc., the practitioner can compare them with the picture presented by the parents via the CBCL and its profile. Disagreements with other types of data do not necessarily mean that parents' reports are wrong — they may accurately reflect the behavior the parents see, but their child may behave differently in other contexts. On the other hand, if the practitioner concludes that parents' perceptions are indeed distorted, then interventions can focus on changing the misperceptions revealed by their responses to the CBCL.

Interventions

From the problems and competencies perceived by parents and other informants, the practitioner needs to answer questions like the following:

1. Is the child's behavior really deviant?

   a. If not, then changes in the child may not be needed, but the parents, family system, teacher, or others may need help.

2. If the child's behavior is in need of change, are the problems confined to particular situations or do they occur in many situations?

   a. If the problems are confined to particular situations, intervention may need to focus on those situations and the people involved in them.

b. If the problems are not confined to particular situations, then the child's overall adaptive pattern may need changing, although interventions may include family therapy, work with parents and teachers, and environmental manipulations, as well as direct work with the child.

3. Which problem areas should receive highest priority for intervention?

  a. The degree of deviance shown by the various scales of the profile can aid the practitioner in deciding whether to focus on those that are most deviant, those that have the most immediate destructive potential (e.g., the behaviors of the Aggressive scale), or competencies that need strengthening (as shown by the Activities, Social, and School scales).

4. What are the goals of intervention in terms of the child's overall adaptive pattern?

  a. Using the child's profile pattern to specify goals can help to avoid an excessively narrow focus on diagnostic constructs such as "attention deficit disorder," "depression," or "conduct disorder." Even children who happen to meet DSM criteria for formal diagnoses of this sort often need help in other areas as well.

  b. By considering the child's entire pattern of competencies and problems, clinicians can tailor goals and interventions to the child's specific needs, rather than aiming interventions at diagnostic categories.

5. Do changes in the child's reported behavior show that the goals of an intervention are met?

a. By having the CBCL (and related instruments) filled out at intervals during and after intervention, changes in reported behavior can be monitored to determine whether the goals are met.

b. Although changes in targeted behaviors may occur, it is equally important to know about unanticipated changes in other behaviors. The profile of a child treated for hyperactivity, for example, may show increases in depression while the targeted hyperactivity declines.

c. The total problem score and certain items that have strong associations with clinical status can serve as general barometers of the child's functioning. Item *103. Unhappy, sad, or depressed,* in particular, is a good indicator of overall functioning, as it has shown a stronger association with clinical status than any other single CBCL item (see Chapter 7). Other common items that have shown especially strong associations with clinical status include: *8. Can't concentrate, can't pay attention for long; 22. Disobedient at home; 23. Disobedient at school; 25. Doesn't get along with other kids; 35. Feels worthless or inferior; 43. Lying or cheating; 45. Nervous, highstrung, or tense;* and *61. Poor school work.*

6. How can experience with previous cases be used to help in choosing an intervention?

a. As research and practical experience grow, knowledge of the course, prognosis, and treatment responsiveness of particular profile patterns can be used to guide the choice of interventions.

b. By having CBCLs sent to parents for completion at regular follow-up intervals (e.g., 6 months, 12 months, 18 months), practitioners can determine outcomes for particular types of cases in their own caseloads.

APPLICATIONS IN SCHOOL CONTEXTS

Assessment in school contexts focuses primarily on school behavior. However, special education evaluations require data from parents to determine eligibility for certain services according to Public Law 94-142 (Education of the Handicapped Act, 1977, 1981). Parents' reports are especially important in justifying eligibility for services for severe emotional disturbance (SED) and in distinguishing between eligibility for SED services and learning disability (LD) services. Disturbed children often have learning problems. Conversely, children with learning disabilities are often disturbed. As a consequence, the administrative distinctions specified by P.L. 94-142 may not correspond very well to real differences among children. Nevertheless, both to meet administrative requirements and to serve children's needs, it is essential to obtain a well-differentiated picture of children's functioning outside as well as in school.

By providing parents' reports in a format similar to the TRF for teachers' reports, the DOF for direct observations, and the SCIC and YSR for self-reports, the CBCL can aid in determining the most appropriate approach to school-based interventions. If the CBCL indicates many behavioral/emotional problems outside of school, for example, this indicates that a focus only on school learning problems would be inadequate. Although some behavioral/emotional problems may arise in reaction to the frustration of school failure, CBCL problem scores in the clinical range would argue in favor of eligibility for SED services. If the CBCL problem scores are all in the normal range and there is no other evidence for behavioral/emotional problems outside of school, this would suggest that school learning and adaptation should be the main focus of intervention.

Sometimes, both school and home ratings show significant problems, but the problem behaviors differ in the two settings. Suppose, for example, that the CBCL profile of an 8-year-old boy scored from his parents' ratings shows deviance mainly on the Anxious/Depressed scale, whereas his TRF and DOF profiles show deviance mainly in attention problems. This may indicate that problems of inattention perceived by the teacher are not due to any basic attention deficit, but to general unhappiness. In another case, aggression seen in school may be accompanied by withdrawal at home, which would require different interventions than if aggression were consistent across situations.

Where the need for a particular service is already clear—such as special education for a retarded child — it is nevertheless important to have a picture of the child's home behavior. For example, CBCL ratings may show that a retarded child has social skills deficits or behavior problems that interfere with adaptation in the home or neighborhood. If so, a school social worker could help the child's family implement training procedures coordinated with the teacher's efforts to train adaptive behavior. During periodic reevaluations of the child, ratings by parents can continue to aid in determining the most appropriate placements and educational objectives for the child.

APPLICATIONS IN MEDICAL CONTEXTS

Medical providers are often in a position to identify children's behavioral/emotional problems and to respond to parents' concerns about them. The CBCL can be obtained routinely by pediatricians, health maintenance organizations, pediatric psychologists, and other medical providers by having parents complete it while waiting for their appointments.   A receptionist can score the CBCL by hand or microcomputer and give the completed form and scored profile to the provider. For 11- to 18-year-olds, it is helpful to obtain the YSR, which can also be filled out in the waiting room and scored by a receptionist.   The YSR provides a basis for comparison with what the parent reports on the CBCL, and it may reveal problems not known to the parent.

A glance at the profile can alert the provider to areas of deviance that need exploration with the parent and/or child. The profile can also be used as a basis for answering questions raised by a parent or child with respect to whether certain problems are normal for the child's age. The problems and competencies of children with physical handicaps and illnesses often require special attention. As such conditions are apt to raise the risk of behavioral/ emotional problems, the profile can be helpful in judging whether the child is generally functioning within the normal range or whether deviance may be associated with the medical condition.

For providers who specialize in a particular type of illness—such as diabetes or leukemia—or handicap—such as deafness, epilepsy, or cerebral palsy—the CBCL can be used to determine what problems are most commonly associated with these conditions and what problems may arise in response to particular treatments, such as drugs. This will make it easier to anticipate problems and to help parents and children cope with them. Advice, therapy, and support programs can be focused on the problems found to accompany particular medical conditions. The outcomes of interventions can be evaluated by readministering the CBCL to assess changes in the reported problems and competencies. Siblings of children with severe physical problems may also show behavioral/emotional reactions that can be assessed with the CBCL.

Pediatricians and pediatric psychologists are often consulted about attention deficits and hyperactivity. If a child attends school, it is usually important to obtain the TRF for comparison with other sources of data. Depending on the picture that emerges from the multiple sources, the provider may opt for a referral to mental health or school psychological services. If multiple sources consistently show an uncomplicated attention deficit, the provider may choose to initiate interventions such as stimulant medication, behavior modification, and/or parent training. As with any other intervention, it would be important to assess the effects periodically, as by readministering the CBCL and/or TRF. At each reassessment point, the different sources could be compared to determine whether all were reporting improvement or whether any source reported failure to improve or worsening.

FORENSIC APPLICATIONS

Children may become involved with the legal system in a variety of ways. In questions of custody and placement, profiles scored from CBCLs completed by relevant adults can be compared to determine how each adult sees the child. In a custody dispute between parents, for example, profiles scored from the CBCL completed by the mother and father can be compared to determine which one corresponds best to all the other findings about the child. If one parent's report differs sharply from everything else that is known about the child, this could raise questions about the parent's knowledge or perceptions of the child. If a foster placement has been made because of a child's behavior problems, profiles scored from CBCLs completed by the foster parents and natural parents can be compared to determine whether the child's behavior improved in the foster home.

If not, more than a change of home environment may be needed. Agencies responsible for foster children can also use the CBCL to survey needs for mental health services among foster children.

When children and youth are brought before juvenile courts, the CBCL can be used to evaluate parents' perceptions of their child and to identify behavioral/emotional problems to be checked against other sources of data, such as the YSR, TRF, and interviews. Rather than focusing only on delinquent behavior, the CBCL profile and other profiles can indicate whether the individual manifests additional problems that may shed light on alleged transgressions. The Thought Problems scale, for example, can indicate whether deficient reality testing may be involved, while the Anxious/Depressed scale may indicate inner discomfort that could motivate efforts to change. It is also important to check specific items for danger signs, such as items *18* and *91*, concerning suicidal behavior and ideation.

CHILD ABUSE

No single measure of children's functioning can infallibly diagnose child abuse, and no single pattern of problems has been found to occur following abuse (LaRiviere, 1990). Abuse may be just one among several factors contributing to a particular pattern of functioning. The possibility of abuse should be considered as one hypothesis for explaining reports obtained with the CBCL. When abuse does occur, the problems reported on the CBCL may be a function of the informant's role in relation to the child, as well as the child's experience of the abuse, pre-existing characteristics of the child, and current strengths, stresses, and supports.

Comparisons of CBCLs from parents and surrogates, the YSR, TRF, interviews, and other sources of data may reveal discrepancies suggesting that a particular informant is minimizing or exaggerating a child's problems. If a suspected abuser reports many fewer problems than all other informants, for example, this might be evidence for the informant's involvement in abuse. If an informant reports far more problems than other informants, on the other hand, this may suggest an effort to blame a suspected abuser.

Children receiving help to remedy the effects of abuse should be periodically reassessed to evaluate their progress. If a child is placed in a foster home, CBCLs can be obtained at regular intervals from the foster parents. For children remaining with their own families, CBCLs can be periodically obtained from adults in the home. Other sources of data, such as the YSR, TRF, and interviews can also be used in conjunction with the CBCL to evaluate children's progress following abuse.

DIAGNOSTIC ISSUES

Because parents can usually provide more information about their children than can any other single source, their reports are important ingredients of the diagnostic process. The data obtained with the CBCL can contribute to diagnosis in various ways. Scores in the normal, borderline, and clinical range provide a basis for judging whether a child is clinically deviant and, if so, in what areas. Each of the problem and competence items is potentially useful in formulating a diagnostic picture of the case as a whole. Certain specific problems, such as suicidal behavior, strange ideas, stealing, and firesetting, for example, are bound to be central foci of diagnostic assessment in their own right. Other specific problems and low competence scores would also be important for diagnostic formulations.

In addition to diagnostic formulations, formal diagnoses are often required for purposes of third party reimbursement and record keeping. (The differences between diagnostic formulations and formal diagnoses are presented in the *Integrative Guide,* Achenbach, 1991a.) The syndrome scales scored from the CBCL reflect syndromes actually found to occur in large clinical samples. Several of the empirically derived syndromes are descriptively similar to DSM categories, as summarized in Table 9-1. When diagnostic categories have been operationally defined in terms of a specific assessment procedure, DSM diagnostic criteria have been significantly associated with our empirically derived syndromes on the CBCL (Edelbrock & Costello, 1988), as well as on the YSR (Weinstein, Noam, Grimes, Stone, & Schwab-Stone, 1990), and TRF (Edelbrock, Costello, & Kessler, 1984). Although the diagnostic categories and criteria change from one edition of the DSM to the next, it is to be hoped that future changes will be based more directly on empirical research.

Because neither diagnostic formulations nor formal diagnoses should be based on a single source of data, the diagnostic process requires coordination of data from multiple sources, such as self-reports, teacher-reports, interviews, tests, observations, and physical exams. If a child is in the clinical range on similar syndrome scales scored from the CBCL, YSR, TRF, and/or DOF, this would argue for a diagnosis corresponding to such syndromes. Because there may be complex variations among the data obtained from multiple sources, the *Integrative Guide* (Achenbach, 1991a) provides various procedures for coordinating multisource data in the diagnostic process.

PLANNING AND ACCOUNTABILITY FOR SERVICES

Documentation of cases is increasingly essential for justifying services, third party payment, protection from

Table 9-1

Approximate Relations Between DSM-III-R and the CBCL, YSR, TRF, and DOF Syndromes

DSM-III-R	CBCL	YSR	TRF	DOF
Avoidant Disorder	Withdrawn	Withdrawn	Withdrawn	Withdrawn-Inattentive
Somatization Disorder	Somatic Complaints	Somatic Complaints	Somatic Complaints	—
Overanxious Disorder	Anxious/Depressed	Anxious/Depressed	Anxious/Depressed	Nervous-Obsessive
Major Depression	"	"	"	Depressed
Dysthymia	"	"	"	"
Schizotypal Personality	Thought Problems	Thought Problems	Thought Problems	—
Psychotic Disorders	"	"	"	
Attention Deficit-Hyperactivity Disorder	Attention Problems	Attention Problems	Attention Problems	Hyperactive
Group Delinquent Conduct Disorder	Delinquent Behavior	Delinquent Behavior	Delinquent Behavior	—
Solitary Aggressive Conduct Disorder	Aggressive Behavior	Aggressive Behavior	Aggressive Behavior	Aggressive Behavior
Oppositional Defiant Disorder	"	"	"	"
Gender Identity Disorder for Males	Sex Problems[a]	Self-Destructive/Identity Problems[b]	—	—

[a] Scored for ages 4-11 only.
[b] Scored for boys only. See YSR Manual (Achenbach, 1991c) for details.

liability, and accreditation of programs. In mental health settings, the CBCL can be made a routine part of the intake process for most or all cases. The completed CBCLs and profiles can then be placed in children's records to provide standardized documentation of the initial problems and competencies. The CBCL can also be readministered periodically to document changes and outcomes, to assist therapists, and to place in the children's records. Where CBCLs are obtained for school evaluations and in other contexts, they can be used in similar ways.

Across the caseload of an agency or multiple agencies, the CBCL can be used to document the prevalence and distribution of problems for purposes of annual reports, requests for funding, and planning for staff and services. Increases and decreases in particular problems and syndrome scores from one period to another can provide a basis for restructuring services. To optimize the allocation of resources, it is especially important to determine whether certain CBCL scores are consistently followed by much worse outcomes than are others. If cases with poor prognoses are identified at intake into a particular service, procedures can be developed to provide and test alternative approaches to such cases rather than continuing to render ineffective services.

Case Registers

At the level of catchment areas or county or state mental health systems, the CBCL, YSR, and TRF can provide the basis for *case registers* that are designed to obtain standardized data on all cases seen in a designated area. When maintained over an extended period, such as a year, a case register provides valuable data on the number of cases having each kind of problem, differences between the problems seen in different facilities, associations of particular problems with variables such as ethnicity and socioeconomic status, seasonal fluctuations, etc.

Our microcomputer programs make it possible for each participating agency to score all forms for its own use and to send diskettes of data to a central facility for aggregation across the entire area served by the case register. No names need to be transmitted, as each agency can use its own code numbers. Each agency can also print profiles and retain computer files of CBCL data for its own use.

If regular follow-ups are done for each clinical service (e.g., at 6-month intervals), the follow-up data can be analyzed to determine the progress of cases seen in the designated area. Follow-up data on the course of particular kinds of problems and cases can aid in planning and justifying agency budgets by answering the frequently asked question, "What happens to these kids later?"

TRAINING OF PRACTITIONERS

The CBCL can contribute to various aspects of training, as exemplified in the following sections.

Training for Intake Assessments

If trainees are taught to use the CBCL as part of the initial assessment, they can learn to use interviews to follow up on the parents' CBCL responses and to focus on matters better dealt with by interviews. Interviewing is costly, as it requires an appointment system, waiting and interview rooms, advance preparation, and the practitioner's time to conduct the interview and compile the interview data. Costs are further increased by the occasional failure of clients to keep appointments. Training of interview skills is still more costly, because cases must be selected for their training value and both the supervisor and trainee must be involved. It is therefore important to make the best possible use of the time for training interviewers, rather than wasting time to get information that can be obtained more cheaply and efficiently with the CBCL.

Selecting Teaching Cases

The lack of a well-validated diagnostic system for childhood disorders makes it hard to select cases that clearly exemplify particular disorders. Extensive assessment is required to determine whether a child truly fits diagnostic categories like those of the DSM. Even when a child does meet the criteria for a DSM category, viewing the child solely in terms of the category may obscure other important facets of the case. The CBCL can therefore be helpful in selecting cases that illustrate complex patterns not adequately subsumed by DSM categories.

Comparing Data From Different Sources

A key objective of training is to help trainees grasp the multifaceted and relativistic nature of children's problems and competencies. The CBCL can be used to compare and contrast behavior reported by a mother and father. If the YSR, TRF, and/or DOF are obtained, these provide a further basis for comparing different viewpoints. This can help the trainee form a more comprehensive picture of the child than by soliciting unstandarized descriptions. It can also pinpoint discrepancies that need exploration to determine whether they reflect differences in the child's behavior in different situations or idiosyncrasies of the informants' reports. Discrepancies between the profiles scored from CBCLs completed by a mother and father can be discussed with the parents to determine why they may see their child differently.

Having Trainees Complete the CBCL

To sharpen trainees' skills in assessing children's problems and competencies, they can be asked to complete the CBCL in the course of evaluating children. Their ratings can then be compared with ratings by parents and experienced practitioners, and the reasons for discrepancies can be explored. This is especially useful for training child care workers who function as surrogate parents. Where multiple workers care for the same child, the profiles scored from their ratings can be compared to provide better perspectives on variations in the child's behavior and in their views of the child.

Having Trainees Evaluate Intervention Effects

By obtaining CBCL ratings at intervals during and after interventions, trainees can learn to document the effects of interventions and to determine whether parents observe the same effects as the trainees believe are occurring. When there are discrepancies between the views of the intervention effects, the trainees can discuss them with the parents to determine the reasons.

SUMMARY

This chapter addressed applications of the CBCL to making *practical decisions* about *particular* cases, groups, programs, policies, etc. The numerous correlates of the CBCL enable practitioners to bring accumulated knowledge to bear on decisions about individual cases and situations.

Applications were described in mental health contexts, including use in intake and evaluation, having both parents fill out CBCLs, clinical interviewing, and interventions. Other applications were described for school contexts, medical contexts, forensic situations, and evaluation of problems related to child abuse.

Implications of the CBCL for diagnostic issues were presented, as were uses of the CBCL in planning and accountability for services, including its use for case registers to provide standardized data on all cases entering a system.

Contributions of the CBCL to training include helping trainees learn to make optimal use of interviews by first obtaining the CBCL as part of the initial assessment; selecting training cases according to problems and patterns manifest on the CBCL profile; teaching trainees to compare data from different sources; having trainees complete the CBCL for comparison with ratings by parents and experienced practitioners; and teaching trainees to evaluate the intervention effects by having parents complete the CBCL during and after interventions.

Chapter 10
Research Use of
the CBCL and Profile

Chapter 9 outlined some ways in which the CBCL can be used for assessment on which to base practical decisions about particular cases and situations. The CBCL, its scales, and profile are products of research designed to improve our ways of helping children. Much remains to be learned, however, and the CBCL can be used in many ways to expand our knowledge through research.

The *Integrative Guide* (Achenbach, 1991a) focuses on multiaxial aspects of research involving the CBCL, YSR, and TRF. Because agreement between different informants may not be very·high, it is desirable to obtain data from multiple sources whenever possible. However, for many purposes, research may center on parents' reports in particular, or parents may happen to be the most feasible and appropriate sources of data. This chapter therefore focuses primarily on research use of the CBCL, although data from parents should be viewed as only one component of comprehensive assessment. The topics generally parallel those presented in the *Integrative Guide*, but with variations specific to the CBCL.

Use of the CBCL is not confined to any single theoretical view, topic, or type of research. Instead, the CBCL provides an assessment procedure and data language that can be shared by workers differing in theoretical persuasions and research interests. Furthermore, the CBCL can be used in conjunction with many other sources of data, such as tests, self-report questionnaires, interviews, direct observations, teachers' ratings, biomedical procedures, and life histories.

Research on a particular type of disorder, such as depression or aggression, typically employs measures specific to that type of disorder. Because the CBCL has eight syndrome scales, it can be used to assess disorders corresponding to any of these eight scales. Even if a more specialized procedure is used to assess a particular type of disorder, the inclusion of the CBCL can reveal problems in other areas that may be equally as important. In research on aggression, for example, both the CBCL and a specialized measure of aggression may identify subjects who obtain high scores for aggression. However, the instrument that measures only aggression will fail to distinguish children whose parents report only aggressive problems from children whose parents would also report significant problems in other areas, if they were asked. The CBCL, by contrast, is designed to simultaneously obtain parents' reports of problems and competencies in many areas in addition to aggression. For research on a particular disorder, such as aggression, the CBCL would thus be useful for distinguishing between children whose parents report problems only in the area of the target disorder and children who present more complex pictures that cannot be discerned via measures that assess only the target disorder.

This chapter first deals with questions arising in the use of raw scores versus T scores for the CBCL scales and in analyzing scores from multiple sex/age groups. Thereafter, it describes applications to research areas including epidemiology, diagnosis, etiology, services, outcomes, child abuse, medical conditions, cross-cultural comparisons, and parental characteristics. Because creative research blends ideas, opportunities, and methods in new ways, readers will no doubt think of many research possibilities beside those mentioned here. To facilitate access to research possibilities and findings, our *Bibliography of Published Studies*

Using the Child Behavior and Related Materials is updated annually. The 1991 edition lists some 200 topics dealt with in over 700 publications (Achenbach & Brown, 1991).

USE OF RAW SCORES VERSUS *T* SCORES IN RESEARCH WITH THE CBCL

Chapters 2 and 3 described the computation of raw scale scores and the assignment of *T* scores to the CBCL scales. The main function of the *T* scores is to facilitate comparisons of the degree of deviance indicated by children's standing on different scales and different instruments. A *T* score of 70, for example, indicates that a child scored at approximately the 98th percentile of our normative sample for that child's age group and sex. Because the *T* scores from 50 to 70 were similarly based on percentiles for the syndrome scales of the CBCL, a child who obtains a *T* score of 70 on the CBCL Aggressive Behavior scale and 55 on the CBCL Somatic Complaints scale is more deviant in reported aggression than in somatic problems, relative to norms based on parents' reports.

Suppose that the child who obtained a *T* score of 70 on the CBCL Aggressive Behavior scale obtained a *T* score of 50 on the TRF Aggressive Behavior scale. This indicates that the child's teacher reported much less aggressive behavior, relative to reports by teachers in our normative sample, than did the child's parents, relative to reports by parents in our normative sample.

By being based on percentiles for the normative sample, the *T* scores provide a convenient way of quickly judging whether a parent reports relatively many or few competencies and problems, as compared to parents of nonreferred children. However, because the distributions of scale scores vary among samples, and because of our method for assigning *T* scores at the extremes of the distributions, the

T scores do not provide a perfectly precise and uniform index of deviance. Furthermore, because we truncated the assignment of T scores at the nondeviant end of the syndrome and competence scales, raw scores can reflect greater differentiation among nondeviant subjects than T scores can on these scales. This is not the case for the total competence, Internalizing, Externalizing, and total problem scores, however, where the T scores were not truncated.

Statistical Analysis of Scale Scores

For statistical analysis of the competence and syndrome scales, it is usually preferable to use the raw scale scores rather than the T scores in order to take account of the full range of variation in these scales. Because T scores were not truncated for the total competence, Internalizing, Externalizing, and total problem scores, statistical analyses using the T scores for these scales should yield results similar to those using the raw scores. In any case, the actual distributions of scores to be analyzed should be checked for compatibility with the statistics to be used. If the obtained distributions depart much from the statistical assumptions, other statistical procedures or transformations of the scores may be needed.

If a researcher wishes to compare a particular sample with our CBCL normative samples, the simplest way is to compare the mean and standard deviation of the sample's raw scores with the mean and standard deviation of the raw scores shown in Table 3-4 for the corresponding normative sample. Because any particular research sample is selected differently than our normative sample, the means and standard deviations are likely to differ between the samples. However, the researcher can determine whether the research sample's scores are similar to, much higher, or much lower than those of our normative sample. Similar comparisons can be made with the scores shown in Appendix B for our clinical samples.

The truncation, normalizing transformation, and equal-interval assignment of extreme T scores in our normative samples make direct comparisons with T scores from a particular research sample more tenuous than comparisons of raw scores. However, if a researcher wishes to describe a sample in terms of our T scores, all the raw scores in the sample should first be individually converted to T scores, as is done by our CBCL computer program. The mean and standard deviation of these T scores can then be compared with the mean and standard deviation of the T scores reported for our normative sample in Table 3-4 or clinical sample in Appendix B. The mean and standard deviation of a raw score distribution should *not* be converted directly to the equivalent T scores shown on the CBCL profile, because this wrongly assumes that the raw score and T score distributions have identical shapes.

RESEARCH SPANNING MULTIPLE SEX/AGE GROUPS

By using a common set of eight syndrome scales for all versions of the 1991 CBCL profiles, we have designed the profiles to facilitate comparisons between both sexes and different ages. A ninth syndrome, Sex Problems, consists of the same set of items for the two groups for which it is scored, i.e., boys and girls at ages 4-11. Because it is specific to these two groups and because the normative sample obtained such low scores, the Sex Problems syndrome is not displayed as a scale on the profile.

The Internalizing, Externalizing, and total problem scales comprise the same items for all sex/age groups, while the competence scales are also uniform for all groups, except that the competence scales are not scored for 4-5-

year-olds. To take account of sex and age differences in scores, percentiles and T scores were based on separate normative samples of each sex within each age range. This makes it possible to compare a child's score on any scale with a normative group of the same sex and age range.

If statistical analyses are to be done on samples that include children of both sexes and/or different age ranges, the sex/age differences in scores must be taken into account. On some scales, a particular raw score may represent a different degree of deviance in one sex/age group than in another. For example, a raw score of 11 is just below the clinical cutpoint on the Anxious/Depressed scale for girls 12-18, but is above the clinical cutpoint for boys 4-11. If we compare the raw scores of two samples that differ greatly in the proportion of girls 12-18 versus boys 4-11, the sample having more girls might appear more deviant. However, because the normative base rate for the problems of the Anxious/Depressed scale is higher for the older girls than for the younger boys, this would be a misleading conclusion.

To prevent sex/age differences from being confounded with other variables, several options are available. For analyses of the Internalizing, Externalizing, total problem, and total competence scores that include multiple sex/age groups, the T scores for the respective sex/age groups can be used. These T scores reflect each subject's deviation from the mean of his/her normative group without losing any of the differentiation that is lost by truncating T scores, as occurs on some of the syndrome and competence scales.

For syndrome and competence scales that have only one raw score assigned to the truncated T score ($T = 50$ on syndrome scales, $T = 55$ on competence scales), the T scores can be used without any loss of differentiation. For syndrome scales that have multiple raw scores assigned to $T = 50$, the loss of differentiation incurred by using T

scores will depend on how many different scores in a research sample would be assigned $T = 50$.

As an example, the Aggressive Behavior scale for boys 4-11 assigns $T = 50$ to raw scores of 0 to 7. If many of the boys in a research sample obtain raw scores of 0 to 7, use of T scores is apt to yield less statistical power than use of raw scores. However, since all scores receiving $T = 50$ are at the low end of the normal range, a researcher may decide that the differences among such scores merely add "noise" to analyses of clinically important variables. The researcher might therefore use T scores to reduce the differentiation among low normal raw scores. On the other hand, if a researcher wishes to preserve all the differentiation in raw scores analyzed for multiple sex/age groups, then the raw scores can be converted to z scores within each of the sex/age groups to be analyzed.

Longitudinal analyses of subjects who are assessed with the CBCL before age 12 and again at ages 12-18 can be handled in the same way as just described for analyses that include multiple sex/age groups. That is, the use of T scores will adjust for the differences between norms for the different age ranges. If a researcher wishes to preserve variations within the normal range on the truncated syndrome scales, then the raw scores can be converted to z scores within each sex/age range to be analyzed.

EPIDEMIOLOGICAL RESEARCH

Epidemiology is the study of the rate and distribution of disorders in populations. It is especially concerned with the *incidence* (rate of onset) of new disorders, and the *prevalence* (percent of the population having disorders) at particular points in time. Knowledge of the incidence, prevalence, and distribution of disorders is important for planning services, developing hypotheses about causal

factors, identifying changes in rates over time, and inter-
preting findings on particular research samples in light of
data from samples of large populations. For instruments
such as the CBCL, epidemiological data are also needed to
provide normative distributions of scores on which to base
cutpoints for discriminating between the normal and clinical
range.

Population Studies

Population studies are typically designed to estimate the
prevalence of disorders or problems in a large population at
a particular point in time. The target population is often
defined as all the children between certain ages living in a
particular geographical area, such as a city, county, state,
region, or country. Because it is seldom feasible to assess
every child in the target population, samples of children are
assessed as a basis for estimating prevalence rates in the
entire population. The sampling procedures must be
carefully designed to obtain samples that are as representative as possible of the population. That is, every child in
the population must have an equal chance of being selected
for assessment. However, it is not only the sampling
procedure, but completion rates in the selected sample and
the quality of the assessment procedures that determine
whether the obtained data validly represent the entire
population.

For population samples of children's behavior-
al/emotional problems, parents are usually a key source of
data. To maximize our chance of obtaining representative
data from parents, it is necessary to use standardized
assessment procedures that are economical, acceptable to
parents, easy to administer, brief, reliable, and efficiently
scored. To maximize the utility of the data, the instruments
should not be narrowly restricted to predetermined concepts
of disorders that are apt to change. The instruments should

also be usable in a similar fashion with different kinds of samples, such as clinical criterion groups.

The CBCL was designed to meet all the foregoing requirements, and it has been used in population studies in several countries (e.g., Achenbach & Edelbrock, 1981; Achenbach, Bird, Canino, Phares, Gould, & Rubio-Stipec, 1990; Achenbach, Hensley, Phares, & Grayson, 1990; Montenegro, 1983; Verhulst, Akkerhuis, & Althaus, 1985; Weisz, Suwanlert, Chaiyasit, Weiss, Achenbach, & Walter, 1987). It has also been used to analyze relations between the prevalence of disorders and patterns of service utilization in general population samples (Sawyer, Sarris, Baghurst, Cornish, & Kalucy, 1990). The methodology used in these studies can be applied to population samples almost anywhere.

Data obtained in new studies using the same methodology can be rigorously compared with data obtained in the previous studies to identify similarities and differences between populations and from one time to another within a population. Population studies in particular areas can also be used to determine base rates for parent-reported problems and competencies in those areas. Comparisons can be made to determine whether rates differ for particular groups within an area, such as children from certain neighborhoods or ethnic groups, or disadvantaged or handicapped children. Mental health agencies may wish to establish local norms for their catchment areas to use as a baseline with which to compare children referred for services.

Case Registers

Research on individuals who are referred for services provides an important complement to population-based studies. Individual clinical services, however, are subject to biases in their caseloads, owing to their specific locations, referral sources that channel cases to one service versus another, admission requirements, economic factors, service philosophies, and the images that they project to consumers. As a consequence, no one service is likely to provide a representative sample of referred children within an area, unless it is the sole service in that area.

Case registers for recording uniform data on all cases referred for services within a delimited area can be extremely valuable for obtaining clinical samples that are less biased than those of any single service. By obtaining data from multiple services, case registers can also yield larger samples of uncommon disorders than can single facilities or general population samples. Furthermore, the variations in cases across multiple services can enable researchers to test associations between disorders and a wider range of case characteristics than in single facilities. Case registers of infectious diseases, for example, provide data on SES, ethnic, age, sex, occupational, and secular variations in the diseases. These data are used to develop hypotheses about etiologies and outcomes.

A comprehensive case register for child psychopathology would include children referred to special education services and juvenile courts, as well as those referred for mental health services, because all three kinds of services deal with an overlapping range of problems. The CBCL can be requested from parents as part of the evaluation process in all services participating in a case register. The register would be designed to obtain other kinds of data according to the aims of the researchers and what can feasibly be obtained in all the participating services. The value of a register can be enhanced by including systematic follow-ups of cases in order to study the course and outcomes of disorders in association with other variables, such as initial case characteristics and type of service received. If the amount and cost of services can be accurately recorded for all cases, case registers can also enable researchers to study the cost of caring for cases that are classified according to the problems reported on the initial CBCL.

DIAGNOSTIC AND TAXONOMIC RESEARCH

To validly distinguish among disorders, a diagnostic system requires a *taxonomy* for grouping disorders according to their distinguishing features. It also requires *assessment procedures* for identifying the features of each case that correspond to the taxonomic groupings. A comprehensive approach to the taxonomic basis for diagnosis should include multiple assessment procedures that converge on the taxonomic groupings from different angles. The *Integrative Guide* (Achenbach, 1991a) discusses coordination of the CBCL, YSR, and TRF in efforts to improve the taxonomic basis for diagnosis of childhood disorders. Because parents are the informants most often involved in clinical referrals of children and are also apt to provide the most comprehensive data, the CBCL can be a key element of diagnostic and taxonomic research.

The eight cross-informant syndromes provide a basis for taxonomy of many childhood problems, as seen by parents. One approach to research is to test the correspondence between the CBCL scores on the eight syndromes and assessment data obtained via other systems based on data from parents. As an example, Edelbrock and Costello (1988) analyzed associations between pre-1991 CBCL syndrome scores and DSM-III diagnoses made from the parent version of the Diagnostic Interview Schedule for Children (DISC-P). Those DSM diagnoses that were defined by multiple descriptive features showed significant associations with the corresponding syndromes of the CBCL.

Because parents continue to be important sources of data for subsequent versions of DSM childhood disorders, it would be worth testing the associations between the 1991 CBCL syndromes and current versions of DSM diagnoses made from data provided by parents. For those DSM disorders that are defined by multiple descriptive features, the number of features that parents report to be present can be summed to provide a quantitative score for each DSM disorder. By testing both this quantitative score and various cutpoints on the score, the researcher can determine whether the standard criteria for DSM diagnoses, other cutpoints, or continuous quantitative scores provide better agreement with the CBCL syndrome scores. Conversely, the CBCL quantitative scores can be compared with various cutpoints on the scores to identify the best basis for agreement with DSM diagnoses.

It should be noted that the cutpoints which maximize agreement between different assessment procedures and different taxonomic criteria may be specific to particular samples. A sample that includes many high scores, for example, may benefit from a higher cutpoint than a sample with few high scores. For cutpoints to have useful generalizability, it is therefore necessary to use samples that are representative of large populations and/or to compare the effects of particular cutpoints when they are applied to samples that differ in important ways. The *Integrative Guide* (Achenbach, 1991a) outlines additional ways in which the CBCL can be used for diagnostic and taxonomic research in conjunction with the YSR, TRF, and other procedures.

ETIOLOGICAL RESEARCH

Etiological research aims to identify the causes of disorders. The behavioral/emotional disorders of childhood are likely to involve many different kinds of causal factors, such as genetic, temperamental, interactions with parents, traumatic, and cultural. Some factors may not ordinarily be causal in themselves, but may raise the risk of behavioral/emotional problems under particular conditions. Children who are cognitively either much more or less advanced than their peers, for example, may face frustrations that spawn behavioral/emotional problems, even though there is nothing pathological about their cognitive functioning per se.

Because the determinants of behavioral/emotional disorders are likely to be complex, it is important to triangulate multiple variables from multiple perspectives. The multiaxial model that was presented in Table 1-1 is therefore relevant to etiological research as well as to clinical assessment of individual children. The *Integrative Guide* outlines approaches to coordinating the CBCL, YSR, and TRF in etiological research. It is recommended that etiological research employ assessment from these different perspectives whenever possible, as well as from other perspectives, such as observations, interviews, tests, laboratory measures, and biomedical assays. For some purposes, however, parents are the only feasible informants about children's typical behavior. For children who do not attend school and cannot provide readily scorable self-reports, the CBCL may be the most feasible way to assess everyday behavioral/emotional problems. Furthermore, if children are to be reassessed longitudinally, the CBCL can provide greater continuity than teacher- or self-report measures from early childhood to later years. Even if children attend school, there may be practical or ethical obstacles to obtaining data from teachers to coordinate with data from parents.

If the CBCL is used as the main means for obtaining standardized ratings from informants who know the child well, it is desirable to have both parents independently complete CBCLs, if possible. If both parents are available for some but not all subjects, the mother's and father's CBCL scale scores can be averaged to provide a single set of scores for analysis in conjunction with subjects for whom only one CBCL is available. On the other hand, if CBCLs are available from both parents of all or nearly all the subjects, separate analyses can be done for the mothers' CBCLs, fathers' CBCLs, the mean of both parents' CBCLs, and combinations of scores from the mothers' and fathers' CBCLs weighted via discriminant, regression, or factor analyses.

Examples of etiological research using the CBCL include the following:

1. Identify children who all manifest a particular CBCL profile pattern and compare them with children who manifest a different profile pattern with respect to hypothesized differences in etiology.

2. If a potential etiological factor, such as a particular type of brain damage, can be identified, compare CBCL scores and profile patterns for subjects who do and do not have the etiological factor to determine whether they differ in parent-reported behavioral/emotional problems. If they do differ, this would be evidence in favor of a causal role for the identified etiological factor.

3. If hypothesized etiological factors can be experimentally manipulated, the CBCL can be completed following different experimental conditions to determine whether problems perceived by parents change in response to the manipulations. If it is hypothesized that a particular food additive is a causal factor in attention problems, for example, CBCLs could be completed by parents after a 2-month period when their children receive food containing the additive and also after a 2-month period when the children's food is free of the

additive. The experimental order should be counter-balanced so that some children receive one condition first, while other children receive the other condition first. To use the CBCL for assessment periods shorter than the usual 6-month period, the instructions need only be changed to specify the target period. Scores obtained at the end of each experimental condition would then be compared to determine whether they differ significantly.

4. If an hypothesized etiological factor is present during a child's early years, the CBCL can be readministered periodically to compare the developmental course of children who have the hypothesized etiological factor and those who do not. If assessment is to begin before age 4, the CBCL for Ages 2-3 can be employed. The CBCL/2-3 has counterparts of 59 CBCL/4-18 problem items, plus 40 items designed specifically for 2- to 3-year-olds. Longitudinal research has demonstrated substantial predictive relations from CBCL/2-3 scores at age 2 to CBCL/4-18 scores at age 5 (Achenbach, Edelbrock, & Howell, 1987).

OUTCOME RESEARCH

If we knew the typical outcome for each childhood disorder following no intervention and following each of several intervention options, we would be in a much better position to make decisions about individual cases. Furthermore, if types of cases were identified that typically had poor outcomes following all available interventions as well as following no intervention, these types of cases should receive high priority for research designed to improve interventions. Because parents are usually involved in the assessment of children for interventions, their reports are a prime source of baseline data with which to compare outcomes. Because parents are also the most likely informants to remain available from initial to outcome assessments, data obtained from them at each point can offer a more rigorous basis for comparing outcomes with initial status than can data from sources that change over time. Because the CBCL can be scored on the same syndrome scales from age 4 to 18, it offers exceptional continuity of assessment for studies of outcomes, over periods ranging from a few months to many years. Furthermore, the CBCL scores and profile patterns obtained at the initial assessment can be tested as potential predictors of outcome.

If we find that particular CBCL scores or profile patterns are typically followed by much worse outcomes than other scores or patterns, then new cases manifesting the prognosticators of poor outcomes can be selected for research efforts to improve their outcomes. Other variables, such as teacher- and self-ratings, interview data, family constellation, cognitive measures, and biomedical conditions, might also be found to augment predictions of outcomes. These variables could then be used in conjunction with the CBCL to identify cases expected to have poor outcomes and to develop better ways of helping them.

Just as additional variables may augment prediction of outcomes from initial characteristics, the outcomes themselves should be evaluated using criteria in addition to the CBCL whenever possible. The additional criteria could include teacher- and self-ratings obtainable with the TRF and YSR, cognitive functioning, new problems, referral for various services, etc.

Groups at Risk

Beside testing predictions of outcomes from child-related variables, outcome research can be useful for determining the relative risk rates for children thought to be predisposed to poor outcomes by certain identifiable background conditions. Children whose family members are alcoholic, schizophrenic, or depressed, for example, are thought to be at elevated risk for behavioral/emotional problems. To determine whether such children have elevated rates of problems in general or the specific problems tapped by particular syndrome scales, CBCLs could be compared from parents of children in each of several risk groups and children not having any of the risk factors. A parent who does not have the target condition should be the informant for all the children in the risk groups. However, it would also be important to obtain data from nonfamily sources as well, such as teachers.

SERVICES RESEARCH

Experimental Intervention Studies

If outcome research identifies case characteristics that predict poor outcomes, this argues for active efforts to improve outcomes for these cases. The most rigorous way to determine whether a particular intervention can improve outcomes is to experimentally manipulate the intervention conditions. Experimental studies require a large enough supply of appropriate cases to be assigned to different experimental conditions, such as by randomized assignment to Intervention A versus Intervention B versus no intervention. For some types of interventions, such as drugs or contingency manipulations designed to alter specific behaviors, it may be possible to test each intervention with the same subjects receiving both interventions in counterbalanced sequences, such as ABAB and BABA.

To warrant the effort and cost of experimental intervention studies, candidate subjects must be assessed in a uniform fashion to identify those who have the target characteristics and to exclude those who do not. If deviant scores on particular CBCL scales were previously found to predict poor outcomes, then these scores could be used to select subjects for an intervention study. Subjects who were not deviant on the target scales or who were deviant on additional scales could be excluded from the study. Moreover, the initial CBCL scores can be used as a baseline against which to measure change by readministering the CBCL again after the experimental conditions and comparing pre- versus post-intervention scores for subjects receiving the different conditions. Other measures, such as direct observations, teacher-reports, self-reports, interviews, and tests could also be used to evaluate the intervention effects. The *Integrative Guide* (Achenbach, 1991a) presents further details of experimental intervention designs using multiple pre- and post-intervention measures.

Operations Research

As discussed in Chapter 9, the CBCL can be applied to planning and accountability for services within a particular caseload or service system. Whether the aim is to make practical decisions about a particular system or to identify general phenomena and principles, a research perspective can aid in promoting rigorous data collection, analysis, and conclusions. Rigorous documentation of the functioning of systems is known as *operations research*, which has been defined as "the application of scientific methods, techniques, and tools to problems involving the operations of a system so as to provide those in control of the operations with optimum solutions to the problems" (Churchman, Ackoff, & Arnoff, 1957, pp. 8-9).

CBCL item scores, scale scores, and profile patterns can be used to document the kinds of problems seen in particular caseloads and the relations of these problems to other variables, such as sex, age, SES, referral source, etc. The CBCL scores and profile patterns can also be used to classify children as they enter, move through, and leave services. By comparing the type, duration, and outcome of services for children who differ in initial CBCL scores and patterns, we can determine whether services, costs, and outcomes vary according to the problems reported by the children's parents.

Another form of operations research involves cross-referencing between empirically based procedures, such as the CBCL, and administrative categories required in particular systems, such as the DSM and International Classification of Disease (ICD; World Health Organization, 1978) in mental health systems and Public Law 94-142 categories for special education. Operations research can be designed to determine how consistently the administrative classifications relate to the empirically based measures. For this type of research to be worthwhile, however, it is important to demonstrate that the administrative classifications are reliable enough to attain significant associations with the CBCL scores. If the administrative classifications are unreliable, this will preclude finding relations to measures such as the CBCL. When DSM diagnoses have been sufficiently reliable, research has shown significant associations between these diagnoses and CBCL scale scores (Edelbrock & Costello, 1988).

RESEARCH ON CHILD ABUSE

Professionals who work with children are expected to detect and report child abuse. When abuse has been detected, assessment of the child is often needed for forensic purposes and as a basis for recommendations and interventions. The CBCL can be useful at all stages of assessment related to abuse. CBCLs from both parents or parent surrogates, for example, may be especially discrepant from each other when one of the informants is involved in or has knowledge of the abuse. Research to date has shown that abused children obtain elevated scores on some CBCL scales and items (see Achenbach & Brown, 1991). In a study comparing sexually abused children with nonabused children referred for mental health services and with nonreferred children, LaRiviere (1990) found that significantly more problems were reported on the CBCL for abused than nonreferred children. However, the comparisons with nonabused referred children showed that few problems were specifically associated with abuse per se.

As with other risk factors, it is important for research on abuse to take account of multiple possibilities. Rather than merely searching for unique symptoms of abuse, for example, it is important to test whether abuse exacerbates pre-existing problems or has different effects on different children. For studies of children known to be abused, comparisons with clinical samples of nonabused children are needed to identify ways in which particular subgroups of abused children may differ from other referred children. The CBCL can also be used in conjunction with other assessment procedures to study the progress of abused children receiving different intervention conditions, such as individual therapy, family therapy, or foster placement.

RESEARCH ON MEDICAL CONDITIONS

Certain behavioral/emotional problems may accompany particular medical conditions. In some cases, a medical condition or a medical treatment may specifically cause problems such as inattention, motor tics, depression, lethargy, or overactivity. In other cases, a medical condition may cause stress that raises the risk of behavioral/emotional problems. To determine whether particular behavioral/emotional problems tend to accompany particular medical conditions, the CBCL can be used to compare children having each medical condition with children having other medical conditions and with physically healthy children.   The comparisons between children having different medical conditions are helpful for avoiding erroneous attributions of elevated rates of problems to a particular condition, when they may actually accompany multiple conditions.

The CBCL can be used as an outcome measure in interventions aimed at reducing behavioral/emotional problems associated with medical conditions.   Afflicted children can be assessed with the CBCL before and after receiving a particular intervention versus a control condition to determine whether the children have fewer behavioral/emotional problems after the intervention than after the control condition. To illustrate the range of possibilities for using the CBCL in research on medical conditions, Table 10-1 summarizes medically related topics from the *Bibliography of Published Studies Using the Child Behavior Checklist and Related Materials* (Achenbach & Brown, 1991).

CROSS-CULTURAL RESEARCH

To advance the study of child psychopathology, it is important to calibrate assessment procedures across different countries and cultures. If similar procedures produce similar results in different cultures, this supports the cross-cultural robustness of the findings and the possibilities for integrating results from the different cultures. If different results are obtained from different cultures, by contrast, the findings may provide clues as to causal factors related to the cultural differences.

Table 10-1
Examples of Medical Conditions for Which
Research has Employed the CBCL, YSR, or TRF[a]

Abdominal pain	Hearing impairment	Obesity
Adrenal hyperplasia	Hemophilia	Pain
Arthritis	Hermaphro-ditism	Phenyl-ketonuria
Asphyxia	Hypospadias	Precocious puberty
Asthma	Hypo-thyroidism	Reyes syndrome
Birth defects	Language disorders	Short stature
Brain damage	Lead Toxicity	Sickle cell anemia
Cancer	Leukemia	Sleep disturbance
Cerebral palsy	Limb deficiency	Spina bifida
Cleft palate	Low birthweight	Tourette's syndrome
Colitis	Meningitis	Trauma
Crohn's disease	Mental retardation	Tracheostomy
Cystic fibrosis	Migraine	Turner's syndrome
Diabetes	Neuro-pathology	Visual impairment
Ear disease		
Epilepsy		
Epstein-Barr virus		
Headaches		

[a]From Achenbach & Brown (1991) *Bibliography of Published Studies Using the Child Behavior Checklist and Related Materials: 1991 Edition.*

The CBCL has been used in numerous studies outside the United States, including epidemiological comparisons with prevalence rates of problems in Australia, Chile, Holland, Puerto Rico, and Thailand, as cited in the earlier section on epidemiological research. The factor structure of the CBCL obtained for American children has also been compared with the factor structures obtained for Israeli (Auerbach & Lerner, 1991) and Dutch children (Achenbach, Verhulst, Baron, & Althaus, 1987; Verhulst, Achenbach, Althaus, & Akkerhuis, 1988). At this writing, we know of translations of the CBCL or its related forms into the 33 languages listed in Table 10-2. The *Bibliography* (Achenbach & Brown, 1991) lists published studies of children in 15 cultures.

RESEARCH ON PARENTAL CHARACTERISTICS

Characteristics of parents may be related to data obtained with the CBCL in various ways. For example, mothers may have a particular condition that is found to be associated with their children's scores on the CBCL. Associations between a maternal condition, such as depression, and CBCL scores may occur for reasons such as the following:

1. The children are responding to the same environmental stressors as their mothers, such as abusive fathers.

2. The children share their mothers' genetic vulnerability to the same depressive disorders.

3. The children are temperamentally like their mothers in displaying proportionally more Internalizing than Externalizing problems.

4. The children are responding to the stress created by their mothers' depression.

Table 10-2
Translations of the CBCL, YSR, and/or TRF

Afrikaans	Korean
Amharic	Norwegian
(Ethiopia)	Papiamento-Aruba
Arabic	Papiamento-Curacao
Bengali	Portuguese
Cambodian	Portuguese Creole
Chinese	Russian
Dutch	Samy
Finnish	(Norwegian Laplanders)
French	Sotho
(Canadian & Parisian)	(South Africa)
German	Spanish
Greek	(Argentina, Chicano,
Haitian Creole	Chile, Puerto Rico,
Hebrew	Spain, & others)
Hindi	Swedish
Hungarian	Thai
Icelandic	Turkish
Italian	Vietnamese
Japanese	Zulu

5. The children model their own behavior on their mothers' depressive behavior.

6. The mothers' behavior toward their children evokes problem behaviors by the children.

7. The children's behavior problems contribute to their mothers' depression.

8. If mothers are the informants, their depressed condition affects their perceptions of their children's behavior.

Correlations between parents' problems and CBCL scores have sometimes been interpreted as reflecting parental "biases." However, parental bias is obviously only one of the many factors that may be at work. When data on the children of depressed mothers were obtained from sources beside the mothers, for example, the other sources also indicated more problems than among control children (Conrad & Hammen, 1989; Richters & Pellegrini, 1989). These findings indicated that the elevated CBCL problem scores were not caused by maternal "biases."

Although conditions that inhere in the parents may well affect parents' perceptions of their children, a full understanding of the relations between child and parent problems requires research on multiple child, parent, environmental, and biological factors that may all contribute and that may involve causation running from child to parent, as well as from parent to child. Rigorous research on associations between child and parent problems therefore requires data from multiple sources, including but not limited to the parents themselves.

For many parental conditions, research is needed to determine whether there is any association at all between parent and child problems. If so, do such associations involve similar or different problems in the parents and their children, and do these associations vary with factors such as the sex of the parent and the sex and age of the child? The *Bibliography of Published Studies* (Achenbach & Brown, 1991) lists some 100 published references to research on parental perceptions and parental characteristics such as psychopathology in relation to the instruments we have developed.

SUMMARY

The CBCL, its scales, and profile are products of research, and they can be used in many ways to expand our knowledge through research. Like practical applications, research should use multiple sources of data about children's functioning. However, parents' reports are usually the most available for child subjects, and the importance of parents' perceptions makes parents' reports a key focus for research. Because the CBCL is not confined to a single theoretical viewpoint, it can be applied to research involving many types of questions, theories, and other assessment procedures.

This chapter presented reasons for using raw scale scores rather than T scores for most statistical purposes and outlined ways of spanning multiple sex/age groups in research with the CBCL. It also addressed applications to research areas including epidemiology, diagnosis, taxonomy, etiology, outcomes, services, child abuse, medical conditions, cross-cultural comparisons, and parental characteristics. Because parental characteristics may be associated with CBCL scores for many different reasons, it is important to rigorously test the various possibilities rather than merely attributing associations to "biases" in parents' reports about their children.

Chapter 11
Assessment Materials
Related to the CBCL/4-18

Although parents' reports are important in the assessment of children's problems and competencies, we have repeatedly stressed the need for multiple sources of data. The relevant and feasible sources of data depend on the age of the children and the conditions under which they are evaluated.

For ages included in those spanned by the CBCL/4-18, the TRF is designed to be closely coordinated with the CBCL for assessing the school behavior of pupils at ages 5 to 18, while the YSR is designed for obtaining self-reports from youths at ages 11 to 18 in a format similar to that of the CBCL and TRF. These three instruments have 89 similar problem items in common, but each instrument also has additional items geared to the type of informant for whom the instrument is designed.

The *Integrative Guide for the 1991 CBCL/4-18, YSR, and TRF Profiles* (Achenbach, 1991a) presents the procedures by which the eight 1991 syndrome scales common to these three instruments were developed. The *Guide* also reports findings on relations among scores from the three instruments and strategies for coordinating their use in practical and research applications. In addition, the *Guide* describes a microcomputer program that is available for entering, scoring, and comparing data from all three instruments. Separate Manuals are available that present detailed information on the development and use of the TRF (Achenbach, 1991b) and YSR (Achenbach, 1991c).

Beside the TRF and YSR, the related instruments described in the following sections have been developed using the same general methodology as the CBCL/4-18.

THE CHILD BEHAVIOR CHECKLIST FOR AGES 2-3 (CBCL/2-3)

The CBCL/2-3 is a 2-page form designed to obtain parents' ratings of the behavioral/emotional problems of 2- and 3-year-old children. It has 99 specific problem items, plus an open-ended item for entering additional problems. Fifty-nine of the items have counterparts on the CBCL/4-18, while 40 items are specifically designed for the younger age group. The 0-1-2 rating scale for the problem items is the same as that for the CBCL/4-18. However, on the CBCL/2-3, parents are asked to base their ratings on a 2-month period, rather than the 6-month period employed on the CBCL/4-18. The 2-month rating period is used in recognition of the faster pace of developmental change characterizing the early years. Figure 11-1 shows the CBCL/2-3, with superscripts indicating items that have counterparts on the CBCL/4-18. Unlike the TRF and YSR, the counterpart problem items of the CBCL/2-3 do not all have the same numbers as those on the CBCL/4-18. The CBCL/2-3 does not have competence items.

Scales of the CBCL/2-3

The 1992 profile for scoring the CBCL/2-3 includes six syndrome scales derived from principal components/varimax analyses of 546 children, including referred children and high scoring nonreferred children. Internalizing, Externalizing, and total problem scores are also computed. Norms were based on 368 nonreferred children randomly selected from the general population. Because no significant sex differences were found in scale scores, the same norms are

CHILD BEHAVIOR CHECKLIST FOR AGES 2-3

	For office use only
	ID #

CHILD'S NAME

PARENTS' USUAL TYPE OF WORK, even if not working now (Please be specific—for example, auto mechanic, high school teacher, homemaker, laborer, lathe operator, shoe salesman, army sergeant.)

SEX	AGE	ETHNIC GROUP OR RACE
☐ Boy ☐ Girl		

FATHER'S TYPE OF WORK: _____

TODAY'S DATE	CHILD'S BIRTHDATE

MOTHER'S TYPE OF WORK: _____

Mo._____ Date_____ Yr._____   Mo._____ Date_____ Yr._____

THIS FORM FILLED OUT BY:

Please fill out this form to reflect *your* view of the child's behavior even if other people might not agree. Feel free to write additional comments beside each item and in the space provided on page 2.

☐ Mother (name): _____

☐ Father (name): _____

☐ Other—name & relationship to child: _____

Below is a list of items that describe children. For each item that describes the child **now or within the past 2 months**, please circle the **2** if the item is **very true** or **often true** of the child. Circle the **1** if the item is **somewhat** or **sometimes true** of the child. If the item is **not true** of the child, circle the **0**. Please answer all items as well as you can, even if some do not seem to apply to the child.

0 = Not True (as far as you know)   1 = Somewhat or Sometimes True   2 = Very True or Often True

0 1 2	^{a}1. Aches or pains (without medical cause)		0 1 2	33. Feelings are easily hurt		
0 1 2	^{a}2. Acts too young for age		0 1 2	^{a}34. Gets hurt a lot, accident-prone		
0 1 2	3. Afraid to try new things		0 1 2	^{a}35. Gets in many fights		
0 1 2	4. Avoids looking others in the eye		0 1 2	36. Gets into everything		
0 1 2	^{a}5. Can't concentrate, can't pay attention for long		0 1 2	37. Gets too upset when separated from parents		
0 1 2	^{a}6. Can't sit still or restless		0 1 2	^{a}38. Has trouble getting to sleep		
0 1 2	7. Can't stand having things out of place		0 1 2	^{a}39. Headaches (without medical cause)		
0 1 2	8. Can't stand waiting; wants everything now		0 1 2	40. Hits others		
0 1 2	9. Chews on things that aren't edible		0 1 2	41. Holds his/her breath		
0 1 2	^{a}10. Clings to adults or too dependent		0 1 2	42. Hurts animals or people without meaning to		
0 1 2	^{a}11. Constantly seeks help		0 1 2	43. Looks unhappy without good reason		
0 1 2	^{a}12. Constipated, doesn't move bowels		0 1 2	44. Angry moods		
0 1 2	^{a}13. Cries a lot		0 1 2	^{a}45. Nausea, feels sick (without medical cause)		
0 1 2	^{a}14. Cruel to animals		0 1 2	^{a}46. Nervous movements or twitching		
0 1 2	15. Defiant			(describe): _____		
0 1 2	^{a}16. Demands must be met immediately					
0 1 2	^{a}17. Destroys his/her own things		0 1 2	^{a}47. Nervous, highstrung, or tense		
0 1 2	^{a}18. Destroys things belonging to his/her family or other children		0 1 2	^{a}48. Nightmares		
			0 1 2	^{a}49. Overeating		
0 1 2	^{a}19. Diarrhea or loose bowels when not sick		0 1 2	^{a}50. Overtired		
0 1 2	^{a}20. Disobedient		0 1 2	^{a}51. Overweight		
0 1 2	21. Disturbed by any change in routine		0 1 2	52. Painful bowel movements		
0 1 2	22. Doesn't want to sleep alone		0 1 2	^{a}53. Physically attacks people		
0 1 2	23. Doesn't answer when people talk to him/her		0 1 2	^{a}54. Picks nose, skin, or other parts of body		
0 1 2	^{a}24. Doesn't eat well (describe): _____			(describe): _____		
0 1 2	^{a}25. Doesn't get along with other children		0 1 2	^{a}55. Plays with own sex parts too much		
0 1 2	26. Doesn't know how to have fun, acts like a little adult		0 1 2	^{a}56. Poorly coordinated or clumsy		
0 1 2	^{a}27. Doesn't seem to feel guilty after misbehaving		0 1 2	^{a}57. Problems with eyes without medical cause (describe): _____		
0 1 2	28. Doesn't want to go out of home					
0 1 2	29. Easily frustrated		0 1 2	58. Punishment doesn't change his/her behavior		
0 1 2	^{a}30. Easily jealous		0 1 2	59. Quickly shifts from one activity to another		
0 1 2	^{a}31. Eats or drinks things that are not food—**don't** include sweets (describe): _____		0 1 2	^{a}60. Rashes or other skin problems (without medical cause)		
0 1 2	^{a}32. Fears certain animals, situations, or places (describe): _____		0 1 2	61. Refuses to eat		
			0 1 2	62. Refuses to play active games		
			0 1 2	63. Repeatedly rocks head or body		
			0 1 2	64. Resists going to bed at night		

Please see other side

Figure 11-1. Page 1 of the Child Behavior Checklist for Ages 2-3. Superscript *a* indicates items that have counterparts on the CBCL/4-18.

0 = Not True (as far as you know)   1 = Somewhat or Sometimes True   2 = Very True or Often True

0	1	2	65. Resists toilet training (describe): _____ _____	0	1	2	a 82. Sudden changes in mood or feelings
				0	1	2	a 83. Sulks a lot
0	1	2	a 66. Screams a lot	0	1	2	a 84. Talks or cries out in sleep
0	1	2	67. Seems unresponsive to affection	0	1	2	a 85. Temper tantrums or hot temper
0	1	2	a 68. Self-conscious or easily embarrassed	0	1	2	a 86. Too concerned with neatness or cleanliness
0	1	2	69. Selfish or won't share	0	1	2	a 87. Too fearful or anxious
0	1	2	70. Shows little affection toward people	0	1	2	88. Uncooperative
0	1	2	71. Shows little interest in things around him/her	0	1	2	a 89. Underactive, slow moving, or lacks energy
0	1	2	72. Shows too little fear of getting hurt	0	1	2	a 90. Unhappy, sad, or depressed
0	1	2	a 73. Shy or timid	0	1	2	a 91. Unusually loud
0	1	2	a 74. Sleeps less than most children during day and/or night (describe): _____ _____	0	1	2	92. Upset by new people or situations (describe): _____ _____
0	1	2	a 75. Smears or plays with bowel movements	0	1	2	a 93. Vomiting, throwing up (without medical cause)
0	1	2	a 76. Speech problem (describe): _____	0	1	2	94. Wakes up often at night
				0	1	2	95. Wanders away from home
0	1	2	a 77. Stares into space or seems preoccupied	0	1	2	96. Wants a lot of attention
0	1	2	a 78. Stomachaches or cramps (without medical cause)	0	1	2	a 97. Whining
				0	1	2	a 98. Withdrawn, doesn't get involved with others
0	1	2	a 79. Stores up things he/she doesn't need (describe): _____ _____	0	1	2	a 99. Worrying
							100. Please write in any problems your child has that were not listed above.
0	1	2	a 80. Strange behavior (describe): _____ _____	0	1	2	_____
				0	1	2	_____
0	1	2	a 81. Stubborn, sullen, or irritable	0	1	2	_____

PLEASE BE SURE YOU HAVE ANSWERED ALL ITEMS.   UNDERLINE ANY YOU ARE CONCERNED ABOUT.

Does your child have any illness, physical disability, or mental handicap?   ☐ No   ☐ Yes — Please describe

---

What concerns you most about your child?

Please describe the best things about your child:

PAGE 2

Figure 11-1 (cont.). Page 2 of the Child Behavior Checklist for Ages 2-3. Superscript *a* indicates items that have counterparts on the CBCL/4-18.

used for 2- and 3-year-olds of both sexes. The *Manual for the CBCL/2-3* provides details of reliability, validity, characteristics of the standardization sample, and other information on the development of the CBCL/2-3, including predictive correlations with CBCL/4-18 scores through age 9. Hand-scored profiles and computer-scoring programs are available. Table 11-1 presents means and standard deviations for demographically matched referred and nonreferred samples described by Achenbach (1992).

Table 11-1
Means and Standard Deviations for CBCL/2-3 Scales

| | T Scores | | | | Raw Scores | | | |
| | Referred | | Nonreferred | | Referred | | Nonreferred | |
Scales	Mean	SD	Mean	SD	Mean	SD	Mean	SD
Anxious/Depressed	60.5	9.8	53.7	5.9	7.7	4.1	4.5	3.0
Withdrawn	63.4	9.9	54.0	5.9	7.9	4.7	3.5	2.8
Sleep Problems	62.7	13.1	54.1	6.2	6.2	3.8	3.2	2.8
Somatic Problems	58.1	7.7	53.9	5.9	4.2	3.1	2.4	2.4
Aggressive Behavior	65.0	12.8	54.2	6.6	16.2	7.2	8.6	5.7
Destructive Behavior	61.0	9.7	54.0	6.2	7.6	4.4	4.1	3.3
Internalizing	62.0	11.4	49.7	9.7	15.6	7.8	8.0	5.2
Externalizing	62.6	12.0	50.0	10.0	23.8	10.6	12.8	8.3
Total Problems	63.8	11.5	50.0	10.3	64.0	26.6	33.8	19.9

Note. N = 321 referred and 321 nonreferred (Achenbach, 1992).

THE DIRECT OBSERVATION FORM (DOF)

The DOF is designed for recording problems and on-task behavior observed in group settings such as school classes and recess. There are 96 specific problem items, plus an open-ended item for entering additional problems. The DOF has 72 problem items corresponding to items on the CBCL/4-18 and 85 corresponding to items on the TRF.

In using the DOF, the observer writes a narrative description of the child's behavior and interactions over a 10-minute interval. The narrative is written in space provided on the DOF while the observer keeps the items to be rated in view. The ratings are made at the end of the 10-minute period. Each item is rated on a 0-1-2-3 scale. The inclusion of one more point than on the CBCL rating scale allows a rating for "a very slight or ambiguous occurrence" of a behavior (scored 1), as well as "a definite occurrence with mild to moderate intensity and less than three minutes duration" (scored 2), and "a definite occurrence with severe intensity or greater than three minutes duration" (scored 3). At the end of each 1-minute interval, the child is also scored as being on task or not on task. The on-task scores are summed at the end of the 10-minute observation session to provide an on-task score ranging from 0 to 10.

To obtain a stable index of problems and on-task behavior, it is recommended that 10-minute samples of behavior be obtained on three to six occasions and that the scores be averaged over those occasions. Because the significance of a child's behavior depends partly on its deviation from the behavior of other children of the same sex under the same conditions, it is recommended that the DOF be completed for one "control" child observed just before the target child and a second "control" child observed just after the target child. Mean scores for the control children can then be compared with mean scores for the target child to identify areas in which the target child's behavior differs from that of children observed under similar conditions.

Scales of the DOF

Six syndrome scales have been derived via principal components/varimax analyses of 212 clinically referred 5- to 14-year-old children. The six syndrome scales, Internalizing, Externalizing, and total problem scores have been normed on 287 children who were observed as controls for referred children in regular classrooms of 45 schools in 23 public and parochial school systems located in Vermont, Nebraska, and Oregon. The means and standard deviations for referred and control samples are shown in Table 11-2. Reliability and validity data have been reported by Achenbach and Edelbrock (1983), McConaughy, Achenbach, and Gent (1988), and Reed and Edelbrock (1983).

Table 11-2
Summary of Cutpoints and Mean Scores for DOF Scales

Scale	Cutpoints[a]		Mean Scores[b]	
	Raw Score	%ile	Clinical	Control
On-Task	No Clinical Cutpoints		6.6 (2.1)	8.9 (1.0)
Total Problems	6.0	93	9.1 (4.1)	3.5 (1.9)
Internalizing	2.0	94	2.4 (1.9)	.6 (.8)
Externalizing	1.0	94	1.6 (1.8)	.2 (.6)
Withdrawn–Inattentive	2.0	98	1.7 (1.7)	.5 (.8)
Nervous-Obsessive	1.0	98	.8 (.8)	.1 (.3)
Depressed	1.0	98	.6 (1.1)	.1 (.4)
Hyperactive	5.0	98	5.0 (2.8)	2.5 (1.6)
Attention Demanding	1.5	98	.7 (1.1)	.1 (.4)
Aggressive	2.0	98	1.2 (1.3)	.2 (.5)

[a]Scores *above* the cutpoints are in the clinical range
[b]Standard deviations are in parentheses. The clinical group comprised 137 elementary school children referred for outpatient mental health or special school services who were observed in 43 schools of 21 Vermont public and parochial school systems. The control group consisted of 274 children observed as controls in the same classrooms as the referred children. The means and standard deviations were obtained by averaging the mean of all boys' scores with the mean of all girls' scores, thus weighting both sexes equally.

Computer-scoring programs are available that average the scores of the target child over multiple occasions and separately average the scores of one or two control children over the same multiple occasions. The programs then print a profile comparing the averaged scores for the target and control children. Similar comparisons can also be made via hand-scored forms for the Internalizing, Externalizing, on-task, and total problem scores, but not for the syndrome scales, which are too laborious to compute and average by hand.

THE SEMISTRUCTURED CLINICAL INTERVIEW FOR CHILDREN (SCIC)

The SCIC has been developed to obtain observational and self-report data in the course of clinical interviews with children at ages 6 to 11. It includes a protocol that provides a detailed outline of questions about important life areas, such as activities, school, friends, family relations, fantasies, self-perceptions, and feelings. It also includes a kinetic family drawing, brief achievement tests, screen for fine and gross motor abnormalities, and probe questions about problems attributed to the child by others, such as parents and teachers.

While administering the SCIC, the interviewer makes brief notes on the protocol regarding observations of the child's behavior and what the child says. Immediately after the interview, the interviewer scores the 117 observational items and 107 self-report items of the SCIC scoring form. Space is also provided for scoring additional problems not specifically listed. Each item is scored on a 4-step scale like that of the DOF.

Principal components analyses of SCIC scores have yielded four syndrome scales based on observational items and four based on self-report items that are scored on a profile using either a computer-scoring program or hand-scoring forms. The *Guide for the Semistructured Clinical Interview for Children* (McConaughy & Achenbach, 1990) provides details of the background, development, scoring, reliability, and validity of the SCIC. Supplementary questions and scoring items are available for use with adolescents through age 18.

FORMS FOR YOUNG ADULTS

To extend our empirically based assessment approach above age 18, we have developed the Young Adult Behavior Checklist (YABCL; Achenbach, 1990b), which is designed to obtain parents' reports of the competencies and problems of their offspring from the age of 19 to 27. The overall format is similar to that of the CBCL, and many of the items have counterparts on the CBCL/4-18. To obtain self-reports from young adults, we have developed the Young Adult Self-Report (YASR; Achenbach, 1990c), which has a format similar to that of the YSR, with many counterpart items. As research on these instruments proceeds, scoring profiles as well as reliability and validity data will be made available.

PARENT'S FOLLOW-UP
REPORT FORM (PFRF)

To facilitate and standardize the assessment of outcomes of clinical services, we have developed the PFRF (Achenbach, 1990a). The PFRF is designed to obtain parents' reports of the functioning of children, youth, and young adults who previously received mental health or similar services. The PFRF requests parents to compare specific aspects of their child's current functioning with the child's functioning at the initiation of services. It also requests information on problems occurring since the initial services, subsequent services received, and contacts with the police and other agencies. In addition, it requests parents to indicate any needs for further help. As research progresses, data will be made available on reliability, validity, and relations to other variables.

SUMMARY

This chapter described several assessment instruments related to the CBCL/4-18. The TRF for obtaining teacher's reports of the school behavior of 5- to 18-year-old pupils and the YSR for obtaining self-reports from 11- to 18-year-old youths are scored for the same eight syndromes as the CBCL/4-18. The *Integrative Guide for the 1991 CBCL/4-18, YSR, and TRF Profiles* (Achenbach, 1991a) describes the coordinated development of the eight syndrome scales, plus procedures for systematically comparing data obtained from parent-, self-, and teacher-reports on the same child.

The CBCL/2-3 includes 59 problems items having counterparts on the CBCL/4-18, plus 40 items designed specifically for ages 2 and 3. It is scored on six syndrome scales, Internalizing, Externalizing, and total problem scores that significantly predict CBCL scale scores obtained at later ages.

The DOF is designed to score direct observations in terms of six syndromes, Internalizing, Externalizing, total problems, and on-task behavior. Scoring profiles provide for averaging scores over multiple occasions and for comparing the scores of the target child with the mean of scores for control children observed under the same conditions. Norms are also provided from randomly selected children observed in many different classrooms.

The SCIC is designed to score observations and self-reports obtained during a standardized semistructured clinical interview. The SCIC profile has four syndrome scales based on observational items, four based on self-report items, Internalizing, Externalizing, and total problem scores.

The YABCL and YASR have been developed to obtain parent- and self-reports for young adults in formats similar to those of the CBCL/4-18 and YSR. The PFRF has been developed to assess the functioning of children, youths, and young adults following mental health and similar services.

Chapter 12
Answers to Commonly
Asked Questions

This chapter answers questions that may arise about the CBCL and the profile on which it is scored. The questions are grouped according to whether they refer mainly to the CBCL/4-18 itself, to scoring the CBCL/4-18, or to the profile on which the scores are displayed. If you have a question that is not found under one heading, look under the other headings. The Table of Contents and Index may also help you find answers to questions not listed here. For questions about relations between the CBCL/4-18 and the 1991 YSR and TRF, consult the *Integrative Guide for the 1991 CBCL/4-18, YSR, and TRF Profiles* (Achenbach, 1991a).

QUESTIONS ABOUT THE CBCL/4-18

1. How does the 1991 CBCL/4-18 differ from previous editions of the CBCL?

Answer: The title has been changed from CBCL/4-16 to CBCL/4-18 in order to reflect the availability of norms through age 18. Small changes in wording have been made to avoid the words "child" and "children" in items where such wording would be anomalous for subjects as old as 18 and to add examples to competence items that are appropriate for 17- and 18-year-olds. Other small changes have been made to clarify the wording of items, such as the following: *Competence Item V.2 (page 2) — the word any* has been inserted before the word *friends* to indicate that not only the "close friends" indicated in Item V.1 are to be included in the frequency of contacts with friends. *Problem Item 42* (page 3) — the wording has been changed to *Would rather be alone than with others*, from *Likes to be alone*. *Problem Item 56a* (page 3) — *(not headaches)* has been added to clarify that headaches should not be included with "aches or pains." These changes do not affect scoring. The 1991 CBCL/4-18 can be scored on the pre-1991 profile. Conversely, the pre-1991 CBCL/4-16 can be scored on the 1991 profile.

2. Why is the CBCL/4-18 said to have 118 problem items when the item numbers only go to 113?

Answer: Item 56 includes seven specific physical complaints designated as *a* through *g*. Combined with the remaining 111 specifically stated problems, this sums to 118 items. In addition, item 56h provides space for parents to enter any physical problems not otherwise listed, and item 113 provides three spaces for parents to add additional problems of any sort. Because Item *2. Allergy* and Item *4. Asthma* were not found to discriminate significantly between clinically referred and nonreferred children on either the CBCL or YSR, they are no longer counted in the total problem score. Total problem scores are computed as the sum of 1s and 2s for the other 116 specific problem items + item 56h + the highest score the respondent gives to any additional items written in for number 113. If a 2 is scored for all 116 items, 56h, and 113, the total score would be 236.

3. Can the CBCL be filled out by people other than parents?

Answer: The CBCL is designed to be filled out by people who know the child well and interact with the child as parents do. Adoptive parents, foster parents, and other adults who live with a child are appropriate respondents. For children in residential care and other institutional settings, child care workers who know the children well would be appropriate respondents for the problem portion of the CBCL. However, they may not know enough of the child's history to complete the competence portion. The TRF, YSR, DOF, and SCIC provide means for obtaining data from other sources in addition to or instead of parents.

4. What if a parent can't read well enough to complete the CBCL?

Answer: The CBCL requires only fifth grade reading skills. It can also be administered orally by an interviewer who writes down the parent's answers. If there is some doubt about a parent's reading skill, embarrassment can be avoided by handing the CBCL to the parent and having the interviewer read each item aloud and record the parent's answers on another copy of the CBCL. Parents who can read will usually start answering spontaneously, without waiting for the questions to be read.

5. What if a parent can't read English but can read a different language?

Answer: At this writing, we know of translations of our forms into the 33 languages listed in Table 10-2. For the current status of translations into a particular language, write to Dr. Achenbach.

6. Don't certain items involve subjective judgments, such as *35. Feels worthless or inferior* and *52. Feels too guilty?*

Answer: Subjectivity is involved in all ratings of any person by another person. Some items of the CBCL are less subjective than others, but we recognize that the scores obtained on all items reflect parents' judgments about what to report. However, parents are usually in a better position than most other people to judge and report their children's expressions of feelings such as inferiority and guilt.

7. Can social desirability, lying, and other informant characteristics such as depression cause biases in CBCL scores?

Answer: Many informant characteristics may be associated with scores on all kinds of questionnaires, including the CBCL. Studies have shown, for example, that CBCL problem scores are correlated with maternal depression. Such correlations do not necessarily indicate a "bias" in parents' reports, however, because other sources of data have also indicated that the children of depressed mothers have more problems than children of nondepressed mothers (Conrad & Hammen, 1989; Richters & Pellegrini, 1989). Because any reports by any informants may be affected by characteristics of the informants, as well as by their own particular knowledge of the child's behavior, no single informant's reports can provide a complete picture. It is the user's task to construct a comprehensive picture of the child from multiple sources and types of data. Questions 7 and 12 in the section on the profile provide guidelines for evaluating scores that are so low or high as to suggest gross distortions or errors. Chapter 5 of this Manual provides data on reliability and inter-parent agreement, while the integrative computer program displays comparisons and correlations between informants' reports for a particular child.

8. Can the CBCL/4-18 be used for ages below 4 and above 18?

Answer: For subjects who are a few months younger than 4 or older than 18, there is not likely to be much error in using the CBCL/4-18 and its norms. The greater the deviation in age from our norms, the less appropriate they will be. This is why we have developed the CBCL/2-3

(Achenbach et al., 1987) for children younger than 4 and the YABCL (Achenbach, 1990b) for young adults older than 18. However, if individuals are to be reassessed over periods that are mainly within the 4-18-year range but include one or two assessments outside this range, it may be preferable to use the CBCL/4-18 at all assessment points to maintain complete continuity of item and scale scores.

9. Page 3 of the CBCL/4-18 instructs the respondent to base ratings on the previous 6 months. What if it is to be readministered over intervals of less than 6 months?

Answer: The 6-month instruction can be changed to suit the interval being used. If the interval is reduced much below 6 months, this may reduce scores on some problem items and scales slightly. Low frequency behaviors such as running away and firesetting, for example, may also be missed if the rating interval is too short. However, if reassessments are planned at intervals of less than 6 months, respondents should use the same shortened interval for the initial ratings as well as each follow-up rating. For example, if follow-up ratings are to be done after a 3-month interval, the initial rating should also be based on a 3-month period, so that initial scores will not be higher than the follow-up scores merely because they encompass a longer rating period. Because of the time required for behavioral changes to stabilize and become clearly recognized by parents, rating periods of less than 2 months are probably not worth using.

10. Is there a short form of the CBCL/4-18 that takes less time to fill out?

Answer: There is no short form as such. However, the competence portion (pages 1 and 2) or problem portion (pages 3 and 4) can be administered alone. Since each of these is brief and each scale's standard scores require that all the constituent items of the scale are considered by the parent, it would not make sense to abbreviate the CBCL any further. A few items can be deleted for certain specific purposes, however. For example, Item *61. Poor school work* can be deleted for children not in school. Item *78. Smears or plays with bowel movements* is of very low frequency and can be deleted for most groups without affecting scale scores much.

11. Is there a machine-readable form of the CBCL?

Answer: We have developed a machine-readable CBCL that can be processed by fax boards and scanners. To employ the machine-readable CBCL, you need either a reflective-read scanner, such as those produced by NCS, Scantron, and Scanning Dynamics, or Teleform software for use with image scanners and fax boards. You also need an IBM-compatible computer with software that is appropriate for your scanner, plus our Scanning Software Package to convert data from the machine-readable CBCL to input for the CBCL or Cross-Informant scoring program. For details, send inquiries to the fax number or address shown on page ii of this Manual.

12. If parents fill out the CBCL, won't this cause them to focus on the child's problems instead of the family system?

Answer: When parents bring their child for help, they expect to provide information about the child. The CBCL is not likely to instigate an exclusive focus on the child, because data on the family will typically be obtained as well. The practitioner's own approach and the specific referral problems usually outweigh the CBCL in determining the degree of focus on the child versus the family system.

13. Can other assessment procedures—such as project-ives, personality inventories, interviews, behavioral observations, and family assessment—be used with the CBCL?

Answer: The CBCL can be used in conjunction with any other assessment procedures. Our multiaxial assessment model (Table 1-1) emphasizes the use of standardized, normed, empirically based procedures to obtain data from multiple sources. However, it does not preclude use of unstandardized procedures or assessment of areas not explicitly included in the model, such as family functioning.

SCORING THE CBCL/4-18

Appendix A contains detailed scoring instructions, including criteria for items the respondent is asked to describe.

1. What if the respondent scores two different items when his/her comments indicate that they refer to exactly the same problem?

Answer: Score only the item that most specifically describes the behavior. For example, if the respondent circled a 2 for Item *1. Acts too young for age* and also circled a 2 for Item *84. Strange behavior*, describing the behavior as "acts very babyish," only Item 1 should be counted.

2. What if the respondent circles two scores for a particular item or otherwise indicates that the item is true of the child but does not clearly indicate a score of 1 or 2?

Answer: Score the item 1.

3. On *Item 113. Please write in any problems your child has that were not listed above*, what if a respondent

describes behavior that is specified elsewhere on the problem list?

Answer: Score the item *only* where it is most precisely specified on the problem list, whether or not the respondent has scored it there as well as in Item *113*. For example, if the respondent wrote "very jealous of younger sister," and scored it 2 for Item *113*, only Item *27*. *Easily jealous* should be scored 2, rather than Item *113*, whether or not the respondent had also scored Item *27*.

4. How is Item 113 figured in the total score?

Answer: If the respondent has entered on Item *113* a problem that is not clearly covered by another item, obtain the total problem score by adding the 1 or 2 scored by the respondent to the sum of 1s and 2s for all other items. If the respondent has entered more than one additional item, count only the one that has received the highest score. Thus, if a respondent has scored one additional item 1 and another item 2, add 2 to the total score. (Adding a maximum of 2 points for Item *113* and 2 for *56h* is intended to limit the amount of variance contributed by items that are not stated for other parents to rate.)

5. Should CBCLs that have many unanswered items be scored?

Answer: The scoring instructions (Appendix A) give rules for dealing with unanswered items. In brief, if one item is omitted from the Activities or Social scale, the mean of the other items of that scale is substituted for the missing item. If more than one item is missing from either of these scales or any item is missing from the School scale, the respective scale is not scored. On the problem portion, if more than 8 items are left blank (excluding Items *2, 4, 56h,* and *113*), do not compute problem scale scores or total scores, unless it is clear that the respondent intends the blanks to be zeroes.

6. How are the total competence and problem scores used?

Answer: These scores provide global indices of the child's competencies and problems, as seen by the respondent. We have found that the competence T scores of 40 and the problem T scores of 60 provide good cutpoints for discriminating between clinically referred and nonreferred children (see Chapter 6 for details of the cutpoints). The total problem score can also be used as a basis for comparing problems in different groups and for assessing change as a function of time or intervention. The total competence score can be used in similar ways, but is not as susceptible to change, because it is determined partly by historical data, such as repetition of grades in school.

THE 1991 CBCL/4-18 PROFILE

1. How does the 1991 profile differ from the previous edition?

Answer: Chapters 2 and 3 describe the 1991 profile scales in detail. Briefly, the main innovations include (*a*) scoring children in terms of the same eight syndromes and the same Internalizing and Externalizing groupings of syndromes for all sex/age groups on the CBCL/4-18 and also on the YSR and TRF; (*b*) use of a new national sample to norm the profiles of all three instruments; (*c*) inclusion of ages 17-18 in the norms; (*d*) changes in normative age ranges to 4-11 and 12-18 years; (*e*) extension of syndrome T scores down to 50; (*f*) demarcation of a borderline clinical range; and (*g*) easier computation of Internalizing and Externalizing scores on the hand-scored profile.

2. Can hand-scoring be made quicker and easier?

Answer: We offer scoring templates that fit over the CBCL to indicate the scales on which the problem items are scored. The 1991 CBCL/4-18 profile is easier than the previous edition to score by hand, because the same templates are used for all four sex/age groups. Furthermore, to compute Internalizing and Externalizing scores, the individual items no longer need to be entered and summed. Instead, the syndrome scores are merely summed and the one redundant item is subtracted. The time taken to score profiles usually decreases with experience. However, we recommend computer-scoring whenever possible, as this is quicker, more accurate, and stores scores for subsequent analysis, as well as printing hard-copy profiles whenever desired.

3. Why are some problem items included on more than one syndrome scale?

Answer: As explained in Chapter 3, problem items are included on each syndrome for which they met criteria for the cross-informant syndrome constructs. In addition, a few items that met criteria for the CBCL core syndromes are included in the CBCL versions of the syndrome scales. Only five items are included in more than one 1991 CBCL syndrome scale. Of these, Item *103. Unhappy, sad, or depressed*, is included on two Internalizing scales, but it is counted only once toward the Internalizing score. No item of the Externalizing scales is included on more than one scale.

4. Why are there no norms for the "Other Problems" listed on the profile?

Answer: The "Other Problems" on the profile do *not* constitute a scale. They are merely the items that were either reported too seldom to be included in the derivation of syndromes or did not qualify for the syndrome scales. There are thus no associations among them to warrant treating them as a scale. However, each of these problems may be important in its own right, and they are all included in the total problem score.

5. Should raw scores or T scores be used to report results?

Answer: Chapter 10 discusses the different uses of raw scores and T scores in detail.

6. Does a high score on the Delinquent Behavior scale mean that a child is a juvenile delinquent?

Answer: The names of the scales are mainly intended to summarize the content of the scales. The term "Delinquent Behavior" literally refers to "conduct that is out of accord with accepted behavior or law" and "offending by neglect or violation of duty or law" (Mish, 1988, p. 336). Although some items of the Delinquent Behavior syndrome, such as stealing, are illegal, a high score on the scale for this syndrome does not necessarily mean that a child has broken laws or will be adjudicated as a delinquent. Instead, it means that the child is reported to engage in more behaviors of the empirically derived Delinquent Behavior syndrome than are reported for normative samples of peers. Similarly, the labels for other syndromes provide summary descriptions for the kinds of problems included in the syndromes, rather than being directly equivalent to any administrative or diagnostic category.

7. Should extremely low scores on problem scales be considered deviant?

Answer: Extremely low scores merely reflect the absence of reported problems. As explained in Chapter 3, the 1991 profile compresses the low end of the problem scales, so that a T score of 50 is the minimum obtainable on any scale. However, nearly all children have at least some problems. The mean problem scores for nonreferred children in our normative samples range from about 22 to 24. In our nonreferred normative samples, total problem scores of 0 and 1 were obtained by only 2% of the children. Such low scores suggest that the respondent has not understood the CBCL, is poorly informed about the child, or is not being candid. Total problem scores of 2 and 3 are also low enough to be questionable.

8. Should there be separate norms for mothers' and fathers' ratings or for different ethnic groups?

Answer: As detailed in Chapter 5, the mean scale scores obtained from mothers' and fathers' ratings did not differ much, on the average. As detailed in Chapter 6, ratings by parents of different ethnic groups matched for socioeconomic status also showed minimal differences. Socioeconomic differences were somewhat larger, but were too small compared to the differences between referred and non-referred children to warrant separate norms.

9. Why are there big gaps between successive raw scores on some scales of the profile?

Answer: Most gaps directly reflect the distributions of scores in the normative samples, where skewed distributions or clusters of individuals at a particular raw score caused a large change in percentiles from one score to the next. Gaps between scores in the clinical range occur in scales where there were only a few possible scores available for assignment to T scores in equal intervals.

10. If a child is in the 4-11 age range at the initial rating and is 12-18 at a subsequent rating, how can the initial and subsequent scores be compared?

Answer: Because the competence and problem scales are the same on the 4-11 and 12-18 profiles, it is easy to compare ratings obtained in the earlier and later age ranges. The T scores show how the child compares with normative samples of peers within either the 4-11 or 12-18 age range. If a CBCL is completed shortly before a child's 12th birthday and a second one is completed shortly after the 12th birthday, it may be desirable to score both of them using the norms for the same age range to provide complete comparability in the T scores. For example, as part of a clinical assessment, a mother may complete the CBCL a few days before her child's 12th birthday, while the father completes the CBCL a few days after the child's 12th birthday. Because children's behavior seldom changes markedly just because they turn 12, it would facilitate comparisons between the mother's and father's CBCLs to score them both on the 12-18 norms. If our computer-scoring program is used, both CBCLs can be scored on the 12-18 norms simply by entering 12 as the age for each of the CBCLs. If hand-scoring profiles are used, the column of scores for age 12-18 can be used for determining the T scores for both CBCLs.

11. How are clinical interpretations of the profile made?

Answer: The profile is intended as a standardized *description* of behavior, as seen by the person filling out the CBCL and compared to reports by parents of children of the same age and sex as the subject. As such, it is to be integrated with everything else that is known about the child, instead of being viewed as a key to hidden entities, as projective tests sometimes are. Rather than being "interpreted," the information from the profile should be *integrated* with other data to provide a picture of the child consisting partly of the child's standing on dimensions assessable for children in general, such as those of the TRF, YSR, and cognitive measures, and partly of unique characteristics of the child and family. Specific guidelines and clinical illustrations are provided in Chapter 9.

12. Is there a "lie" scale for the profile?

Answer: Deliberate lying is only one factor that can lead to excessively low or high scores, depending on whether the informant denies or exaggerates problems. Social desirability sets, over-scrupulousness, and misunderstandings can also affect ratings. Because of the variety of possible influences and our desire to restrict the CBCL to items that are meaningful in themselves, we did not add items designed to detect all such influences. Instead, we stress that profile scores should never be used to make clinical judgments in isolation from other information about the child and the informant; the scores should always be compared with other data in order to identify major distortions and to determine the possible reason for distortions. Extremely low or high total scores for problems or competence should always be followed up to determine whether they accurately reflect the informant's view of the child, and, if so, whether this view differs markedly from other people's view of the child.

In our answer to Question 7 above, we listed problem scores that are so low as to invite further inquiry. Based on the distributions of problem scores in the clinical samples from which our scales were derived, the following raw scores are so *high* as to raise questions about exaggeration or misunderstanding: Boys aged 4-11 >156; 12-18 >140; girls aged 4-11 >140; 12-18 >135.

Because the competence scores have a much smaller range, they do not lend themselves to consideration of response biases as well as the total problem scores do. However, a total competence score equivalent to a T score < 13 suggests an unusually negative picture of the child, whereas a competence score equivalent to a T score > 78 suggests an unusually favorable picture.

REFERENCES

Abramowitz, M., & Stegun, I.A. (1968). *Handbook of mathematical functions*. Washington, D.C.: National Bureau of Standards.

Achenbach, T.M. (1966). The classification of children's psychiatric symptoms: A factor-analytic study. *Psychological Monographs, 80* (No. 615).

Achenbach, T.M. (1978). The Child Behavior Profile: I. Boys aged 6-11. *Journal of Consulting and Clinical Psychology, 46*, 478-488.

Achenbach, T.M. (1990a). *Parent's Follow-up Report Form*. Burlington, VT: University of Vermont Department of Psychiatry.

Achenbach, T.M. (1990b). *Young Adult Behavior Checklist*. Burlington, VT: University of Vermont Department of Psychiatry.

Achenbach, T.M. (1990c). *Young Adult Self-Report*. Burlington, VT: University of Vermont Department of Psychiatry.

Achenbach, T.M. (1991a). *Integrative guide for the 1991 CBCL/4-18, YSR, and TRF profiles*. Burlington, VT: University of Vermont Department of Psychiatry.

Achenbach, T.M. (1991b). *Manual for the Teacher's Report Form and 1991 Profile*. Burlington, VT: University of Vermont Department of Psychiatry.

Achenbach, T.M. (1991c). *Manual for the Youth Self-Report and 1991 Profile*. Burlington, VT: University of Vermont Department of Psychiatry.

Achenbach, T.M. (1992). *Manual for the Child Behavior Checklist/2-3 and 1992 Profile*. Burlington, VT: University of Vermont Department of Psychiatry.

Achenbach, T.M., Bird, H.R., Canino, G.J., Phares, V., Gould, M., & Rubio-Stipec, M. (1990). Epidemiological comparisons of Puerto Rican and U.S. mainland children: Parent, teacher, and self reports. *Journal of the American Academy of Child and Adolescent Psychiatry, 29*, 84-93.

Achenbach, T.M., & Brown, J.S. (1991). *Bibliography of published studies using the Child Behavior Checklist and related materials: 1991 edition*. Burlington, VT: University of Vermont Department of Psychiatry.

Achenbach, T.M., Conners, C.K., Quay, H.C., Verhulst, F.C., & Howell, C.T. (1989). Replication of empirically derived syndromes as a basis for taxonomy of child/adolescent psychopathology. *Journal of Abnormal Child Psychology, 17*, 299-323.

Achenbach, T.M., & Edelbrock, C. (1978). The classification of child psychopathology: A review and analysis of empirical efforts. *Psychological Bulletin, 85*, 1275-1301.

Achenbach, T.M., & Edelbrock, C. (1979). The Child Behavior Profile: II. Boys aged 12-16 and girls aged 6-11 and 12-16. *Journal of Consulting and Clinical Psychology, 47,* 223-233.

Achenbach, T.M., & Edelbrock, C. (1981). Behavioral problems and competencies reported by parents of normal and disturbed children aged four to sixteen. *Monographs of the Society for Research in Child Development, 46* (Serial No. 188).

Achenbach, T.M., & Edelbrock, C. (1983). *Manual for the Child Behavior Checklist and Revised Child Behavior Profile.* Burlington, VT: University of Vermont, Department of Psychiatry.

Achenbach, T.M., Edelbrock, C., & Howell, C.T. (1987). Empirically based assessment of the behavioral/emotional problems of 2-3-year-old children. *Journal of Abnormal Child Psychology, 15,* 629-650.

Achenbach, T.M., Hensley, V.R., Phares, V.S., & Grayson, D. (1990). Problems and competencies reported by parents of Australian and American children. *Journal of Child Psychology and Psychiatry, 31,* 265-286.

Achenbach, T.M., Howell, C.T., Quay, H.C., & Conners, C.K. (1991). National survey of competencies and problems among 4- to 16-year-olds: Parents' reports for normative and clinical samples. *Monographs of the Society for Research in Child Development,* in press.

Achenbach, T.M., & Lewis, M. (1971). A proposed model for clinical research and its application to encopresis and enuresis. *Journal of the American Academy of Child Psychiatry, 10,* 535-554.

Achenbach, T.M., McConaughy, S.H., & Howell, C.T. (1987). Child/adolescent behavioral and emotional problems: Implications of cross-informant correlations for situational specificity. *Psychological Bulletin, 101,* 213-232.

Achenbach, T.M., Phares, V., Howell, C.T., Rauh, V.A., & Nurcombe, B. Seven-year outcome of the Vermont intervention program for low-birth-weight infants. *Child Development,* 1990, *61,* 1672-1681.

Achenbach, T.M., Verhulst, F.C., Baron, G.D., & Althaus, M. (1987). A comparison of syndromes derived from the Child Behavior Checklist for American and Dutch boys aged 6-11 and 12-16. *Journal of Child Psychology and Psychiatry, 28,* 437-453.

American Psychiatric Association (1952, 1968, 1980, 1987). *Diagnostic and statistical manual of mental disorders* (1st ed., 2nd ed., 3rd ed., 3rd ed. rev.). Washington, D.C.: Author.

Auerbach, J.G. & Lerner, Y. (1991). Syndromes derived from the Child Behavior Checklist for clinically referred Israeli boys aged 6-11. *Journal of Child Psychology and Psychiatry*, in press.

Bartko, J.J. (1976). On various intraclass correlation reliability coefficients. *Psychological Bulletin, 83*, 762-765.

Bernstein, G.A., & Garfinkel, D.B. (1986). School phobia: The overlap of affective and anxiety disorders. *Journal of the American Academy of Child Psychiatry, 25*, 235-241.

Churchman, C.W., Ackoff, R.L., & Arnoff, E.L. (1957). *Introduction to operations research*. New York: Wiley.

Cohen, J. (1988). *Statistical power analysis for the behavioral sciences* (2nd ed.). New York: Academic Press.

Cole, D.A. (1987). Methodological contributions to clinical research: Utility of confirmatory factor analysis in test validation research. *Journal of Consulting and Clinical Psychology, 55*, 584-594.

Conners, C.K. (1973). Rating scales for use in drug studies with children. *Psychopharmacology Bulletin: Pharmacotherapy with children*. Washington, DC: U.S. Government Printing Office.

Conrad, M., & Hammen, C. (1989). Role of maternal depression in perceptions of child maladjustment. *Journal of Consulting and Clinical Psychology, 57*, 663-667.

Crocker, L., & Algina, J. (1986). *Introduction to classical and modern test theory*. New York: Holt, Rinehart, & Winston.

Cronbach, L.J. (1951). Coefficient alpha and the internal structure of tests. *Psychometrika, 16*, 297-334.

Cronbach, L.J., & Meehl, P.E. (1955). Construct validity in psychological tests. *Psychological Bulletin, 52*, 281-302.

Doll, E.A. (1965). *Vineland Social Maturity Scale*. Circle Pines, MN: American Guidance Service.

Edelbrock, C., & Costello, A.J. (1988). Convergence between statistically derived behavior problem syndromes and child psychiatric diagnoses. *Journal of Abnormal Child Psychology, 16*, 219-231.

Edelbrock, C., Costello, A.J., Dulcan, M.K., Kalas, R., & Conover, N.C. (1985). Age differences in the reliability of the psychiatric interview of the child. *Child Development, 56*, 265-275.

Edelbrock, C., Costello, A.J., & Kessler, M.D. (1984). Empirical corroboration of attention deficit disorder. *Journal of the American Academy of Child Psychiatry, 23*, 285-290.

Education of the Handicapped Act. (1977). *Federal Register, 42*, p. 42478. Amended in *Federal Register*, (1981), *46*, p. 3866.

Evans, W.R. (1975). The Behavior Problem Checklist. Data from an inner city population. *Psychology in the Schools, 12*, 301-303.

Fleiss, J.L. (1981). *Statistical methods for rates and proportions* (2nd ed.). New York: Wiley.

Gorsuch, R.L. (1983). *Factor analysis* (2nd ed.). Hillsdale, NJ: Erlbaum.

Guilford, J.P. (1965). *Fundamental statistics in psychology and education* (4th ed.). New York: McGraw-Hill.

Hollingshead, A.B. (1975). *Four factor index of social status.* Unpublished paper. New Haven, CT: Yale University, Department of Sociology.

Katz, P.A., Zigler, E., & Zalk, S.R. (1975). Children's self-image disparity: The effects of age, maladjustment and action-thought orientation. *Developmental Psychology, 11*, 546-550.

Kazdin, A.E., Esveldt-Dawson, K., French, N.H., & Unis, A.S. (1987). Problem-solving skills training and relationship therapy in the treatment of antisocial child behavior. *Journal of Consulting and Clinical Psychology, 55*, 76-85.

LaRiviere, C.L. (1990). Behavioral and emotional correlates of child sexual abuse. Unpublished Ph.D. dissertation. Nova University, Davie, Florida.

Mash, E.J. & Johnston, C. (1983). Parental perceptions of child behavior problems, parenting self-esteem, and mothers' reported stress in younger and older hyperactive and normal children. *Journal of Consulting and Clinical Psychology, 51*, 86-99.

McConaughy, S.H., & Achenbach, T.M. (1988). *Practical guide for the Child Behavior Checklist and related materials.* Burlington, VT: University of Vermont, Department of Psychiatry.

McConaughy, S.H., & Achenbach, T.M. (1990). *Guide for the Semi-structured Clinical Interview for Children Aged 6-11.* Burlington, VT: University of Vermont, Department of Psychiatry.

McConaughy, S.H., Achenbach, T.M., & Gent, C.L. (1988). Multiaxial empirically based assessment: Parent, teacher, observational, cognitive, and personality correlates of Child Behavior Profiles for 6-11-year-old boys. *Journal of Abnormal Child Psychology, 16*, 485-509.

McConaughy, S.H., Stanger, C., & Achenbach, T.M. (1991). Three-year prediction of behavioral/emotional problems and signs of disturbance in a national sample of 4- to 16-year-olds: I. Categorical versus quantitative predictive relations. Submitted for publication.

Mezzich, A.C., Mezzich, J.E., & Coffman, G.A. (1985). Reliability of DSM-III vs. DSM-II in child psychopathology. *Journal of the American Academy of Child Psychiatry, 24*, 273-280.

Milich, R., Roberts, M., Loney, J., & Caputo, J. (1980). Differentiating practice effects and statistical regression on the Conners Hyperkinesis Index. *Journal of Abnormal Child Psychology, 8,* 549-552.

Miller, L.C. (1967). Louisville Behavior Checklist for males, 6-12 years of age. *Psychological Reports, 21,* 885-896.

Miller, L.C., Hampe, E., Barrett, C.L., & Noble, H. (1972). Test-retest reliability of parent ratings of children's deviant behavior. *Psychological Reports, 31,* 249-250.

Mish, F.C. (Ed.). (1988). *Webster's ninth new collegiate dictionary.* Springfield, MA: Merriam-Webster.

Montenegro, H. (1983). *Salud mental del escolar. Estandarización del inventario de problemas conductuales y destrezas sociales de T. Achenbach en niños de 6 a 11 años.* Santiago, Chile: Centro de Estudios de Desarollo y Estimulacion Psicosocial.

Peterson, D.R. (1961). Behavior problems of middle childhood. *Journal of Consulting Psychology, 25,* 205-209.

Quay, H.C., & Peterson, D.R. (1983). *Interim Manual for the Revised Behavior Problem Checklist.* Coral Gables, FL: University of Miami, Applied Social Sciences.

Reed, M.L. & Edelbrock, C. (1983). Reliability and validity of the Direct Observation Form of the Child Behavior Checklist. *Journal of Abnormal Child Psychology, 11,* 521-530.

Richters, J., & Pellegrini, D. (1989). Depressed mothers' judgments about their children: An examination of the depression-distortion hypothesis. *Child Development, 60,* 1068-1075.

Robins, L.N. (1985). Epidemiology: Reflections on testing the validity of psychiatric interviews. *Archives of General Psychiatry, 42,* 918-924.

Sakoda, J.M., Cohen, B.H., & Beall, G. (1954). Test of significance for a series of statistical tests. *Psychological Bulletin, 51,* 172-175.

SAS Institute, (1988). *SAS/STAT User's Guide, Release 6.03 Edition.* Cary, NC: SAS Institute.

Sawyer, M.G. (1990). Childhood behavior problems: Discrepancies between reports from children, parents, and teachers. Unpublished Ph.D. dissertation. University of Adelaide, Australia.

Sawyer, M.G., Sarris, A., Baghurst, P.A., Cornish, C.A., & Kalucy, R.S. (1990). The prevalence of emotional and behaviour disorders and patterns of service utilization in children and adolescents *Australian and New Zealand Journal of Psychiatry, 24,* 323-330.

Saylor, C.F., Finch, A.J., Spirito, A., & Bennett, B. (1984). The children's depression inventory: A systematic evaluation of psychometric properties. *Journal of Consulting and Clinical Psychology, 52,* 955-967.

Snook, S.C., & Gorsuch, R.L. (1989). Component analysis versus common factor analysis: A Monte Carlo study. *Psychological Bulletin, 106,* 148-154.

Sparrow, S., Cicchetti, D.V., & Balla, D. (1984). *Vineland Social Maturity Scale-Revised.* Circle Pines, MN: American Guidance Service.

Stanger, C., McConaughy, S.H., & Achenbach, T.M. (1991). Three-year prediction of behavioral/emotional problems and signs of disturbance in a national sample of 4- to 16-year-olds: II. Path analyses. Submitted for publication.

Strauss, C.C., Last, C.G., Hersen, M., & Kazdin, A.E. (1988). Association between anxiety and depression in children and adolescents with anxiety disorders. *Journal of Abnormal Child Psychology, 16,* 57-68.

Swets, J.E., & Pickett, R.M. (1982). *Evaluation of diagnostic systems: Methods from signal detection theory.* New York: Academic Press.

Treiber, F.A. & Mabe, P.A. (1987). Child and parent perceptions of children's psychopathology in psychiatric outpatient children. *Journal of Abnormal Child Psychology, 15,* 115-124.

Verhulst, F.C., Achenbach, T.M., Althaus, M., & Akkerhuis, G.W. (1988). A comparison of syndromes derived from the Child Behavior Checklist for American and Dutch girls aged 6-11 and 12-16. *Journal of Child Psychology and Psychiatry, 29,* 879-895.

Verhulst, F.C., Akkerhuis, G.W., & Althaus, M. (1985). Mental health in Dutch children: (I) A cross-cultural comparison. *Acta Psychiatrica Scandinavica, 72* (Suppl. 323).

Wechsler, D. (1989). *Wechsler Preschool and Primary Scale of Intelligence-Revised.* San Antonio: Psychological Corporation.

Weinstein, S.R., Noam, G.G., Grimes, K., Stone, K., & Schwab-Stone, M. (1990). Convergence of DSM-III diagnoses and self-reported symptoms in child and adolescent inpatients. *Journal of the American Academy of Child and Adolescent Psychiatry, 29,* 627-634.

Weintraub, S.A. (1973). Self-control as a correlate of an internalizing-externalizing symptom dimension. *Journal of Abnormal Child Psychology, 1,* 292-307.

Weissman, M.M., Orvaschel, H., & Padian, N. (1980). Children's symptoms and social functioning self-report scales. Comparison of mothers' and children's reports. *Journal of Nervous and Mental Disease, 168,* 736-740.

Weisz, J.R., Suwanlert, S., Chaiyasit, W., Weiss, B., Achenbach, T.M., & Walter, B.R. (1987). Epidemiology of behavioral and emotional problems among Thai and American children: Parent reports for ages 6-11. *Journal of the American Academy of Child and Adolescent Psychiatry, 26,* 890-897.

Weisz, J.R., & Weiss, B. (1989). Assessing the effects of clinic-based psychotherapy with children and adolescents. *Journal of Consulting and Clinical Psychology, 57,* 741-746.

World Health Organization (1978). *Mental disorders: Glossary and guide to their classification in accordance with the Ninth Revision of the International Classification of Diseases.* Geneva: Author.

APPENDIX A
INSTRUCTIONS FOR HAND SCORING
THE CHILD BEHAVIOR CHECKLIST/4-18

Note. There are some small differences between the hand-scored and computer-scored data entry formats, but they produce the same results. Templates are available to assist in transferring data from pp. 3-4 of the CBCL to the profile. The same 1991 templates are used for all four sex/age groups on the CBCL. Be sure to use the profile form appropriate for the child's sex. Competence scales are *not* scored for 4-5-year-olds. For information on computer-scoring programs, write to Dr. Achenbach.

Scoring the Competence Scales

The following item is *not* scored on the 1991 competence scales but its score can be entered in the space provided below the profile:

II-A. # of nonsports activities. If parent reported:

> 0 or 1 activity — enter 0 below profile
> 2 activities — enter 1 below profile
> 3 or more activities — enter 2 below profile

Do not count listening to radio or TV, goofing off, or the like as activities.

ACTIVITIES SCALE

Do *not* score if data are missing for more than 1 of the 5 scores indicated beside the Roman numerals below. The Roman numerals correspond to those on pages 1 and 2 of the CBCL and on the profile scoring form. If a parent checked more than 1 box where only 1 should be checked, score the box closest to "average."

I-A. # of sports.

> If a parent reported 0 or 1 sport — enter 0 on profile
> 2 sports — enter 1 on profile
> 3 or more sports — enter 2 on profile

I-B. Mean of participation & skill in sports. If parent reported no sports, enter 0.

> For each response of *less than average* or *below average* — score 0
> *average* — score 1
> *more than average* or *above average* — score 2

Excluding blanks and "don't know" responses, compute the *mean* of these scores by summing them and dividing by the number of scores you have summed. Enter this mean on the profile.

II-B. Mean of participation & skill in activities. Compute in the same way as specified in I-B for sports.

246

IV-A. # of jobs. If parent reported 0 or 1 job — enter 0 on profile
2 jobs — enter 1 on profile
3 or more jobs — enter 2 on profile

IV-B. Mean job quality. Compute as specified in I-B.

Total score for Activities Scale. Sum the 5 scores just entered for the items of the Activities scale. If missing data prevent computation of 1 score, substitute the *mean* of the other 4 scores for the missing score in computing the total. Round off total to nearest .5.

SOCIAL SCALE

Do *not* score if data are missing for more than 1 of the 6 scores.

III-A. # of organizations. If parent reported 0 or 1 — enter 0 on profile
2 — enter 1 on profile
3 or more — enter 2 on profile

III-B. Mean of participation in organizations. Compute as specified in I-B.

V-1. # of friends. If parent checked *0 or 1* — enter 0 on profile
2 or 3 — enter 1 on profile
4 or more — enter 2 on profile

V-2. Contacts with friends. (On the 1991 profile, Item V-2 can be scored 1 or 2 even if no close friends were reported in Item V-1.)
If parent checked *less than 1* — enter 0 on profile
1 or 2 — enter 1 on profile
3 or more— enter 2 on profile

VI-A. Behavior with others. For each of the first three items (items a, b, & c):
If the parent checked *worse* — score 0
about the same — score 1
better — score 2
Excluding any items for which the parent did not check a box, compute the *mean* of these scores and enter it on the profile.

VI-B. Play/work by self. (Item d)
If the parent checked *worse* — enter 0 on profile
about the same— enter 1 on profile
better— enter 2 on profile

Total score for Social Scale. Sum the 6 scores just entered for the items of the Social scale. If missing data prevent computation of 1 score, substitute the *mean* of the other 5 scores for the missing score in computing the total. Round off total to nearest .5.

SCHOOL SCALE

Do *not* score if the child does not attend school or if data are missing for any of the 4 scores indicated below for Items VII-1 through VII-4, which appear on Page 2 of the CBCL and on the *School* scale of the profile scoring form.

VII-1. Academic performance. For each academic subject checked:

failing — score 0
below average — score 1
average — score 2
above average — score 3

Enter the *mean* of these scores on the profile. (Academic subjects include reading, writing, arithmetic, spelling, science, English, foreign language, history, social studies, and similar subjects. Do *not* count physical education, art, music, home economics, driver education, industrial arts, typing, or the like.)

VII-2. Special Class. For any type of remedial special class (for retarded, emotionally disturbed, learning disabled, perceptual-motor handicapped, reading readiness, resource room, behavior problems, etc):   — enter 0 on profile
not in remedial class — enter 1 on profile

VII-3. Repeated Grade.   If any grades were repeated — enter 0 on profile
no grades repeated — enter 1 on profile

VII-4. School Problems. If the parent entered any school problem that was present in the last 6 months but not already scored above: — enter 0 on profile
no problem beside those scored above — enter 1 on profile

Total score for School Scale. Sum the 4 scores just entered on the *School* scale of the profile, unless any score is missing. After computing the total, round off to the nearest .5.

TOTAL COMPETENCE SCORE

A total competence score is obtained by summing the totals of the 3 scales. *T* scores for total competence scores are listed in the box on the right-hand side of the hand-scored competence profile. *Be sure to look at the column for the age of the child being scored (6-11 or 12-18).*

Problem Scales

Do *not* score if data are missing for more than 8 items, not counting #2, 4, 56h and 113. If a parent circled two numbers for an item, score the item 1. Note that there are 120 problem items, even though the numbers range from 1-113 (items 56a-h comprise 8 items).

ITEM SCORES

Place the 1991 CBCL/4-18 Page 3 template over Page 3 of the CBCL. The Roman numerals beside each item number on the template indicate the syndrome scales on which the item is scored. If the parent circled 0, 1, or 2 beside an item, enter the 0, 1, or 2 on the appropriate syndrome scale of the profile. If the item is not on any syndrome scale, the *Other Problems* on the template indicates that you should enter the item's score in the list of *Other Problems* to the right of the profile. Repeat, using the Page 4 template on Page 4 of the CBCL. Comments written by the parent should be used in judging whether items deserve to be scored, with the following guidelines:

a. For each problem reported by the parent, only the CBCL item that most specifically describes the problem should be scored. If the parent's comments show that more than one item has been scored for a particular behavior, or if the parent wrote in a problem for #56h or 113 that is specifically covered elsewhere, count only the most specific item.

b. For extreme behaviors (e.g., sets fires, attempts suicide) — if parent noted that it happened once but circled 0 or left it blank, score 1 unless it clearly happened earlier than the interval specified in the rating instructions (6 months, unless user specifies a different interval).

c. For items on which parent notes "used to do this," score as the parent scored it, unless it clearly occurred earlier than the interval specified in the instructions.

d. When in doubt, score item the way the parent scored it, except on the following items:

9. Obsessions — exclude anything that is clearly *not* obsessional; e.g., do *not* score "won't take no for an answer."

28. Eats or drinks things that are not food — do *not* count sweets & junk food.

40. Hears sounds and **70. Sees things** — do *not* score anxiousness about sounds and sights that others notice too; e.g., afraid noises at night might be burglars; do *not* score experiences while under the influence of drugs or alcohol.

46. Nervous movements — if "can't sit still" or anything entirely covered by item 10 is entered here, score *only* item 10.

56d. Problems with eyes — do *not* score "wears glasses," "near-sighted," and other visual problems having an organic basis.

66. Compulsions — do *not* score noncompulsive behavior; e.g., "keeps hitting brother."

72. Sets fires — score playing with matches or lighter if parent reported it.

77. Sleeps more than most — do *not* score "wants to stay in bed," but score difficulties in waking child.

83. Stores up things —do *not* score hobby collections, such as stamps, dolls.

84. Strange behavior and **85. Strange ideas** — if what the parent describes is specifically covered by another item, score the more specific item instead.

105. Alcohol or drugs — do *not* score tobacco or medication.

113. Additional problems — score only if *not* specifically covered by another item; if parent listed more than 1 "other" item, count only highest toward total problem score. For example, if a parent scored one additional problem "2" and another additional problem "1," add 2 to the total problem score.

SYNDROME SCALE SCORES

To obtain the total raw score for each syndrome scale, sum the 0s, 1s, and 2s you have entered for the scale.

GRAPHIC DISPLAY AND T SCORES

To complete the graphic displays for the competence and syndrome scales, make an X on the number above each scale that equals the score obtained for that scale. *Be sure to mark the number in the column that includes the child's age.* Then draw a line to connect the Xs in the graphic display. Percentiles based on nonreferred children can be read from the left side of the graphic display. *T* scores can be read from the right side.

INTERNALIZING AND EXTERNALIZING

A box at the bottom of the problem profile outlines the computation of Internalizing and Externalizing scores as follows: *Internalizing* = the sum of raw scores for syndrome scales I + II + III, minus the score for Item 103 to avoid counting Item 103 twice, because it is on both Scale I and III. *Externalizing* = the sum of raw scores for syndrome Scales VII + VIII. A *T* score for each Internalizing and Externalizing raw score is listed in the box to the right of the profile. *Be sure to look at the raw score column for the age of the child being scored (age 4-11 or 12-18).*

TOTAL PROBLEM SCORE

To compute the total problem score, sum the 1s and 2s on the CBCL and enter the sum in the box to the far right of the profile. **Omit Items 2.** *Allergy* **and 4.** *Asthma.* If the parent has entered a problem for Item 56h or 113 that is not covered by another item, include the score for 56h or 113. If more than one problem has been entered for item 113, count only the one having the highest score. The total problem score can be cross-checked by subtracting the number of items scored as present from the sum of 1s and 2s. The difference should equal the number of 2s, omitting Items 2 and 4. (The number and sum of items can *not* be computed by adding scale totals, because some items appear on more than one scale.) A *T* score for each total problem score is listed in the box to the right of the profile. *Be sure to look at the total score column for the age of the child being scored (age 4-11 or 12-18).*

SCALE *IX. SEX PROBLEMS* FOR AGES 4-11 (OPTIONAL)

To obtain the raw scale score for the Sex Problems syndrome, sum the 0s, 1s, and 2s for problem Items *5, 59, 60, 73, 96,* and *110.* These 6 items are marked with superscript *S* on the hand-scored profile. Item 96 is also scored on Scale *VII. Delinquent Behavior*, while the remaining 5 items are listed under the *Other Problems* heading. The *T* score for each raw score is listed below. The raw score and *T* score can be entered in the box at the bottom of the hand-scored profile.

Boys				Girls			
Raw Score	*T*	Raw Score	*T*	Raw Score	*T*	Raw Score	*T*
0	50	7	85	0	50	7	85
1	65	8	88	1	64	8	88
2	70	9	91	2	70	9	91
3	73	10	94	3	73	10	94
4	76	11	97	4	76	11	97
5	79	12	100	5	79	12	100
6	82			6	82		

APPENDIX B
Mean Scale Scores for Matched Referred and Nonreferred Boys 4-11

Scale	T Score Referred Mean	SD	T Score Nonreferred Mean	SD	Raw Score Referred Mean	SD	Raw Score Nonreferred Mean	SD	SE of Mean[a] Ref	Nonref	SE of Meas[b] Ref	Nonref	Cronbach's alpha
Activities	45.5	7.3	48.0	7.1	5.9	1.8	6.4	1.7	.08	.08	.83	.80	.46
Social	40.3	9.0	48.0	7.3	5.0	2.1	6.9	2.0	.10	.10	.71	.67	.54
School	36.1	8.6	48.4	7.1	3.4	1.3	5.1	.9	.06	.04	.29	.20	.59
Total Competence	39.3	8.8	50.3	9.6	14.5	3.6	18.5	3.3	.18	.16	1.10	1.02	.57
Withdrawn	61.0	9.8	54.0	5.6	4.1	3.3	1.8	1.9	.14	.08	1.65	.92	.76
Somatic Complaints	57.7	8.1	53.8	5.8	1.7	2.2	.8	1.3	.09	.06	.35	.22	.68
Anxious/Depressed	63.3	11.2	54.0	5.9	7.9	5.8	3.1	3.1	.24	.13	2.10	1.11	.87
Social Problems	62.6	9.9	53.9	5.6	4.7	3.0	2.0	1.9	.12	.08	1.06	.67	.72
Thought Problems	60.4	9.1	53.4	5.5	1.9	2.0	.5	.9	.08	.04	.59	.26	.62
Attention Problems	64.7	10.6	54.0	5.8	8.2	4.4	3.3	2.8	.18	.12	1.53	.98	.84
Delinquent Behavior	62.3	9.4	53.8	5.7	4.3	3.3	1.6	1.7	.14	.07	1.21	.63	.74
Aggressive Behavior	64.1	11.9	54.0	6.0	16.6	8.8	8.2	5.8	.37	.24	2.65	1.73	.92
Sex Problems	54.9	8.8	51.6	5.0	.5	1.1	.1	.5	.05	.02	.42	.18	.56
Internalizing	61.7	11.8	50.2	9.6	13.1	8.7	5.5	4.7	.36	.19	2.78	1.49	.89
Externalizing	62.5	11.6	49.9	9.8	20.9	11.3	9.8	7.0	.47	.29	3.40	2.12	.93
Total Problems	64.4	10.7	50.0	9.8	54.5	26.6	24.2	15.6	1.10	.65	7.66	4.48	.96

Note. N = 582 each in demographically-matched referred and nonreferred samples described in Chapter 6.
[a]Standard error of mean raw scores. [b]Standard error of measurement = SD √1-reliability (Guilford, 1965) computed from reliability of raw scores shown in Table 5-1.

APPENDIX B (Continued)
Mean Scale Scores for Matched Referred and Nonreferred Boys 12-18

Scale	T Score Referred Mean	SD	T Score Nonreferred Mean	SD	Raw Score Referred Mean	SD	Raw Score Nonreferred Mean	SD	SE of Mean[a] Ref	Nonref	SE of Meas[b] Ref	Nonref	Cronbach's alpha
Activities	44.5	8.4	48.4	7.0	5.8	1.9	6.7	1.6	.09	.08	.87	.75	.42
Social	37.8	8.8	48.3	7.2	5.0	2.0	7.6	2.0	.10	.10	.68	.68	.60
School	37.7	8.6	48.3	6.9	3.1	1.3	4.8	1.1	.07	.05	.31	.26	.61
Total Competence	37.7	8.1	50.8	9.7	14.0	3.6	19.1	3.5	.19	.18	1.11	1.08	.64
Withdrawn	62.2	11.1	54.0	6.2	5.3	3.7	2.4	2.2	.17	.10	1.84	1.10	.80
Somatic Complaints	58.3	9.3	54.1	5.8	2.2	2.6	1.0	1.4	.12	.07	.43	.23	.72
Anxious/Depressed	62.4	10.1	54.2	6.1	7.7	5.4	3.2	3.3	.26	.15	1.98	1.20	.86
Social Problems	62.0	10.0	54.0	6.1	4.1	3.2	1.6	1.9	.15	.09	1.14	.67	.76
Thought Problems	60.6	9.5	53.3	5.4	2.0	2.2	.5	.9	.10	.04	.64	.27	.68
Attention Problems	64.8	10.0	54.0	5.9	8.5	4.3	3.4	3.1	.20	.14	1.48	1.06	.83
Delinquent Behavior	63.3	9.1	53.9	5.8	6.1	4.5	1.9	2.4	.21	.12	1.65	.89	.83
Aggressive Behavior	62.5	11.1	54.2	6.2	14.2	8.5	7.0	5.7	.40	.27	2.55	1.71	.92
Internalizing	61.5	11.1	50.5	9.7	14.4	9.2	6.5	5.3	.43	.25	2.94	1.70	.90
Externalizing	62.6	10.7	50.5	9.7	20.3	11.8	8.9	7.5	.55	.35	3.55	2.27	.93
Total Problems	64.0	9.5	50.5	9.8	52.5	26.4	23.0	16.7	1.25	.79	7.61	4.81	.96

Note. N = 450 each in demographically matched referred and nonreferred samples described in Chapter 6. [a]Standard error of mean raw scores. [b]Standard error of measurement = SD $\sqrt{1\text{-reliability}}$ (Guilford, 1965) computed from reliability of raw scores shown in Table 5-1.

APPENDIX B (Continued)

Mean Scale Scores for Matched Referred and Nonreferred Girls 4-11

Scale	T Score				Raw Score				SE of Mean[a]		SE of Meas[b]		Cronbach's alpha
	Referred Mean	SD	Nonreferred Mean	SD	Referred Mean	SD	Nonreferred Mean	SD	Ref	Nonref	Ref	Nonref	
Activities	44.6	7.6	47.8	7.3	5.6	1.8	6.4	1.8	.08	.08	1.16	1.16	.54
Social	41.2	8.7	48.1	7.2	5.1	2.1	6.9	2.1	.10	.10	.50	.48	.58
School	37.4	9.0	48.4	6.9	3.8	1.3	5.3	.8	.06	.04	.44	.25	.62
Total Competence	39.8	8.8	50.2	9.8	14.6	3.8	18.7	3.6	.18	.17	1.61	1.53	.62
Withdrawn	61.4	9.5	54.0	5.7	4.6	3.4	2.0	2.0	.13	.08	1.22	.73	.77
Somatic Complaints	58.0	8.7	53.9	5.7	2.3	2.8	1.0	1.6	.11	.07	.81	.48	.76
Anxious/Depressed	62.9	10.0	54.0	5.7	8.5	5.6	3.4	3.3	.23	.13	2.21	1.31	.87
Social Problems	64.6	11.4	54.0	5.9	4.9	3.2	1.9	1.7	.13	.07	1.19	.64	.74
Thought Problems	60.2	9.3	53.2	5.7	1.8	2.1	.5	1.0	.08	.04	1.26	.59	.66
Attention Problems	65.7	11.1	54.1	5.9	7.3	4.6	2.5	2.5	.19	.10	1.30	.69	.84
Delinquent Behavior	60.8	9.5	53.8	5.7	3.3	3.1	1.2	1.4	.12	.06	1.17	.54	.73
Aggressive Behavior	62.9	11.8	54.0	5.8	14.2	8.7	7.0	5.2	.35	.21	2.59	1.54	.92
Sex Problems	55.6	8.9	52.0	5.4	.6	1.2	.2	.5	.05	.02	.53	.22	.54
Internalizing	61.4	10.9	50.1	9.7	14.6	9.2	6.3	5.5	.37	.22	3.26	1.96	.90
Externalizing	61.2	12.3	50.0	9.6	17.5	11.1	8.2	6.1	.45	.24	2.54	1.39	.93
Total Problems	63.8	11.3	50.1	9.9	52.1	27.3	23.1	15.5	1.10	.62	6.63	3.76	.96

Note. $N = 619$ each in demographically-matched referred and nonreferred samples described in Chapter 6. [a]Standard error of mean raw scores. [b]Standard error of measurement = SD $\sqrt{1\text{-reliability}}$ (Guilford, 1965) computed from reliability of raw scores shown in Table 5-1.

APPENDIX B (Continued)
Mean Scale Scores for Matched Referred and Nonreferred Girls 12-18

Scale	T Score Referred Mean	SD	T Score Nonreferred Mean	SD	Raw Score Referred Mean	SD	Raw Score Nonreferred Mean	SD	SE of Mean[a] Ref	Nonref	SE of Meas[b] Ref	Nonref	Cronbach's alpha
Activities	44.1	8.2	48.3	7.1	5.6	1.9	6.6	1.7	.09	.08	1.21	1.10	.48
Social	39.9	9.5	48.3	7.1	5.1	2.3	7.4	2.1	.11	.11	.54	.50	.61
School	38.9	9.1	48.5	7.1	3.8	1.4	5.2	.9	.07	.04	.45	.30	.62
Total Competence	39.7	9.5	50.9	9.8	14.8	4.1	19.3	3.5	.21	.18	1.72	1.50	.64
Withdrawn	62.5	10.2	53.8	6.0	5.9	3.7	2.6	2.4	.17	.11	1.35	.88	.81
Somatic Complaints	59.1	9.3	53.9	6.2	3.2	3.2	1.4	2.0	.15	.10	.93	.59	.79
Anxious/Depressed	62.7	9.7	54.1	6.1	9.0	5.7	3.8	3.8	.27	.18	2.26	1.49	.88
Social Problems	60.2	9.6	54.2	6.0	3.9	3.3	1.8	2.1	.15	.10	1.22	.78	.76
Thought Problems	60.4	9.5	53.4	5.6	2.0	2.2	.5	1.0	.10	.05	1.35	.62	.70
Attention Problems	63.5	9.6	54.1	5.9	7.1	4.5	2.6	2.8	.21	.13	1.27	.79	.84
Delinquent Behavior	64.4	10.6	54.1	5.8	5.5	4.7	1.4	1.9	.22	.09	1.79	.72	.84
Aggressive Behavior	63.0	10.3	54.4	6.5	12.9	8.3	6.0	5.4	.39	.25	2.46	1.59	.92
Internalizing	62.0	11.5	50.1	10.0	17.1	10.1	7.5	6.6	.47	.31	3.59	2.35	.92
Externalizing	62.8	11.4	50.8	9.8	18.4	11.8	7.4	6.7	.55	.31	2.70	1.53	.93
Total Problems	63.8	10.9	50.4	10.1	53.1	28.7	22.7	17.8	1.34	.83	6.98	4.32	.96

Note. N = 459 each in demographically matched referred and nonreferred samples described in Chapter 6. [a]Standard error of mean raw scores. [b]Standard error of measurement = SD $\sqrt{1\text{-reliability}}$ (Guilford, 1965) computed from reliability of raw scores shown in Table 5-1.

APPENDIX C
Pearson Correlations Among *T* Scores for Boys Aged 4-11
Clinical Sample above Diagonal, Nonclinical Sample below Diagonal

	Act	Soc	Sch	Tot Comp	With-drn	Som	Anx/ Dep	Soc Prob	Tht Prob	Att	Del	Agg	Sex Prob	Int	Ext	Tot Prob
Activities		.30	.10	.69	-.06	-.02	.06	-.07	-.18	-.16	-.12	-.12	-.04	-.01	-.15	-.13
Social	.35		.18	.79	-.17	-.01	-.19	-.37	-.26	-.32	-.29	-.36	-.14	-.20	-.38	-.36
School	.16	.16		.50	-.17	-.07	-.07	-.26	-.23	-.43	-.21	-.20	-.01	-.15	-.23	-.28
Tot. Competence	.72	.77	.45		-.20	-.05	-.13	-.39	-.34	-.46	-.31	-.37	-.12	-.21	-.41	-.42
Withdrawn	.03	.03	-.10	-.05		.27	.61	.42	.53	.47	.30	.36	.19	.78	.37	.61
Somatic Comp.	.06	.09	-.04	.04	.22		.36	.22	.30	.28	.22	.29	.09	.56	.29	.43
Anx/Depressed	.07	.02	-.10	-.01	.46	.26		.50	.48	.52	.38	.54	.28	.88	.53	.74
Social Problems	-.11	-.08	-.19	-.18	.42	.19	.46		.42	.63	.41	.53	.25	.51	.54	.68
Thought Prob.	.07	.02	-.09	.03	.30	.19	.45	.32		.58	.40	.49	.27	.53	.49	.63
Attention	-.06	-.09	-.29	-.17	.38	.19	.50	.53	.44		.45	.52	.19	.56	.54	.71
Delinquent	-.01	-.09	-.25	-.16	.28	.19	.28	.37	.29	.39		.65	.24	.40	.79	.67
Aggressive	-.03	-.12	-.13	-.15	.33	.22	.42	.45	.37	.52	.62		.28	.51	.92	.80
Sex Problems	-.01	.01	-.07	-.04	.17	.13	.28	.22	.21	.21	.35	.29		.25	.27	.33
Internalizing	.12	.10	-.09	.04	.69	.52	.78	.49	.46	.49	.35	.46	.27		.55	.82
Externalizing	.05	-.04	-.17	-.10	.37	.26	.43	.46	.40	.53	.70	.85	.29	.56		.87
Total Problems	.06	.01	-.20	-.07	.55	.40	.64	.62	.53	.66	.60	.75	.32	.81	.89	

Note: Samples are demographically-matched referred and nonreferred children. $N = 582$ in each sample for problem scales, N ranged from 392 to 450 for competence scales, $rs > .10$ were significant at $p < .05$. $rs > .09$ were significant at $p < .05$; $rs > .09$ were significant at $p < .05$.

APPENDIX C (Continued)
Pearson Correlations Among *T* Scores for Boys Aged 12-18
Clinical Sample above Diagonal, Nonclinical Sample below Diagonal

	Act	Soc	Sch	Tot Comp	With-drn	Som	Anx/Dep	Soc Prob	Tht Prob	Att	Del	Agg	Int	Ext	Tot Prob
Activities		.25	.11	.67	-.04	.04	.02	-.09	.00	-.04	-.06	-.06	.00	-.05	-.04
Social	.32		.20	.75	-.29	-.08	-.26	-.44	-.17	-.30	-.18	-.28	-.29	-.27	-.36
School	.21	.32		.56	-.10	-.05	-.14	-.26	-.13	-.35	-.28	-.29	-.14	-.32	-.32
Tot. Competence	.68	.78	.56		-.21	-.03	-.20	-.40	-.13	-.37	-.24	-.31	-.21	-.31	-.36
Withdrawn	-.09	-.15	-.18	-.17		.30	.61	.31	.49	.41	.30	.29	.78	.34	.61
Somatic Comp.	.02	-.04	.01	-.03	.27		.45	.27	.26	.31	.16	.29	.60	.24	.49
Anx/Depressed	.00	-.13	-.18	-.11	.58	.28		.42	.53	.54	.25	.47	.88	.43	.74
Social Problems	-.02	-.27	-.24	-.22	.41	.19	.50		.38	.61	.21	.53	.43	.46	.65
Thought Prob.	-.03	-.11	-.16	-.10	.43	.19	.49	.42		.55	.25	.41	.53	.39	.62
Attention	-.13	-.30	-.33	-.31	.53	.21	.60	.60	.56		.38	.53	.54	.53	.75
Delinquent	-.21	-.23	-.32	-.31	.37	.17	.41	.33	.32	.50		.59	.31	.80	.61
Aggressive	-.05	-.21	-.22	-.20	.41	.21	.59	.49	.49	.61	.64		.45	.90	.79
Internalizing	.02	-.15	-.11	-.12	.71	.55	.80	.49	.45	.56	.41	.53		.45	.80
Externalizing	-.06	-.24	-.24	-.24	.43	.26	.55	.47	.44	.58	.74	.85	.59		.84
Total Problems	-.05	-.25	-.25	-.24	.60	.41	.72	.62	.55	.71	.63	.76	.83	.88	

Note: Samples are demographically-matched referred and nonreferred children. *N* = 450 in each sample for problem scales; *N* ranged from 359 to 441 for competence scales, *r*s >.10 were significant at *p* <.05.

APPENDIX C (Continued)
Pearson Correlations Among T Scores for Girls Aged 4-11
Clinical Sample above Diagonal, Nonclinical Sample below Diagonal

	Act	Soc	Sch	Tot Comp	With-drn	Som	Anx/ Dep	Soc Prob	Tht Prob	Att	Del	Agg	Sex Prob	Int	Ext	Tot Prob
Activities		.32	.14	.70	-.24	-.08	-.07	-.21	-.17	-.27	-.22	-.24	-.03	-.15	-.26	-.26
Social	.43		.22	.78	-.23	-.04	-.21	-.41	-.19	-.36	-.35	-.38	-.20	-.22	-.39	-.37
School	.26	.21		.54	-.04	-.02	-.02	-.33	-.20	-.46	-.18	-.22	-.09	-.06	-.25	-.27
Tot. Competence	.77	.79	.47		-.25	-.08	-.14	-.45	-.24	-.49	-.35	-.39	-.15	-.20	-.42	-.41
Withdrawn	.00	-.12	.01	-.10		.36	.59	.44	.42	.46	.41	.38	.21	.77	.44	.63
Somatic Comp.	-.02	-.06	-.05	-.08	.36		.46	.27	.27	.27	.25	.28	.06	.64	.29	.48
Anx/Depressed	.05	-.04	-.01	-.03	.56	.42		.52	.38	.47	.39	.47	.14	.89	.50	.71
Social Problems	-.04	-.11	-.20	-.15	.38	.23	.41		.46	.66	.48	.61	.30	.54	.62	.74
Thought Prob.	.00	-.06	-.08	-.07	.36	.32	.40	.30		.55	.42	.47	.29	.45	.47	.60
Attention	-.08	-.17	-.29	-.23	.39	.33	.48	.49	.50		.53	.58	.30	.52	.62	.75
Delinquent	-.04	-.14	-.09	-.14	.35	.26	.32	.34	.33	.38		.73	.37	.44	.81	.71
Aggressive	-.04	-.15	-.18	-.16	.35	.29	.53	.47	.41	.57	.53		.35	.49	.93	.80
Sex Problems	.00	-.07	-.08	-.04	.14	.09	.21	.25	.31	.27	.25	.29		.18	.37	.37
Internalizing	.05	-.06	.02	-.04	.72	.63	.80	.42	.43	.49	.37	.50	.17		.56	.82
Externalizing	-.03	-.11	-.14	-.14	.40	.31	.52	.47	.42	.55	.62	.86	.27	.56		.88
Total Problems	.02	-.09	-.12	-.10	.60	.49	.70	.57	.52	.65	.55	.75	.30	.82	.88	

Note: Samples are demographically-matched referred and nonreferred children. $N = 619$ in each sample for problem scales, N ranged from 425 to 486 for competence scales, $rs > .10$ were significant at $p < .05$ $rs > .08$ were significant at $p < .05$; N ranged from 425 to 486 for competence scales, $rs > .10$ were significant at $p < .05$

APPENDIX C (Continued)
Pearson Correlations Among *T* Scores for Girls Aged 12-18
Clinical Sample above Diagonal, Nonclinical Sample below Diagonal

	Act	Soc	Sch	Tot Comp	With-drn	Som	Anx/ Dep	Soc Prob	Tht Prob	Att	Del	Agg	Int	Ext	Tot Prob
Activities		.38	.18	.70	-.15	-.07	-.04	-.08	-.11	-.20	-.26	-.10	-.10	-.18	-.15
Social	.38		.28	.81	-.32	-.07	-.26	-.41	-.25	-.35	-.30	-.33	-.29	-.36	-.39
School	.21	.29		.58	-.07	-.17	-.14	-.30	-.18	-.47	-.30	-.24	-.16	-.28	-.33
Tot. Competence	.71	.79	.51		-.23	-.15	-.20	-.35	-.21	-.44	-.37	-.28	-.24	-.37	-.37
Withdrawn	-.10	-.23	-.29	-.24		.38	.65	.35	.49	.48	.34	.42	.80	.45	.66
Somatic Comp.	.01	.00	-.16	-.02	.40		.48	.25	.32	.36	.27	.35	.68	.34	.54
Anx/Depressed	.03	-.11	-.21	-.11	.65	.43		.41	.54	.54	.30	.51	.88	.49	.74
Social Problems	-.07	-.22	-.37	-.24	.46	.33	.51		.39	.59	.18	.46	.43	.40	.58
Thought Prob.	-.07	-.15	-.27	-.20	.53	.33	.54	.39		.61	.48	.57	.56	.56	.68
Attention	-.09	-.15	-.50	-.25	.52	.37	.55	.60	.56		.54	.65	.58	.66	.78
Delinquent	-.04	-.21	-.36	-.24	.45	.29	.44	.42	.39	.52		.65	.39	.82	.65
Aggressive	-.01	-.18	-.34	-.23	.53	.35	.63	.53	.52	.65	.63		.55	.90	.81
Internalizing	.01	-.11	-.22	-.13	.73	.63	.81	.50	.54	.57	.48	.59		.58	.85
Externalizing	.01	-.16	-.33	-.21	.49	.36	.57	.49	.49	.61	.70	.85	.63		.86
Total Problems	-.02	-.16	-.37	-.23	.66	.54	.72	.64	.60	.72	.63	.76	.87	.87	

Note. Samples are demographically-matched referred and nonreferred children. $N = 459$ for problem scales; N ranged from 389 to 450 for competence scales, $rs > .10$ were significant at $p < .05$.

APPENDIX D

Scores For Referred and Nonreferred Children on Each CBCL Problem Item

Item	Group[a]	N	Age 4-11					N	Age 12-18				
			1	2	1+2	Mean	SE[b]		1	2	1+2	Mean	SE[b]
1. Acts too young	RB	582	41%	22%	63%	.85	.03	450	39%	23%	62%	.86	.04
	RG	619	39	18	57	.76	.03	459	32	17	50	.68	.04
	NB	582	31	4	34	.38	.02	450	28	5	33	.38	.03
	NG	619	24	2	26	.28	.02	459	20	4	24	.28	.02
2. Allergy	RB		10	13	23	.36	.03		13	13	26	.40	.03
	RG		10	10	20	.30	.03		13	14	27	.42	.03
	NB		14	12	25	.37	.03		17	16	32	.48	.04
	NG		13	9	22	.31	.03		17	16	33	.49	.04
3. Argues a lot	RB		36	50	86	1.36	.03		36	50	86	1.36	.03
	RG		36	47	83	1.31	.03		37	48	85	1.34	.03
	NB		48	21	70	.91	.03		51	20	71	.92	.03
	NG		48	18	66	.84	.03		48	21	69	.90	.03
4. Asthma	RB		5	3	8	.12	.02		6	4	10	.14	.02
	RG		4	2	6	.08	.01		4	3	7	.10	.02
	NB		4	5	9	.14	.02		4	5	9	.14	.02
	NG		4	4	8	.12	.02		4	4	8	.12	.02

[a]RB = referred boys; RG = referred girls; NB = nonreferred boys; NG = nonreferred girls.
[b]SE = standard error of the mean.

APPENDIX D (Continued)

Item	Group[a]	Age 4-11					Age 12-18				
		1	2	1+2	Mean	SE[b]	1	2	1+2	Mean	SE[b]
5. Acts like opposite sex	RB	8	1	8	.09	.01	3	1	4	.04	.01
	RG	12	3	15	.18	.02	9	3	12	.15	.02
	NB	3	1	4	.04	.01	1	1	2	.03	.01
	NG	8	1	10	.11	.01	4	1	5	.05	.01
6. BM outside toilet	RB	7	3	10	.13	.02	1	1	2	.03	.01
	RG	5	2	7	.10	.01	1	1	2	.03	.01
	NB	2	1	3	.03	.01	0	0	0	.00	.00
	NG	2	0	2	.02	.01	0	0	0	.00	.00
7. Brags	RB	43	18	61	.79	.03	41	19	61	.80	.03
	RG	37	11	48	.60	.03	29	11	40	.51	.03
	NB	41	5	46	.52	.02	42	10	53	.63	.03
	NG	32	4	36	.40	.02	26	4	30	.34	.03
8. Can't concentrate	RB	37	44	81	1.26	.03	40	40	80	1.21	.04
	RG	36	37	72	1.09	.03	36	26	62	.89	.04
	NB	38	8	47	.55	.03	32	8	41	.49	.03
	NG	32	4	36	.40	.02	24	4	28	.32	.03
9. Can't get mind off thoughts	RB	29	20	49	.71	.03	27	24	51	.77	.04
	RG	26	21	47	.71	.03	30	27	57	.86	.04
	NB	18	6	24	.29	.02	22	5	26	.31	.03
	NG	18	2	20	.22	.02	20	7	27	.34	.03

APPENDIX D (Continued)

Item	Group[a]	Age 4-11					Age 12-18				
		1	2	1+2	Mean	SE[b]	1	2	1+2	Mean	SE[b]
10. Can't sit still	RB	40	39	79	1.19	.03	40	26	67	.94	.04
	RG	34	30	64	.94	.03	29	18	47	.65	.04
	NB	37	13	50	.63	.03	27	10	36	.46	.03
	NG	31	8	39	.47	.03	20	5	25	.30	.03
11. Too dependent	RB	34	16	50	.66	.03	21	8	29	.37	.03
	RG	37	22	59	.82	.03	22	11	33	.45	.03
	NB	23	4	27	.32	.02	12	3	15	.17	.02
	NG	29	5	33	.38	.02	14	3	18	.21	.02
12. Lonely	RB	30	10	41	.51	.03	19	8	27	.36	.03
	RG	34	13	47	.61	.03	33	14	47	.63	.03
	NB	19	2	20	.22	.02	15	2	16	.18	.02
	NG	25	3	27	.30	.02	22	5	26	.31	.03
13. Confused	RB	28	11	39	.50	.03	30	12	42	.54	.03
	RG	28	9	37	.45	.03	30	12	42	.55	.03
	NB	8	0	8	.09	.01	11	1	12	.12	.02
	NG	7	0	7	.08	.01	9	1	10	.11	.02
14. Cries a lot	RB	31	14	45	.59	.03	13	3	16	.20	.02
	RG	36	18	55	.73	.03	28	8	36	.44	.03
	NB	16	2	18	.20	.02	4	1	4	.05	.01
	NG	21	4	25	.28	.02	9	2	11	.13	.02

APPENDIX D (Continued)

Item	Group[a]	Age 4-11					Age 12-18				
		1	2	1+2	Mean	SE[b]	1	2	1+2	Mean	SE[b]
15. Cruel to animals	RB	15	3	18	.21	.02	14	2	16	.18	.02
	RG	9	2	11	.13	.02	8	2	9	.11	.02
	NB	5	1	6	.07	.01	3	0	3	.04	.01
	NG	2	0	2	.02	.01	1	0	1	.01	.00
16. Mean to others	RB	35	13	48	.62	.03	35	12	47	.60	.03
	RG	31	11	42	.54	.03	31	8	40	.48	.03
	NB	18	2	20	.22	.02	17	1	17	.18	.02
	NG	11	1	12	.13	.01	8	2	10	.11	.02
17. Daydreams	RB	34	15	49	.65	.03	40	18	57	.75	.03
	RG	32	15	47	.62	.03	39	19	57	.77	.04
	NB	29	5	34	.38	.02	31	6	37	.43	.03
	NG	27	3	30	.32	.02	29	4	33	.37	.03
18. Harms self	RB	6	2	8	.11	.02	7	2	9	.11	.02
	RG	5	2	7	.09	.01	13	5	18	.23	.02
	NB	1	0	1	.01	.00	0	0	0	.00	.00
	NG	1	0	1	.01	.00	1	0	1	.01	.01
19. Demands attention	RB	37	43	80	1.23	.03	38	26	64	.90	.04
	RG	38	42	81	1.23	.03	36	28	64	.93	.04
	NB	41	11	52	.63	.03	25	5	30	.35	.03
	NG	43	11	54	.65	.03	27	8	35	.43	.03

APPENDIX D (Continued)

Item	Group[a]	Age 4-11					Age 12-18				
		1	2	1+2	Mean	SE[b]	1	2	1+2	Mean	SE[b]
20. Destroys own things	RB	34	17	50	.68	.03	27	11	38	.50	.03
	RG	23	11	34	.45	.03	18	4	22	.26	.02
	NB	17	2	19	.21	.02	8	1	9	.11	.02
	NG	7	1	8	.09	.01	1	0	2	.02	.01
21. Destroys others' things	RB	33	14	47	.62	.03	26	10	37	.47	.03
	RG	23	8	31	.40	.03	19	5	23	.28	.03
	NB	14	1	15	.16	.02	7	1	8	.09	.02
	NG	8	1	9	.10	.01	3	0	3	.03	.01
22. Disobeys at home	RB	54	29	83	1.12	.03	52	22	75	.98	.03
	RG	52	25	77	1.03	.03	50	25	75	1.01	.03
	NB	50	3	53	.56	.02	38	3	40	.43	.03
	NG	47	1	48	.49	.02	32	3	35	.38	.03
23. Disobeys at school	RB	42	18	60	.82	.03	41	21	62	.86	.04
	RG	33	11	44	.57	.03	37	14	52	.66	.03
	NB	25	1	26	.27	.02	23	3	26	.30	.02
	NG	12	0	12	.12	.01	14	1	15	.16	.02
24. Doesn't eat well	RB	23	10	33	.43	.03	21	6	27	.34	.03
	RG	26	10	36	.46	.03	25	10	36	.46	.03
	NB	22	6	27	.33	.02	15	3	18	.22	.02
	NG	26	4	30	.34	.02	19	5	24	.29	.03

APPENDIX D (Continued)

Item	Group[a]	Age 4-11					Age 12-18				
		1	2	1+2	Mean	SE[b]	1	2	1+2	Mean	SE[b]
25. Doesn't get along	RB	47	15	62	.77	.03	41	11	52	.63	.03
	RG	45	14	59	.73	.03	34	11	45	.56	.03
	NB	19	0	19	.19	.02	13	0	13	.13	.02
	NG	16	1	17	.18	.02	12	1	12	.13	.02
26. Lacks guilt	RB	37	22	59	.82	.03	36	26	62	.89	.04
	RG	32	18	50	.69	.03	29	24	53	.77	.04
	NB	24	4	28	.33	.02	28	4	32	.36	.03
	NG	20	3	23	.26	.02	23	3	26	.30	.02
27. Jealous	RB	41	24	65	.89	.03	34	18	51	.69	.04
	RG	40	33	74	1.07	.03	39	23	62	.85	.04
	NB	39	7	46	.53	.03	26	5	31	.36	.03
	NG	40	8	48	.56	.03	29	8	37	.44	.03
28. Eats nonfood	RB	4	2	6	.08	.01	2	1	3	.05	.01
	RG	4	1	5	.07	.01	3	1	4	.05	.01
	NB	2	0	2	.02	.01	1	0	1	.01	.01
	NG	2	0	2	.03	.01	2	0	2	.02	.01
29. Fears	RB	27	12	39	.51	.03	13	6	19	.25	.03
	RG	29	15	44	.59	.03	22	9	31	.40	.03
	NB	26	5	31	.36	.02	16	2	18	.21	.02
	NG	32	6	37	.43	.02	22	7	29	.36	.03

APPENDIX D (Continued)

Item	Group[a]	Age 4-11					Age 12-18				
		1	2	1+2	Mean	SE[b]	1	2	1+2	Mean	SE[b]
30. Fears school	RB	15	4	19	.23	.02	12	9	21	.30	.03
	RG	15	5	20	.25	.02	16	7	23	.30	.03
	NB	4	1	5	.05	.01	3	1	5	.06	.01
	NG	4	0	5	.05	.01	3	1	4	.04	.01
31. Fears impulses	RB	28	5	34	.39	.02	22	4	26	.30	.03
	RG	26	7	33	.41	.03	23	6	29	.35	.03
	NB	18	2	19	.21	.02	11	1	11	.12	.02
	NG	18	1	19	.20	.02	14	1	15	.17	.02
32. Needs to be perfect	RB	29	12	42	.55	.03	27	13	40	.53	.03
	RG	28	17	45	.63	.03	33	15	47	.63	.03
	NB	25	7	32	.39	.03	31	8	39	.47	.03
	NG	29	8	37	.45	.03	33	12	45	.57	.03
33. Feels unloved	RB	36	16	51	.68	.03	34	12	46	.60	.03
	RG	39	20	59	.80	.03	42	19	61	.81	.03
	NB	22	2	24	.26	.02	19	3	22	.24	.02
	NG	30	2	32	.34	.02	25	3	28	.32	.03
34. Feels persecuted	RB	27	11	38	.50	.03	32	15	48	.63	.03
	RG	23	9	32	.41	.03	31	10	41	.51	.03
	NB	10	1	10	.11	.01	15	1	16	.16	.02
	NG	8	0	8	.09	.01	9	1	10	.12	.02

APPENDIX D (Continued)

Item	Group[a]	Age 4-11					Age 12-18				
		1	2	1+2	Mean	SE[b]	1	2	1+2	Mean	SE[b]
35. Feels worthless	RB	39	15	54	.69	.03	42	19	61	.81	.03
	RG	34	15	48	.64	.03	46	18	64	.84	.03
	NB	12	1	13	.14	.02	19	1	20	.20	.02
	NG	13	1	14	.15	.02	17	3	19	.22	.02
36. Accident-prone	RB	24	9	33	.43	.03	18	6	24	.31	.03
	RG	20	11	31	.43	.03	17	6	23	.29	.03
	NB	14	2	16	.17	.02	10	2	12	.14	.02
	NG	14	3	16	.19	.02	10	2	12	.14	.02
37. Fighting	RB	40	15	55	.70	.03	28	11	39	.50	.03
	RG	24	11	35	.46	.03	23	11	34	.46	.03
	NB	15	1	17	.18	.02	11	1	12	.13	.02
	NG	10	1	11	.11	.01	8	1	9	.10	.02
38. Is teased	RB	37	24	61	.86	.03	34	20	54	.75	.04
	RG	37	20	56	.77	.03	30	15	45	.60	.03
	NB	29	5	34	.39	.02	22	6	28	.34	.03
	NG	25	3	28	.32	.02	23	10	33	.42	.03
39. Hangs around kids who get in trouble	RB	21	10	31	.42	.03	30	20	50	.70	.04
	RG	13	4	17	.21	.02	31	17	48	.65	.04
	NB	11	1	12	.13	.02	14	3	17	.20	.02
	NG	5	0	5	.05	.01	11	2	14	.16	.02

APPENDIX D (Continued)

Item	Group[a]	Age 4-11					Age 12-18				
		1	2	1+2	Mean	SE[b]	1	2	1+2	Mean	SE[b]
40. Hears things	RB	6	1	7	.09	.01	4	2	6	.07	.01
	RG	5	2	7	.08	.01	6	1	7	.08	.01
	NB	1	0	1	.01	.00	0	0	0	.00	.00
	NG	2	1	3	.03	.01	1	0	1	.01	.00
41. Acts without thinking	RB	46	29	76	1.06	.03	44	32	76	1.08	.03
	RG	39	22	61	.84	.03	42	25	67	.92	.04
	NB	41	4	45	.48	.02	37	4	42	.46	.03
	NG	32	2	35	.37	.02	32	4	36	.41	.03
42. Would rather be alone	RB	37	9	47	.56	.03	42	16	58	.74	.03
	RG	37	7	44	.51	.03	48	15	63	.78	.03
	NB	31	3	34	.37	.02	45	7	52	.59	.03
	NG	39	3	42	.44	.02	48	7	54	.61	.03
43. Lying, cheating	RB	47	15	61	.76	.03	45	22	66	.88	.03
	RG	36	18	54	.73	.03	37	23	61	.85	.04
	NB	29	2	31	.33	.02	25	2	27	.28	.02
	NG	23	1	24	.26	.02	17	1	18	.20	.02
44. Bites fingernails	RB	14	18	31	.50	.03	16	17	33	.50	.04
	RG	21	21	42	.62	.03	24	22	45	.68	.04
	NB	13	7	20	.27	.02	14	11	25	.36	.03
	NG	21	9	30	.39	.03	21	14	35	.48	.03

APPENDIX D (Continued)

Item	Group[a]	Age 4-11					Age 12-18				
		1	2	1+2	Mean	SE[b]	1	2	1+2	Mean	SE[b]
45. Nervous	RB	36	26	62	.90	.03	36	26	62	.89	.04
	RG	35	26	61	.88	.03	40	27	67	.95	.04
	NB	22	3	26	.29	.02	24	2	26	.28	.02
	NG	15	3	17	.20	.02	25	4	29	.32	.03
46. Nervous movements	RB	18	13	31	.45	.03	17	13	30	.44	.03
	RG	16	9	26	.36	.03	15	8	23	.31	.03
	NB	6	2	8	.10	.02	8	2	10	.12	.02
	NG	4	1	5	.06	.01	6	1	7	.08	.01
47. Nightmares	RB	34	5	39	.44	.02	16	3	19	.22	.02
	RG	35	9	44	.53	.03	24	5	28	.33	.03
	NB	23	1	24	.25	.02	7	0	8	.08	.01
	NG	26	2	27	.29	.02	12	2	14	.15	.02
48. Not liked	RB	34	9	43	.53	.03	33	6	39	.46	.03
	RG	30	9	39	.49	.03	32	7	39	.47	.03
	NB	8	0	9	.09	.01	7	0	7	.08	.01
	NG	8	0	9	.09	.01	9	0	9	.10	.01
49. Constipated	RB	10	2	11	.13	.02	7	1	8	.10	.02
	RG	12	3	14	.17	.02	11	1	12	.14	.02
	NB	5	1	5	.06	.01	5	0	5	.05	.01
	NG	8	1	9	.10	.01	5	1	5	.06	.01

APPENDIX D (Continued)

Item	Group[a]	Age 4-11					Age 12-18				
		1	2	1+2	Mean	SE[b]	1	2	1+2	Mean	SE[b]
50. Fearful, anxious	RB	35	10	45	.56	.03	27	9	36	.46	.03
	RG	37	11	48	.59	.03	31	11	42	.54	.03
	NB	13	2	14	.16	.02	13	1	14	.15	.02
	NG	14	1	15	.16	.02	12	1	13	.14	.02
51. Dizzy	RB	5	0	6	.06	.01	11	3	13	.16	.02
	RG	6	1	7	.09	.01	20	3	23	.27	.02
	NB	1	0	1	.01	.00	6	0	6	.06	.01
	NG	3	0	3	.03	.01	7	1	8	.08	.01
52. Feels too guilty	RB	22	5	27	.33	.02	19	4	23	.28	.03
	RG	23	4	27	.32	.02	23	7	30	.37	.03
	NB	7	0	7	.08	.01	7	1	8	.10	.02
	NG	5	0	5	.05	.01	8	0	9	.09	.01
53. Eats too much	RB	11	7	18	.24	.02	14	10	25	.35	.03
	RG	13	10	23	.34	.03	21	14	35	.48	.03
	NB	12	2	14	.16	.02	18	5	23	.27	.03
	NG	14	3	17	.20	.02	17	7	24	.31	.03
54. Overtired	RB	27	6	33	.39	.02	29	12	41	.54	.03
	RG	27	7	34	.42	.03	30	16	46	.62	.03
	NB	18	0	18	.18	.02	25	2	28	.30	.02
	NG	17	1	18	.19	.02	25	3	27	.30	.02

APPENDIX D (Continued)

Item	Group[a]	Age 4-11					Age 12-18				
		1	2	1+2	Mean	SE[b]	1	2	1+2	Mean	SE[b]
55. Overweight	RB	5	3	8	.11	.02	8	6	14	.21	.03
	RG	7	7	14	.20	.02	15	12	27	.39	.03
	NB	7	3	10	.13	.02	8	5	14	.19	.02
	NG	9	3	12	.15	.02	15	5	21	.26	.03
56a. Aches, pains	RB	13	5	18	.24	.02	16	4	20	.24	.02
	RG	16	8	24	.33	.03	23	8	31	.40	.03
	NB	9	0	9	.09	.01	11	1	11	.12	.02
	NG	13	1	14	.16	.02	14	1	15	.17	.02
56b. Headaches	RB	21	4	24	.28	.02	22	8	30	.38	.03
	RG	22	8	30	.38	.03	32	12	44	.57	.03
	NB	12	2	13	.15	.02	21	2	23	.26	.02
	NG	15	2	17	.18	.02	22	3	25	.28	.02
56c. Nausea, feels sick	RB	9	2	11	.12	.02	14	3	17	.19	.02
	RG	13	5	18	.23	.02	19	5	24	.29	.03
	NB	7	0	7	.07	.01	4	0	5	.05	.01
	NG	8	0	9	.09	.01	8	2	10	.11	.02
56d. Eye problems	RB	6	3	10	.13	.02	8	4	11	.15	.02
	RG	6	4	11	.15	.02	10	5	15	.20	.02
	NB	3	1	4	.05	.01	3	0	4	.04	.01
	NG	3	1	4	.05	.01	6	2	8	.10	.02

APPENDIX D (Continued)

Item	Group[a]	Age 4-11					Age 12-18				
		1	2	1+2	Mean	SE[b]	1	2	1+2	Mean	SE[b]
56e. Skin problems	RB	8	3	11	.14	.02	12	4	16	.20	.02
	RG	13	5	18	.22	.02	12	5	17	.23	.03
	NB	4	1	5	.07	.01	8	2	10	.12	.02
	NG	7	1	8	.10	.01	8	2	10	.11	.02
56f. Stomachaches	RB	20	5	24	.29	.02	18	4	22	.25	.02
	RG	22	9	31	.40	.03	31	9	40	.49	.03
	NB	11	1	12	.13	.01	8	0	8	.09	.01
	NG	18	1	19	.21	.02	18	3	21	.24	.02
56g. Vomiting	RB	6	1	8	.09	.01	6	1	7	.08	.01
	RG	8	1	9	.10	.01	10	2	12	.13	.02
	NB	3	0	3	.04	.01	2	0	2	.02	.01
	NG	3	0	3	.04	.01	2	1	3	.04	.01
56h. Other physical problems	RB	3	2	5	.08	.01	4	2	6	.08	.02
	RG	3	2	5	.08	.01	2	3	5	.09	.02
	NB	1	1	2	.02	.01	2	0	3	.03	.01
	NG	1	0	1	.02	.01	2	0	2	.02	.01
57. Attacks people	RB	29	9	39	.49	.03	26	4	30	.34	.03
	RG	17	6	23	.30	.02	20	5	25	.30	.03
	NB	11	1	11	.12	.01	5	0	5	.05	.01
	NG	6	1	7	.08	.01	3	1	4	.05	.01

APPENDIX D (Continued)

Item	Group[a]	Age 4-11					Age 12-18				
		1	2	1+2	Mean	SE[b]	1	2	1+2	Mean	SE[b]
58. Picking	RB	29	10	39	.49	.03	16	7	23	.31	.03
	RG	26	9	35	.45	.03	12	6	18	.24	.03
	NB	22	2	24	.25	.02	12	3	15	.18	.02
	NG	21	2	23	.24	.02	8	2	9	.11	.02
59. Plays with sex parts in public	RB	7	1	8	.09	.01	2	0	2	.03	.01
	RG	3	1	4	.06	.01	1	0	1	.02	.01
	NB	2	0	2	.02	.01	0	0	0	.00	.00
	NG	1	0	1	.01	.00	0	0	0	.00	.00
60. Plays with sex parts too much	RB	8	3	10	.13	.02	3	1	4	.05	.01
	RG	6	2	8	.10	.02	1	0	1	.02	.01
	NB	2	0	2	.02	.01	0	0	0	.00	.00
	NG	1	0	1	.01	.00	0	0	0	.00	.00
61. Poor school work	RB	34	21	55	.78	.03	34	43	78	1.23	.04
	RG	29	17	46	.65	.03	34	27	62	.90	.04
	NB	16	2	17	.19	.02	28	9	37	.46	.03
	NG	8	2	10	.12	.02	19	4	23	.27	.02
62. Clumsy	RB	26	7	33	.39	.03	23	6	29	.35	.03
	RG	26	11	37	.49	.03	19	5	24	.29	.03
	NB	11	1	12	.12	.01	9	1	10	.10	.02
	NG	10	1	11	.11	.01	9	1	11	.12	.02

APPENDIX D (Continued)

Item	Group[a]	Age 4-11					Age 12-18				
		1	2	1+2	Mean	SE[b]	1	2	1+2	Mean	SE[b]
63. Prefers older kids	RB	40	18	57	.76	.03	30	17	47	.65	.04
	RG	34	13	47	.61	.03	26	15	41	.57	.03
	NB	35	8	44	.52	.03	26	7	33	.41	.03
	NG	33	7	40	.47	.03	22	7	29	.36	.03
64. Prefers younger kids	RB	39	9	48	.59	.03	28	12	40	.53	.03
	RG	37	15	51	.67	.03	25	10	35	.46	.03
	NB	32	2	34	.36	.02	19	2	21	.23	.02
	NG	33	2	36	.38	.02	25	2	27	.29	.02
65. Refuses to talk	RB	27	8	35	.43	.03	35	12	47	.59	.03
	RG	29	9	38	.48	.03	37	13	50	.63	.03
	NB	12	1	12	.13	.01	18	1	19	.20	.02
	NG	13	1	14	.14	.02	16	2	18	.19	.02
66. Repeats actions	RB	14	12	26	.39	.03	14	11	25	.37	.03
	RG	15	10	24	.35	.03	10	7	17	.25	.03
	NB	4	2	5	.07	.01	4	2	5	.07	.01
	NG	4	2	6	.07	.01	5	1	5	.06	.01
67. Runs away from home	RB	6	2	8	.10	.02	11	5	16	.21	.02
	RG	4	2	7	.09	.01	19	7	26	.32	.03
	NB	1	0	1	.01	.01	2	0	2	.02	.01
	NG	0	0	0	.00	.00	2	0	2	.02	.01

APPENDIX D (Continued)

Item	Group[a]	Age 4-11					Age 12-18				
		1	2	1+2	Mean	SE[b]	1	2	1+2	Mean	SE[b]
68. Screams a lot	RB	25	17	42	.60	.03	19	8	28	.36	.03
	RG	28	19	47	.66	.03	31	15	46	.61	.03
	NB	18	2	20	.23	.02	11	1	12	.12	.02
	NG	20	3	24	.27	.02	15	3	18	.21	.02
69. Secretive	RB	32	16	48	.65	.03	45	28	73	1.01	.03
	RG	32	16	48	.63	.03	41	32	72	1.05	.04
	NB	20	2	22	.24	.02	43	5	48	.54	.03
	NG	21	2	23	.25	.02	34	6	40	.46	.03
70. Sees things	RB	5	1	6	.07	.01	3	0	4	.04	.01
	RG	4	1	5	.06	.01	5	1	5	.06	.01
	NB	1	1	1	.02	.01	1	0	1	.01	.00
	NG	2	0	2	.02	.01	1	0	1	.01	.00
71. Self-conscious	RB	37	18	55	.74	.03	40	21	60	.82	.04
	RG	42	20	61	.81	.03	41	23	64	.87	.04
	NB	44	6	50	.57	.03	44	8	52	.60	.03
	NG	46	9	54	.63	.03	46	11	56	.67	.03
72. Sets fires	RB	7	3	10	.13	.02	8	2	10	.12	.02
	RG	2	1	3	.05	.01	3	0	3	.04	.01
	NB	3	0	3	.03	.01	2	1	2	.03	.01
	NG	0	0	0	.00	.00	1	0	1	.01	.00

APPENDIX D (Continued)

Item	Group[a]	Age 4-11					Age 12-18				
		1	2	1+2	Mean	SE[b]	1	2	1+2	Mean	SE[b]
73. Sex problems	RB	4	1	4	.05	.01	7	3	10	.14	.02
	RG	5	2	7	.08	.01	8	5	13	.18	.02
	NB	0	0	0	.00	.00	1	0	1	.01	.00
	NG	0	0	0	.00	.00	1	0	1	.01	.01
74. Shows off	RB	47	31	78	1.09	.03	44	23	67	.90	.03
	RG	45	16	62	.78	.03	36	10	46	.55	.03
	NB	55	11	66	.77	.03	50	9	60	.69	.03
	NG	44	5	48	.53	.02	29	2	32	.34	.02
75. Shy	RB	35	8	43	.51	.03	30	8	38	.47	.03
	RG	43	11	54	.65	.03	35	12	47	.59	.03
	NB	41	4	45	.50	.02	34	5	38	.43	.03
	NG	41	8	49	.56	.03	39	7	46	.53	.03
76. Sleeps little	RB	16	13	30	.43	.03	15	7	22	.29	.03
	RG	16	9	25	.34	.03	14	9	23	.32	.03
	NB	12	4	16	.19	.02	10	2	12	.15	.02
	NG	8	3	11	.14	.02	8	2	10	.11	.02
77. Sleeps much	RB	7	3	11	.14	.02	17	9	26	.35	.03
	RG	9	4	12	.16	.02	15	9	25	.34	.03
	NB	4	2	6	.08	.01	11	1	12	.14	.02
	NG	8	1	10	.11	.01	9	3	13	.16	.02

APPENDIX D (Continued)

Item	Group[a]	Age 4-11					Age 12-18				
		1	2	1+2	Mean	SE[b]	1	2	1+2	Mean	SE[b]
78. Smears BM	RB	3	0	3	.03	.01	1	0	1	.01	.01
	RG	1	0	1	.01	.01	0	0	1	.01	.01
	NB	0	0	0	.00	.00	0	0	0	.00	.00
	NG	0	0	0	.00	.00	0	0	0	.00	.00
79. Speech problem	RB	14	11	25	.36	.03	9	4	13	.18	.02
	RG	10	9	19	.29	.03	4	4	8	.12	.02
	NB	5	3	8	.11	.02	2	0	3	.03	.01
	NG	5	1	6	.07	.01	2	0	2	.02	.01
80. Stares blankly	RB	19	4	23	.27	.02	19	4	23	.27	.03
	RG	20	4	24	.28	.02	23	3	26	.30	.02
	NB	6	0	6	.06	.01	4	0	5	.05	.01
	NG	5	1	6	.06	.01	6	0	7	.07	.01
81. Steals at home	RB	15	5	20	.25	.02	22	8	30	.39	.03
	RG	15	5	20	.25	.02	20	7	27	.34	.03
	NB	3	0	3	.03	.01	3	1	4	.04	.01
	NG	2	0	2	.02	.01	2	0	2	.02	.01
82. Steals outside home	RB	17	3	21	.25	.02	20	8	28	.37	.03
	RG	12	4	16	.20	.02	12	4	16	.21	.02
	NB	2	0	2	.03	.01	3	0	4	.04	.01
	NG	1	0	2	.02	.01	1	0	1	.01	.01

APPENDIX D (Continued)

Item	Group[a]	Age 4-11					Age 12-18				
		1	2	1+2	Mean	SE[b]	1	2	1+2	Mean	SE[b]
83. Stores up unneeded things	RB	17	10	28	.38	.03	13	8	21	.29	.03
	RG	19	11	30	.42	.03	19	11	30	.41	.03
	NB	17	7	25	.32	.03	16	7	23	.30	.03
	NG	21	8	29	.37	.03	17	9	26	.35	.03
84. Strange behavior	RB	12	6	18	.25	.02	13	6	19	.25	.03
	RG	11	4	15	.20	.02	12	6	18	.25	.03
	NB	2	0	2	.02	.01	1	0	1	.02	.01
	NG	1	0	1	.02	.01	2	0	2	.02	.01
85. Strange thoughts	RB	10	4	14	.18	.02	13	5	18	.23	.03
	RG	11	2	13	.16	.02	12	5	17	.23	.03
	NB	4	0	4	.05	.01	4	0	4	.05	.01
	NG	3	0	3	.03	.01	2	1	3	.04	.01
86. Stubborn	RB	46	31	77	1.10	.03	52	28	80	1.09	.03
	RG	45	32	77	1.10	.03	51	28	78	1.07	.03
	NB	50	8	58	.66	.03	48	5	53	.58	.03
	NG	47	7	53	.60	.02	46	7	52	.59	.03
87. Moody	RB	35	22	57	.79	.03	42	21	62	.84	.04
	RG	40	21	61	.83	.03	44	29	73	1.03	.04
	NB	25	2	26	.28	.02	26	2	28	.30	.02
	NG	30	1	31	.32	.02	31	5	36	.41	.03

APPENDIX D (Continued)

Item	Group[a]	Age 4-11					Age 12-18				
		1	2	1+2	Mean	SE[b]	1	2	1+2	Mean	SE[b]
88. Sulks a lot	RB	33	13	46	.60	.03	34	12	46	.58	.03
	RG	34	17	51	.69	.03	38	19	57	.77	.04
	NB	22	2	24	.26	.02	15	3	18	.21	.02
	NG	19	2	21	.23	.02	18	2	20	.23	.02
89. Suspicious	RB	16	6	22	.28	.02	23	8	32	.41	.03
	RG	19	5	24	.28	.02	28	9	37	.46	.03
	NB	4	1	5	.06	.01	12	1	13	.14	.02
	NG	7	1	8	.09	.01	9	1	10	.10	.02
90. Swearing	RB	34	12	46	.58	.03	38	20	58	.79	.04
	RG	19	4	23	.27	.02	32	18	50	.68	.04
	NB	15	1	16	.17	.02	21	3	24	.27	.02
	NG	7	0	8	.08	.01	14	2	15	.17	.02
91. Suicidal thoughts	RB	13	3	16	.19	.02	13	2	15	.18	.02
	RG	10	2	12	.14	.02	18	4	22	.27	.02
	NB	3	0	3	.03	.01	2	0	2	.02	.01
	NG	2	0	2	.02	.01	3	0	4	.04	.01
92. Talks, walks in sleep	RB	18	5	23	.28	.02	13	3	16	.20	.02
	RG	22	5	27	.32	.02	16	3	20	.24	.02
	NB	16	2	19	.21	.02	12	2	14	.15	.02
	NG	15	2	17	.20	.02	11	1	12	.14	.02

APPENDIX D (Continued)

Item	Group[a]	Age 4-11					Age 12-18				
		1	2	1+2	Mean	SE[b]	1	2	1+2	Mean	SE[b]
93. Talks too much	RB	36	21	57	.78	.03	26	13	38	.51	.03
	RG	32	21	53	.74	.03	30	10	40	.51	.03
	NB	35	10	45	.55	.03	27	7	34	.41	.03
	NG	41	11	52	.64	.03	33	8	41	.49	.03
94. Teases a lot	RB	41	21	61	.82	.03	34	21	56	.77	.04
	RG	34	12	45	.57	.03	30	8	39	.47	.03
	NB	37	5	43	.48	.02	43	11	54	.66	.03
	NG	32	3	35	.38	.02	27	6	33	.39	.03
95. Hot temper	RB	35	33	68	1.02	.03	38	26	64	.90	.04
	RG	34	27	61	.88	.03	36	24	59	.84	.04
	NB	33	10	42	.52	.03	26	7	33	.40	.03
	NG	30	5	35	.40	.02	23	5	27	.32	.03
96. Thinks about sex	RB	7	2	9	.11	.02	12	4	17	.22	.02
	RG	6	2	9	.11	.02	15	7	21	.29	.03
	NB	2	0	3	.03	.01	5	2	6	.08	.02
	NG	2	0	2	.03	.01	6	1	7	.08	.01
97. Threatens people	RB	26	9	34	.43	.03	24	7	32	.39	.03
	RG	15	4	19	.24	.02	17	7	24	.31	.03
	NB	7	1	8	.08	.01	4	1	5	.06	.01
	NG	3	0	3	.03	.01	4	1	4	.05	.01

APPENDIX D (Continued)

Item	Group[a]	Age 4-11					Age 12-18				
		1	2	1+2	Mean	SE[b]	1	2	1+2	Mean	SE[b]
98. Thumbsucking	RB	4	8	12	.20	.02	2	1	3	.05	.01
	RG	7	14	21	.35	.03	3	3	5	.08	.02
	NB	4	4	8	.12	.02	1	0	1	.01	.01
	NG	5	8	13	.21	.02	2	2	4	.06	.01
99. Concerned with neat, clean	RB	14	3	16	.19	.02	11	4	15	.19	.02
	RG	11	4	14	.18	.02	14	5	19	.24	.02
	NB	11	2	13	.14	.02	14	2	17	.19	.02
	NG	16	3	19	.22	.02	15	6	22	.28	.03
100. Trouble sleeping	RB	18	9	27	.36	.03	13	6	20	.26	.03
	RG	16	9	25	.34	.03	17	7	24	.31	.03
	NB	6	1	7	.08	.01	5	0	6	.06	.01
	NG	7	1	7	.08	.01	7	0	7	.07	.01
101. Truancy	RB	2	2	4	.07	.01	14	14	28	.42	.03
	RG	2	1	4	.05	.01	17	14	31	.45	.03
	NB	1	0	1	.01	.00	4	2	6	.08	.02
	NG	0	0	0	.01	.00	5	1	6	.07	.01
102. Lacks energy	RB	9	3	12	.15	.02	20	9	29	.39	.03
	RG	14	4	18	.22	.02	20	10	30	.41	.03
	NB	4	1	4	.05	.01	10	1	12	.13	.02
	NG	8	0	8	.08	.01	12	2	15	.17	.02

APPENDIX D (Continued)

Item	Group[a]	Age 4-11					Age 12-18				
		1	2	1+2	Mean	SE[b]	1	2	1+2	Mean	SE[b]
103. Unhappy, sad, depressed	RB	39	11	50	.61	.03	45	17	62	.80	.03
	RG	44	13	58	.71	.03	48	23	71	.95	.03
	NB	12	1	12	.13	.01	16	0	17	.17	.02
	NG	12	0	13	.13	.01	18	1	19	.21	.02
104. Loud	RB	39	18	57	.76	.03	30	11	41	.52	.03
	RG	30	14	44	.59	.03	29	10	39	.49	.03
	NB	23	3	26	.30	.02	20	1	21	.22	.02
	NG	22	1	24	.25	.02	16	2	18	.21	.02
105. Alcohol, drugs	RB	1	1	1	.02	.01	18	7	25	.33	.03
	RG	0	0	0	.00	.00	19	6	24	.31	.03
	NB	0	0	0	.00	.00	3	2	4	.06	.01
	NG	0	0	0	.00	.00	3	0	3	.03	.01
106. Vandalism	RB	5	2	7	.10	.01	12	3	15	.18	.02
	RG	3	1	3	.04	.01	4	1	5	.06	.01
	NB	1	0	1	.01	.00	2	0	2	.02	.01
	NG	0	0	0	.00	.00	0	0	0	.01	.00
107. Wets during day	RB	7	3	10	.12	.02	1	0	1	.01	.00
	RG	10	2	13	.15	.02	2	0	2	.03	.01
	NB	2	0	2	.02	.01	0	0	0	.00	.00
	NG	2	0	2	.02	.01	0	0	0	.00	.00

APPENDIX D (Continued)

Item	Group[a]	Age 4-11					Age 12-18				
		1	2	1+2	Mean	SE[b]	1	2	1+2	Mean	SE[b]
108. Wets bed	RB	13	10	22	.32	.03	4	2	6	.08	.02
	RG	12	10	22	.31	.03	4	1	5	.06	.01
	NB	9	3	12	.15	.02	1	0	1	.01	.01
	NG	8	2	11	.13	.02	1	0	1	.01	.01
109. Whining	RB	39	11	50	.61	.03	13	2	16	.18	.02
	RG	37	17	54	.72	.03	21	3	24	.27	.02
	NB	31	3	34	.37	.02	9	2	11	.13	.02
	NG	42	3	45	.47	.02	15	1	16	.17	.02
110. Wishes to be opposite sex	RB	3	1	3	.04	.01	2	0	2	.02	.01
	RG	5	1	5	.07	.01	5	0	5	.05	.01
	NB	1	0	1	.01	.00	0	0	0	.00	.00
	NG	0	0	1	.01	.01	0	0	0	.00	.00
111. Withdrawn	RB	24	7	31	.38	.03	30	10	40	.50	.03
	RG	26	7	33	.40	.02	25	11	36	.47	.03
	NB	7	1	8	.08	.01	8	1	9	.10	.02
	NG	6	0	6	.07	.01	8	1	8	.09	.01
112. Worries	RB	39	11	49	.61	.03	39	13	52	.65	.03
	RG	38	16	54	.70	.03	40	16	55	.72	.03
	NB	24	2	26	.28	.02	30	2	33	.35	.02
	NG	28	2	30	.31	.02	34	3	37	.40	.03

APPENDIX D (Continued)

Item	Group[a]	Age 4-11					Age 12-18				
		1	2	1+2	Mean	SE[b]	1	2	1+2	Mean	SE[b]
113. Other problems	RB	3	9	13	.48	.05	3	12	15	.46	.05
	RG	6	11	17	.57	.05	4	12	17	.53	.05
	NB	1	2	3	.06	.01	2	3	6	.11	.02
	NG	1	1	3	.05	.01	2	3	4	.09	.02